FIFTY STRATEGIES
for TEACHING
ENGLISH LANGUAGE
LEARNERS

SECOND EDITION

ADRIENNE HERRELL
California State University, Fresno

MICHAEL JORDAN
California State University, Fresno

PEARSON

Merrill
Prentice Hall

Upper Saddle River, New Jersey
Columbus, Ohio

Library of Congress Cataloging-in-Publication Data

Herrell, Adrienne L.
    Fifty strategies for teaching English language learners/Adrienne L. Herrell, Michael
Jordan.—2nd ed.
        p. cm.
    Includes bibliographical references.
    ISBN 0-13-098462-0
    1. English language—Study and teaching—Foreign speakers. I. Jordan, Michael II. Title.
PE1128.A2 H467 2004

428.2'4—dc21

2002043114

Vice President and Executive Publisher: Jeffery W. Johnston
Acquisitions/Executive Editor: Debra A. Stollenwerk
Editorial Assistant: Mary Morrill
Production Editor: Kris Robinson
Production Coordination: Carlisle Publishers Services
Design Coordinator: Diane C. Lorenzo
Cover Designer: Keith Van Norman
Cover Art: Getty One
Production Manager: Pamela D. Bennett
Director of Marketing: Ann Castel Davis
Marketing Manager: Darcy Betts Prybella
Marketing Coordinator: Tyra Poole

This book was set in New Caledonia by Carlisle Communications, Ltd. It was printed and bound by Courier
Kendallville, Inc. The cover was printed by The Lehigh Press, Inc.

Pearson Prentice Hall™ is a trademark of Pearson Education, Inc.
Pearson® is a registered trademark of Pearson plc
Prentice Hall® is a registered trademark of Pearson Education, Inc.
Merrill® is a registered trademark of Pearson Education, Inc.

Pearson Education Ltd.   Pearson Education Australia Pty. Limited
Pearson Education Singapore Pte. Ltd.   Pearson Education North Asia Ltd.
Pearson Education Canada, Ltd.   Pearson Educación de Mexico, S.A. de C.V.
Pearson Education—Japan   Pearson Education Malaysia Pte. Ltd.

10 9 8 7 6
ISBN: 0-13-098462-0

To Connor Jacob, and Megan Jade. . .
Our favorite active learners. . .

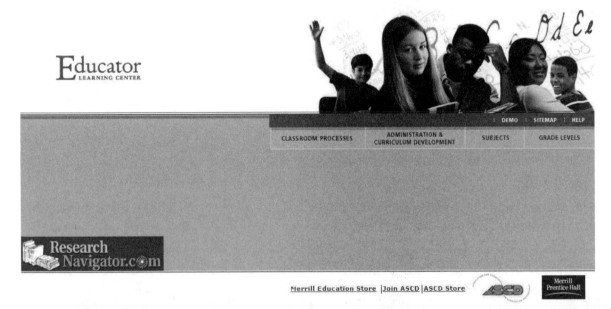

CONTENTS

SECTION IV

STRATEGIES FOR BUILDING VOCABULARY AND FLUENCY

SECTION V

STRATEGIES FOR BUILDING COMPREHENSION

ABOUT THE AUTHORS

Adrienne Herrell is a professor of reading/language arts at California State University, Fresno, where she teaches classes in early literacy, assessment, and strategies for teaching English language learners. *Fifty Strategies for Teaching English Language Learners,* Second Edition, is Dr. Herrell's fifth book for Merrill/Prentice Hall. Her previous books include *Camcorder in the Classroom* with Joel Fowler; *Fifty Strategies for Teaching English Language Learners; Reflective Planning, Teaching, and Evaluation: K–12* with Judy Eby and Jim Hicks; and *Fifty Active Learning Strategies for Improving Comprehension* with Michael Jordan. Dr. Herrell's writing and research are built on her experiences teaching in Florida's public schools for 23 years. She and co-author Dr. Jordan are currently engaged in research in public schools in California, Florida, and Alaska validating the effectiveness of the strategies described in this text.

Michael Jordan is an assistant professor in the Department of Curriculum and Instruction and Coordinator of the Multiple Subject Credential Program (Elementary Credential) at California State University, Fresno. He has taught primary grades through high school in Georgia, Alabama, Florida, and California. Dr. Jordan is an actor, education director, and board member of Theatre Three Repertory Company in Fresno and is dedicated to providing children and youth access to live theater. He and Dr. Herrell incorporate many dramatic reenactment strategies in their joint research working with vocabulary and comprehension development in children learning English in Fresno public schools. *Fifty Strategies for Teaching English Language Learners,* Second Edition, is Dr. Jordan's second book for Merrill/Prentice Hall. His previous book is *Fifty Active Learning Strategies for Improving Comprehension* with Adrienne Herrell. He has published several articles on interactive script writing and vocabulary development to enhance reading comprehension for children.

Drs. Herrell and Jordan serve as educational consultants to a number of school districts across the nation and have presented widely on the subject of reading and comprehension at national and international conferences.

PREFACE

The United States becomes more ethnically and linguistically diverse every year. More than 90 percent of new residents come from non-English-speaking countries. The number of students with non-English-speaking backgrounds represents the fastest growing group of this population. In the last decade, the total student enrollment in public schools increased by only 14 percent, while the number of English learners grew 70 percent and is projected to grow even more (National Clearinghouse for Bilingual Education, 1999). The 2000 U.S. Census identified 20 percent of school-age children as non-native English speakers (Jamieson, Curry, & Martinez, 2001).

Teachers everywhere are faced with enormous challenges in their classrooms. They are expected to meet the needs of an increasingly diverse population each year. There is more content to teach each year, as well. Teachers are now expected to integrate technology and teach to myriad standards, and they are judged by the standardized test scores achieved by their students, with no excuses tolerated and little understanding of the challenges they face daily in the classroom.

This second edition of *Fifty Strategies for Teaching English Language Learners* includes a number of features to support teachers in meeting some of the more daunting challenges of the 21st century classroom.

WHAT'S NEW IN THE SECOND EDITION?

Organization

This edition is organized to serve as a resource book, not just a text. The book is arranged in five sections.

Section I: Theoretical Overview supports the teacher in understanding the basic principles of teaching and assessing English learners.

Section II: Strategies for Enhancing Instruction through Planning gives suggestions of ways to integrate the basic principles addressed in Section I into effective classroom lessons. This section focuses on the adaptations necessary in making ordinary lessons extraordinary in helping ELL students understand the content being taught and acquire the English necessary for successful participation in English-only classrooms. The last three sections in the book address specific learning goals.

Section III: Strategies for Supporting Student Involvement supports the teacher in ensuring active participation by all students. This is an important factor in enhancing the success of English learners in the classroom.

Section IV: Strategies for Building Vocabulary and Fluency gives a number of vocabulary and fluency-building approaches.

Section V: Strategies for Building Comprehension completes the text by providing active-learning approaches to helping students make sense of the instruction and readings they encounter. Each section begins with easy-to-implement strategies and progresses to more involved approaches. It should be noted that all 50 strategies have been thoroughly field-tested in highly diverse classrooms in California, Florida, and Alaska.

Standards Base

The national TESOL (Teachers of English to Students of Other Languages) Standards are used as the standards base for this text (TESOL, 1997). A matrix of the TESOL Standards and the 50 strategies in the text demonstrates the standards supported by each strategy (see Standards Matrix in Table P.1 on page xii). At the beginning of each strategy there is a list of the TESOL Standards supported by that strategy. In addition, there are examples of the outcome behaviors that could be expected as a result of the teaching strategy listed for each of the three grade-level ranges (pre-K–3, 4–8, and 9–12) of the TESOL Standards at the conclusion of each strategy. These are included to help teachers visualize the type of student behaviors they should begin to see in their English learners as a result of lessons planned to enhance both content knowledge and English development.

Assessment

In addition to the assessment strategies explained in the theoretical overview in Section I, suggestions for assessment are integrated into many of the strategies in this edition. Teachers are encouraged to use anecdotal records, performance samples, and portfolios in an ongoing way with English learners since the more traditional evaluation methods are often primarily language-based and prove difficult for English learners to use in demonstrating their growing skills.

Technology

Suggestions for integrating technology and using it to enhance learning are also integrated into the strategies. Technology can serve as an enormous support to students and teachers alike because of easy access to the Internet and resources such as visuals and even bilingual teaching materials.

New Strategies

Several new strategies are included in this edition. The authors are actively involved in diverse classrooms on a weekly basis and are continually discovering new approaches and enhancing old ones. These discoveries and redefined approaches are included in this edition. There is an increased emphasis on vocabulary development in the strategies due to an ongoing research study we have been conducting, which is providing convincing evidence of the importance of this focus in supporting the success of English learners in the classroom.

HOW TO USE THIS TEXT

Reading and understanding the theoretical overview (Section I) is vital to understanding the basic principles of instructing and assessing English learners. This should be approached first. The other sections can be approached one strategy at a time, but one or two strategies from each section should be tried first before working through each section. Strategies that are the easiest to implement are listed first in each category. It makes sense for student or beginning teachers to build their repertoire of strategies gradually, sampling from all five sections. After that, the text can easily be used as a resource book.

When you notice a need in your students, look for a strategy to meet that need. Keep in mind the basic principles of teaching English learners. You must support their understanding with realia, visuals, and contextualized language. It is vital to emphasize vocabulary, fluency, and building background knowledge for comprehension. Students must be actively engaged to benefit fully from instruction. They must be given opportunities to demonstrate their growing skills in authentic tasks and in a nonstressful environment. We recognize the complexity of teaching in effective ways and have written this text with the goal of providing this type of classroom for all students.

We wish to thank the following teachers for the use of their classrooms in validating strategies and for their ongoing implementation of the strategies in support of their students.

Susan McCloskey, K–1 teacher, Greenberg Elementary School, Fresno, California

Vince Workman, intermediate literacy coach, Greenberg Elementary School, Fresno, California

Scott Benning, primary literacy coach, Greenberg Elementary School, Fresno, California

David Reynolds, 10th-grade English teacher, Avenal High School, Avenal, California

Diana Bateman, third grade teacher, Lewis Carroll Elementary School, Merritt Island, Florida

Teachers at Rosa Parks Elementary School, Clark Middle School, and Hoover High School—San Diego, CA

Teachers at Tanaina Elementary School—Wasilla, AK

We appreciate the comments and suggestions of the following individuals who reviewed the manuscript; Imelda Basurto, California State University–Fresno; Julie Coppola, Boston University; Glenn DeVoogd, California State University–Fresno; Dana L. Grisham, San Diego State University; and Rafael Lara-Alecio, Texas A&M University.

ESL STANDARDS AND THIS TEXT

This second edition of *Fifty Strategies for Teaching English Language Learners* has been aligned with *ESL Standards for Pre-K–12 Students* published by Teachers of English to Speakers of Other Languages (TESOL). The TESOL publication is organized around three overarching goals: the development of (a) social language, (b) academic language, and (c) sociocultural knowledge. Each goal supports three standards, the attainment of which means that students will become proficient English speakers, writers, and readers.

The TESOL standards are divided into three grade-level groupings: pre-K–3, 4–8, and 9–12. These grade-level groupings and the nine standards—three for each overarching goal—are aligned in Table P. 1 with the 50 strategies explained in this book. In addition to this matrix of strategies and standards, each strategy begins with a graphic that indicates the standards and grade levels for which it is appropriate. In the current emphasis on standards-based education, this addition to the second edition will support teachers in their documentation of standards-based planning and teaching as well as the monitoring and individualization of instruction for English language learners.

The ESL Standards for Pre-K–12 Students is available to read or order online at **www.tesol.org/.** (To read, click on "standards and initiatives" under "advancing the profession of TESOL." To order a copy, click on "publications and products.")

References

Jamieson, A., Curry, A., & Martinez, G. (2001). School enrollment in the United States—Social and economic characteristics of students. *Current Population Report* (Report Number P20533). Washington, DC: U.S. Government Printing Office.

National Clearinghouse for Bilingual Education. (1999). K–12 and LEP enrollment trends. Retrieved from http://www.ncbe.gwu.edu/ncbepubs/reports/state-data/index.htm.

TESOL. (1997). *ESL standards for pre-K–12 students*. Alexandria, VA: Author.

Table P.1

TESOL Standards / Chapters	Goal #1—Use English to communicate in social settings	Standard 1: Use English to participate in social interactions.	Standard 2: Interact in, through, and with spoken and written English.	Standard 3: Use learning strategies to extend communicative competence.	Goal #2—Use English to achieve academically.	Standard 1: Use English to interact in the classroom.	Standard 2: Use English to obtain, process, construct, and provide subject matter information in spoken and written form.	Standard 3: Use appropriate learning strategies to construct and apply academic knowledge.	Goal #3—Use English in socially and culturally appropriate ways.	Standard 1: Use the appropriate language variety, register, and genre according to audience, purpose, and setting.	Standard 2: Use nonverbal communication appropriate to audience, purpose, and setting.	Standard 3: Use appropriate learning strategies to extend sociolinguistic and sociocultural competence.
1				x			x					
2				x			x	x			x	
3							x	x				
4			x			x	x	x		x	x	
5							x	x				
6						x	x	x				x
7			x	x		x	x	x		x		
8						x	x	x				
9						x	x	x				
10		x				x	x	x			x	
11				x							x	x
12	x	x		x		x	x	x				
13						x	x	x				
14						x	x	x				
15		x	x	x		x	x					
16		x	x			x	x	x				
17		x	x			x	x	x		x		
18				x		x	x	x			x	x
19						x	x	x		x	x	x
20						x	x	x				
21						x	x	x			x	x
22	x					x	x	x		x		
23						x	x	x				
24						x	x	x				
25						x	x	x			x	x
26						x	x	x		x		
27						x	x	x				
28						x	x	x				
29				x		x	x	x			x	
30	x	x		x				x				
31				x		x	x	x				x
32	x	x		x		x	x	x		x	x	
33	x	x		x		x	x	x		x	x	x
34	x	x		x		x	x	x		x	x	x
35						x	x	x		x	x	
36						x	x	x				
37						x	x	x				
38						x	x	x				
39						x	x	x				
40				x		x	x	x				
41						x	x	x				
42						x	x	x				
43						x	x	x				
44				x		x	x	x				x
45						x	x	x		x		x
46			x			x	x	x		x		x
47						x	x	x				
48						x	x	x		x		x
49		x	x	x		x	x	x		x		x
50		x	x	x		x	x	x		x	x	x

THEORETICAL OVERVIEW

In this section of *Fifty Strategies for Teaching English Language Learners,* you are introduced to the basic theory, principles, and assessment strategies underlying the effective teaching of students who are in the process of acquiring English as a second language.

This section provides the research and exemplary practices on which the 50 teaching strategies are built. It is vital that teachers make good choices in their everyday interactions with students, particularly students for whom English is not their first language. To make good choices in the way they plan instruction, interact verbally, correct mistakes, and assess English language learners, teachers must understand how language is acquired.

This second edition of *Fifty Strategies for Teaching English Language Learners* is aligned with the national standards for teaching English language learners published by Teachers of English for Speakers of Other Languages (TESOL). These standards provide teachers with clear guidelines in supporting English language learners as they become more proficient in speaking, writing, and comprehending social and academic English. This ongoing quest for ways to build and maintain proficient bilingual students in schools can only be achieved with teachers who understand the value of good teaching. These are teachers who produce academically successful students who stay in school and are given every opportunity to participate fully and equitably.

THEORETICAL OVERVIEW

The research in language acquisition has been rich and productive during the past 20 years. Linguists and educators working together (Krashen & Terrell, 1983) have discovered effective ways to support students in their acquisition of new languages and content knowledge. It is vital that classroom teachers understand the implications of the language acquisition research so they can provide the scaffolding necessary for their students to be successful in the classroom.

LANGUAGE ACQUISITION THEORY AND THE CLASSROOM TEACHER

For classroom teachers to make good decisions about instructional practices for English language learners, they must understand how students acquire English and how this acquisition differs from the way foreign languages have traditionally been taught in the United States (Collier, 1995). Many teachers have experienced classes in Spanish, French, or other languages in which they have practiced repetitive drills and translated long passages using English–French (or Spanish) dictionaries. While these approaches have been used for many years in the United States without much success, it should be noted that linguists such as Jim Cummins and Stephen Krashen have been researching new approaches to language acquisition.

Krashen (1982), in his study of language acquisition, makes a distinction between language acquisition and language learning that is vital to the support of students' gradual acquisition of fluency in a new language. Krashen states that language acquisition is a natural thing. Young children acquire their home language easily without formal teaching.

This acquisition is gradual, based on receiving and understanding messages, building a listening (receptive) vocabulary, and slowly attempting verbal production of the language in a highly supportive, nonstressful situation. It is exactly these same conditions that foster the acquisition of a second language. The teacher is responsible for providing the understandable language (comprehensible input), along with whatever supports are necessary for the students to understand the messages. Using approaches and materials that add context to the language—props, gestures, pictures—all contribute to the child's acquisition and eventually to the production of language.

Krashen and Terrell (1983) also stress the need for English language learners to be allowed to move into verbal production of the new language at a comfortable rate. Students must hear and understand messages in the target language and build a listening vocabulary before being expected to produce spoken language. This does not mean that the English language learners should be uninvolved in classroom activities, but that the activities should be structured so that English language learners can participate at a level of comfort. Questions asked of them should be answerable at first with gestures, nods, or other physical responses. This language acquisition stage is called the silent or preproduction period, and it is a vital start to language acquisition. The subsequent stages and implications for teaching and learning are explained in Chapter 13, Leveled Questions.

The role of the classroom environment in supporting children's language acquisition cannot be ignored. Meaningful exposure to language is not enough. Students need many opportunities for language interaction. Swain (1993) proposes that a classroom where children work together to solve problems and produce projects supports their language development in several ways. It gives them authentic reasons to communicate and support in refining their language production. It also provides students with the realization that their verbal communication is not always understood by others. This realization helps to move the child from receptive, semantic processing (listening to understand) to expressive, syntactic processing (formation of words and sentences to communicate). If children are left to simply listen and observe without the opportunity or necessity to communicate they remain in the preproductive stage for an extended period of time. The structure of communicative classroom activities, those that necessitate communication and verbal interaction, prevents this from happening.

Another important component supportive of children's language acquisition is their discovery of what they can do with language. Halliday (1978) identified seven functions of language or purposes for using language, which provide impetus for children's verbal communication. The functions that Halliday identified are the following:

1. *Instrumental.* The use of language to cause things to happen. For example, "Bathroom" causes the teacher to take notice and excuse the student to use the bathroom.
2. *Regulatory.* The use of language to control events or the behavior of others. For example, "He hit me!" causes the teacher to intervene on the child's behalf.
3. *Representation.* The use of language to communicate facts or knowledge. For example, "I have two pennies" tells the teacher that the child understands the number concept.
4. *Interactional.* The use of language to get along with others. For example, "Sit with me" is used to make a friend.
5. *Personal.* The use of language to express personality, feelings, or emotions. For example, "I sad" is used to convey feelings.
6. *Heuristic.* The use of language to acquire knowledge. For example, "Show me" is used to gain access to information.
7. *Imaginative.* The use of language to create an imaginative world for pleasure or play. For example, "Pretend we are on a train" is used to create a fantasy play situation.

Many researchers (Krashen, 1982; Krashen & Terrell, 1983; McLaughlin, 1990) have studied the role of emotions on the acquisition of language. Krashen calls the effect of emotions on learning the "affective filter." When a learner is placed in a stressful situation in which language production or performance is demanded, the student's ability to learn or produce spoken language is impaired. This underscores the responsibility of the teacher to provide a supportive classroom environment in which students can participate at a comfortable level without having to worry about being embarrassed or placed in a situation where they will be made to feel foolish. Krashen's Affective Filter Hypothesis stresses that for the student to learn effectively the student's motivation and self-esteem must be supported while anxiety is diminished. This provides an opportunity for the English language learner to take in information, process vocabulary, and eventually produce language because stress levels are low and the affective filter is not interfering with thinking or learning.

Jim Cummins's research (1986) contributes to the understanding of language acquisition and effective classroom practice in several ways. First, Cummins differentiates between social language, called basic interpersonal communication skills (BICS), and academic language, called cognitive academic language proficiency (CALP). While students may acquire BICS and be able to communicate in English while on the playground or in asking and answering simple questions, this is not the same thing as having the level of language proficiency necessary to benefit fully from academic English instruction (CALP) without additional support.

Cummins also helps us understand what must be added to instruction to make it comprehensible to students. He identifies two dimensions of language, its cognitive demand and its context embeddedness. Using a quadrant matrix, Cummins demonstrates how the addition of context supports the students' understanding of more cognitively demanding language such as the language of content instruction in the classroom (see Figure TO.1).

By examining Cummins's quadrant the teacher can see that even social language is made more understandable by the addition of context. Directions given orally with gestures are more easily understood than the same words spoken over the telephone without the aid of gestures. This becomes even more important in the classroom, where teachers are using academic terms that may be unfamiliar to the English language learner or using them in a different way from the customary social

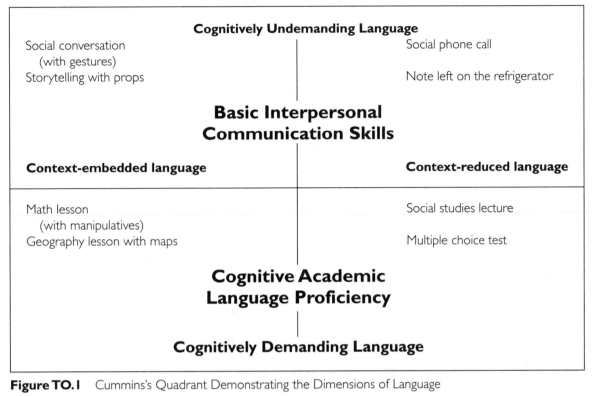

Figure TO.1 Cummins's Quadrant Demonstrating the Dimensions of Language

Adapted from "Primary Language Instruction and the Education of Language Minority Students" by J. Cummins, 1996. *Schooling and Language Minority Students: A Theoretical Framework,* 2nd ed. (p. 10). Los Angeles: Evaluation, Dissemination and Assessment Center, School of Education, California State University, Los Angeles. Copyright © 1996 by Charles F. Leyba, Reprinted with permission.

meaning. This is demonstrated by one English language learner's illustration of a riverbed in response to a geography lesson (see Figure TO.2). The student's understanding of the word *bed* was linked to his prior knowledge of the word and did not support his understanding of the term when used to describe a geographic feature.

THE UNDERLYING THEORY BASE OF INSTRUCTION FOR ENGLISH LANGUAGE LEARNERS

Strategies are defined in this book as approaches that can be used across curricular areas to support the learning of students. The strategies described in this book are based on the theories of the linguists described in this introductory section. The goals of the strategies are to enhance learning. To provide this enhancement, one or more of the underlying premises of effective instruction of English language learners are emphasized in each of the strategies. These premises are the following:

1. Teachers should provide instruction in a way that ensures that students are given *comprehensible input* (material presented in a manner that leads to the student's understanding of the content, i.e., visual, manipulative, scaffolded in L1(the child's first language), and so on).
2. Teachers should provide opportunities to *increase verbal interaction* in classroom activities.
3. Teachers should provide instruction that *contextualizes language* as much as possible.
4. Teachers should use teaching strategies and grouping techniques that *reduce the anxiety* of the students as much as possible.
5. Teachers should provide activities in the classroom that offer opportunities for *active involvement* of the students.

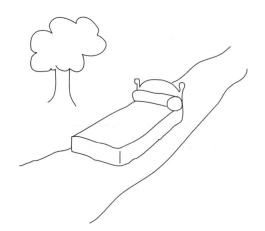

Figure TO.2 An English Language Learner's Concept of a Riverbed.

As teaching strategies are explained in the following chapters, the reader will be reminded of the national TESOL standards by means of a graphic box at the beginning of each chapter, which connects the strategy to the reasons for its appropriateness to English language learners. Strategies will be related to the goals established by TESOL as important to the support of students acquiring English. This will enable the teacher to select activities that best suit the needs of the learners being taught. In addition, the outcome behaviors to be expected from students after the use of the strategies are enumerated at the conclusion of each chapter. The strategies in this book are not meant to be used in isolation. By combining strategies the teacher can plan innovative lessons, which will motivate the students to learn. The examples that are included in each chapter will demonstrate ways the strategies can be combined and used effectively.

THE ROLE OF ASSESSMENT IN TEACHING ENGLISH LANGUAGE LEARNERS

Students in the process of acquiring English often have difficulty expressing themselves to convey the understanding they have of the content they are learning. Beginning English learners often understand much more than they are able to express. Their receptive English grows at a much faster rate than their expressive English. For this reason, teachers must create a variety of ways for English learners to demonstrate their understanding. It is important that teachers provide ways to document the learning of English learners so that appropriate lessons can be planned. It is also vital that English learners be able to show that they are learning and for them to be included in the classroom interactions. Assessment strategies are included as a part of this theoretical overview because teachers will need to adjust their teaching strategies on the basis of their knowledge of the students' growing competencies. Because assessment can be extremely language-based, requiring exact vocabulary to read and answer questions, assessment strategies must be adjusted to find out how well the students understand the concepts being taught. Less formal assessment also provides an opportunity for teachers to learn more about the learners' understanding of English vocabulary and use of sentence structure.

Assessment strategies appropriate for English learners include the use of observation and anecdotal records by the classroom teacher and paraprofessionals, watching the students' reactions and responses, and documenting their growth. In addition, performance sampling, where students are asked to perform certain tasks and teachers observe and document their responses, are very effective in monitoring and documenting growth. The third assessment strategy, portfolio assessment, is a way of maintaining records of observations, performance sampling and ongoing growth. These three assessment strategies, when combined, provide a rich store of information about English learners which give a more complete picture of their individual growth and learning development.

ANECDOTAL RECORDS

Anecdotal records (Rhodes & Nathenson-Mejia, 1993) are a form of assessment that allow the teacher to document the growth and accomplishments of students. They are based on the teacher's observations as the students engage in classroom activities. This form of assessment and documentation is especially appropriate for English language learners because the teacher can ask questions of the student, record language samples and note ways in which the student demonstrates understanding (Genishi & Dyson, 1984).

The teacher is free to discuss the observations with the student and celebrate the growth that is documented. This encourages and motivates the student and may even serve to lower classroom anxiety, thereby increasing participation and learning (Garcia, 1994). An anecdotal record always includes the student's name, the date of the observation, and a narrative of what was seen and heard by the teacher. It is not intended to be a summary of behavior but instead a record of one incident or anecdote observed by the teacher. Such things as quotes, descriptions of interactions with other students or teachers, and demonstration of knowledge through use of manipulatives or learning centers are easily documented through these narratives. If anecdotal records are taken regularly and placed in sequential order, they provide a good indication of the student's progress and a basis for instructional planning. A sample of an anecdotal record of a first-grade child working at the writing center is shown in Figure TO.3.

STEP BY STEP

The steps in implementing anecdotal records are the following:

• *Deciding on a system*—Decide what system you will use for keeping anecdotal records. They can be kept on index cards, in a notebook, on peel-off mailing labels (later transferred in sequence to an anecdotal record form), or in any format that helps the teacher keep track of student progress.

• *Choosing what to document and scheduling*—Decide what you want to document and make a schedule for observing the students. A sample schedule allowing a teacher to observe a class of 20 students—four per day—in four areas a month is shown in Figure TO.4.

• *Conferencing and goal-setting*—Set up a conference schedule and discuss your observations with the students and/or parents. This is also a good time to discuss language development and the setting of language and content-area goals.

• *Using records for planning*—Use the records to plan appropriate lessons for your students or to focus on language acquisition goals and progress. See the Language Framework Planning section in Chapter 9 for an example of how this could be done.

Maria	**4/15**	**Writing Center with Dolores**

Maria and Dolores are sitting at the writing center looking at labeled pictures of birds. On the table is a collection of books about birds. The students are to write one page for a book about birds they are compiling this week.

"What this word?" Maria asks Dolores, pointing to the word *eagle*. Dolores answers "eagle." Maria: "That a pretty bird. I write about eagle." She writes, "Eagle is a prty brd." and draws a very detailed picture of the eagle. The teacher asks her why she thinks the eagle is pretty. Maria says, "Eagle have shiny feathers." The teacher asks if she can write that. Maria smiles, and says, "I try." She writes, "Eagle hv shne fethrs."

Figure TO.3 Anecdotal Record for an English Language Learner

Focus Area	Monday	Tuesday	Wednesday	Thursday	Friday
Writing Center	Ana Blia Carol Helen	Dan Irana Maria Susana	Jose Earl Patrick Wally	Luis Rosa Tomas Franco	Gina Karen Ned Pablo
Literature Circles					
Writing Conference					
Guided Reading					

Figure TO.4 Schedule for Conducting Observations for Anecdotal Records

PERFORMANCE SAMPLING

Performance sampling is a form of authentic assessment where the student is observed in the process of accomplishing academic tasks and is evaluated on how the tasks are done. The word *authentic* indicates that the tasks the students are asked to do are similar or identical to actual tasks that students routinely accomplish in the classroom setting, unlike more traditional forms of assessment, which tend to be unlike everyday classroom activities.

Performance samples are well-named because the teacher observes a sample of the student's performance in a given academic task. Examples of the types of tasks used in performance sampling are the following:

• Working a mathematics problem that involves reading the problem, setting up an approach to finding a solution, and finding a reasonable solution

• Responding to a writing prompt by webbing a short piece of writing, writing a draft of a written piece, working with a peer to elicit feedback on the draft, revising the piece, and working with a peer to edit the piece for mechanics and spelling

• Researching a topic in social studies and documenting the information gained by completing a data chart

Performance samples are documented in several ways. The teacher might write an anecdotal record of the observation. The teacher might design a scoring rubric and evaluate the student's performance on the rubric (see Figure TO.5 for an example). The teacher might design a checklist and evaluate the student's performance on the basis of the items on the checklist. (See Figure TO.6 for an example of a checklist that might be used in this way.)

Performance sampling is a particularly appropriate form of assessment for English language learners because their approach to academic tasks is observed and documented and their assessment is based on their ability to perform the task rather than their fluency in English, which is sometimes the case in more traditional forms of assessment (Hernandez, 1997).

5   Exemplary Performance
     The student:
            planned the task in an outstanding way
            followed the plan to achieve a high-level product
            proofread and corrected all errors
            produced a unique product

4   Strong Performance
     The student:
            planned the task
            followed the plan to complete the product
            proofread and corrected the majority of errors
            produced a good product

3   Acceptable Performance
     The student:
            performed the task to an acceptable end
            corrected some errors
            showed some understanding of what was required

2   Weak Performance
     The student:
            showed some confusion about what was expected
            left out some important steps in the process or didn't finish the task completely
            failed to correct errors

1   Very Weak Performance
     The student:
            showed only minimal understanding of the task
            completed a very small portion of the task

0   No Performance
     The student failed to complete the task

Figure TO.5   Example of a Scoring Rubric for Performance Sampling

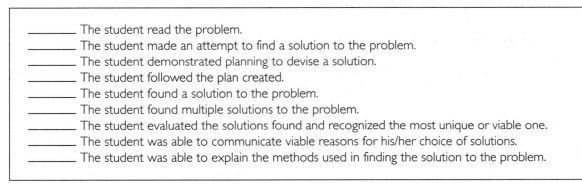

_____ The student read the problem.
_____ The student made an attempt to find a solution to the problem.
_____ The student demonstrated planning to devise a solution.
_____ The student followed the plan created.
_____ The student found a solution to the problem.
_____ The student found multiple solutions to the problem.
_____ The student evaluated the solutions found and recognized the most unique or viable one.
_____ The student was able to communicate viable reasons for his/her choice of solutions.
_____ The student was able to explain the methods used in finding the solution to the problem.

Figure TO.6   Example of a Checklist for the Assessment of Performance Sampling

STEP BY STEP

The steps in performance sampling are the following:

• *Choosing an assessment task*—Decide on the academic area to be assessed and choose a task for the students to perform that will demonstrate their understanding of the content that has been studied. Design an observation instrument such as a rubric or checklist (see Figures TO.5 and Figure TO.6) or structure an anecdotal record that will itemize the abilities documented by the student.

• *Setting up a schedule*—Set up a schedule so that you can observe all the students within a reasonable amount of time.

• *Designing the task*—Gather materials and set up the task so that you can observe the students and document their performance. Plan an assignment for the rest of the class to do so that you will be able to observe without interruption.

• *Observing and giving feedback*—Observe the students, complete the observation instrument, and give them feedback on their performances.

PORTFOLIO ASSESSMENT

Portfolio assessment refers to a system for gathering observations, performance samples, and work samples in a folder or portfolio; analyzing the contents of the portfolio regularly; and summarizing the students' progress as documented by the contents of the portfolio (Herrell, 1996). Often students are involved in selecting the work to be kept in the portfolio. Students are also involved in the review and summarization of the work, setting goals for future work, and sharing the contents of the portfolio with parents (Farr & Tone, 1994).

This approach to assessment is particularly appropriate for English language learners because it allows assessment based on actual sampling of the students' work and the growth they are experiencing with less dependence on scores on standardized tests, which are often difficult for English language learners to understand (Hernandez, 1997). Portfolio assessment allows the students to demonstrate their content knowledge without being so dependent on English fluency. The focus in this approach to assessment is celebration of progress rather than focus on weaknesses (See Figure TO.7).

STEP BY STEP

The steps in implementing portfolio assessment are the following:

• *Choosing portfolio contents*—Decide what curricular areas you want to include in the portfolio and obtain baseline work samples, performance samples, or observations for each student, in each area to be included.

• *Introducing the portfolio to students*—Explain the portfolio system to the students, stressing their active involvement in the selection of materials to be included in the portfolio. Also explain the use of baseline samples and the fact that future work samples will be selected to demonstrate the students' progress. Involve them in setting up the portfolio and labeling the samples of work that will be used as baseline samples.

• *Scheduling performance and work samples*—Establish a schedule of observations and performance and work sampling that will serve to document periodic checks on the students' progress and provide updated samples of their work.

• *Scheduling conferences*—Schedule periodic conferences with the students and their parents to review the contents of their portfolios, celebrate their growth, and involve them in setting goals for themselves.

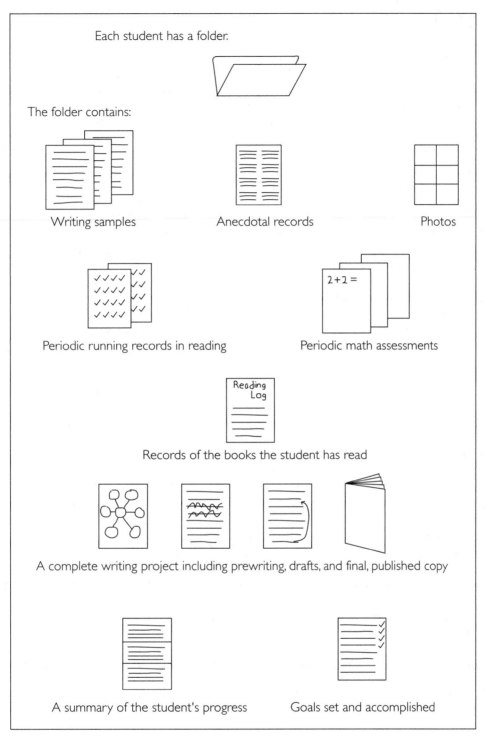

Figure TO.7   An Example of the Contents of a Student Portfolio

CONCLUSION

It is important for teachers of English language learners to recognize the essential ways in which they must adapt lessons and assessment to meet the unique needs of these students. Teachers need to understand the basic support that must be provided for English language acquisition in the context of the classroom. English learners can comprehensively acquire language and content if they are given the appropriate scaffolding and are assessed in ways that allow them to demonstrate their understanding and knowledge.

The format of this new edition of *Fifty Strategies for Teaching English Language Learners* is arranged to help teachers recognize how these students must be supported so that they can be successful in classes taught in English. The strategies are arranged in four sections: *Strategies for Enhancing Instruction Through Planning,* which focuses on the ways in which teachers must adapt their lesson plans and add supports for English learners; *Strategies for Supporting Student Involvement,* which focuses on active-learning strategies to provide English language learners with more oral and written practice in English; *Strategies for Building Vocabulary and Fluency,* which focuses on strategies for helping students to gain enriched understanding of English vocabulary and oral and written fluency in English; and *Strategies for Building Comprehension,* which emphasizes ways teachers can support students' understanding of written and spoken English and curricular content.

The strategies in each section are arranged beginning with the most basic, both in meeting student needs and in ease of implementation, and moving to the more sophisticated and involved strategies.

References

Collier, V. P. (1995). Acquiring a second language for school. *Directions in Language & Education,* Vol.1, No.4. National Clearinghouse for Bilingual Education.

Cummins, J. (1986). Empowering minority students: A framework for interaction. *Harvard Review, 56,* 18–36.

Farr, R., & Tone, B. (1994). *Portfolio performance assessments.* Fort Worth, TX: Harcourt Brace.

Garcia, G. E. (1994). Assessing the literacy development of second-language students: A focus on authentic assessment. In K. Spangenberg-Urbaschat & R. Pritchard (Eds.), *Kids come in all languages: Reading instruction for ESL students* (pp. 180–205). Newark, DE: International Reading Association.

Genishi, C., & Dyson, A. H. (1984). *Language assessment in the early years.* Norwood, NJ: Ablex.

Halliday, M. (1978). *Language as a social semiotic.* Baltimore: University Park Press.

Hernandez, H. (1997). *Teaching in multicultural classrooms.* Upper Saddle River, NJ: Merrill/Prentice Hall.

Herrell, A. (1996). Portfolios and young children, a natural match. *Kindergarten Education: Research, Theory, and Practice, 1,* 1–10.

Krashen, S. (1982). *Principles and practices of second language acquisition.* Oxford: Pergamon Press.

Krashen, S., & Terrell, T. (1983). *The natural approach: Language acquisition in the classroom.* Oxford: Pergamon Press.

McLaughlin, B. (1990). *Myths and misconceptions about second language learning: What every teacher needs to unlearn.* Santa Cruz, CA: National Center for Research on Cultural Diversity and Second Language Learning.

Rhodes, L., & Nathenson-Mejia, S. (1993). Anecdotal records: A powerful tool for ongoing literacy assessment. *The Reading Teacher, 15,* 503–509.

Swain, M. (1993). The output hypothesis: Just speaking and writing aren't enough. *The Canadian Modern Language Review, 50,* 158–164.

TESOL. (1997). *ESL standards for pre-K-12 students.* Alexandria, VA: author.

STRATEGIES FOR ENHANCING INSTRUCTION THROUGH PLANNING

The 10 strategies contained in this section range from simple classroom procedures to formats designed to support English learners in their successful participation in the classroom.

Many of the approaches that teachers use can be more successful with English learners simply with the addition of some planning. Some of the basic principles reviewed in Section I, the theoretical overview for teaching English learners, are exemplified in these 10 strategies. English learners are most successful when they are:

- supported by language that is contextualized (connected to real objects, visuals, actions).
- able to see and experience connections between new English vocabulary and their past experiences.
- actively involved in authentic learning situations.
- participating in classroom situations without fear of embarrassment.

The strategies included in this section are arranged beginning with the easiest to implement and build in complexity. Conscientious teachers will be constantly building their repertoire of teaching strategies. The purpose of this book is to support that endeavor.

The national TESOL standards addressed by each of the strategies are listed at the beginning of each. Depending on the grade level and curricular focus, the standards will be met at various levels. The TESOL publication, *ESL Standards for Pre-K–12 Students* (TESOL, 1997), is very helpful in suggesting progress indicators at various grade levels (pre-K–3, 4–8, and 9–12) for each of the nine standards. These progress indicators make excellent benchmarks to be documented in individual student portfolios.

Appropriate assessment strategies as described in the theoretical overview section of this text are also integrated into the step-by-step sections of individual strategies as appropriate. By using the teaching strategies in this section assessing student growth and understanding in a variety of authentic formats, teachers will be well on their way to providing English learners with the type of instruction and assessment necessary to help them be successful participants in ongoing learning sequences.

PREDICTABLE ROUTINES AND SIGNALS:
Reducing Anxiety

This strategy addresses the following TESOL Standards:

Goal 1: To use English to communicate in social settings

Standard 3: Students will use learning strategies to extend their communicative competence

Goal 2: To use English to achieve academically in all content areas

Standard 2: Students will use English to obtain, process, construct, and provide subject matter information in spoken and written form

Predictable routines and signals in the classroom are among the easiest strategies to implement and yet extremely important in reducing the anxiety of English language learners (Krashen, 1982). Because English language learners do not always understand everything that is said in the classroom, having set patterns, routines, and signals helps them relax and not worry as much about being able to follow the sequence of events and activities during the school day. If they know what to expect, they can focus more of their energy on the instruction and less on what they will be expected to do next. Routines that can be set and predictable include the sequence of the subjects to be taught, places within the classroom where certain things are stored and accessible to students, a certain spot on the chalkboard or bulletin board where reading or homework assignments are posted, a daily list posted that gives the routine in sequence, and hand or flashing light signals that indicate the close of one activity and the beginning of another. See Figure 1.1 for a list of predictable routines and signals that support English language learners in the classroom.

STEP BY STEP

The steps in implementing predictable routines and signals are:

• **Setting up your room**—Set up your room with certain areas designated for group activities, free reading, and partner work. Establish these areas with the students by modeling their use and asking questions like, "Will you work with other people in this area?" or "Where will you sit if you want to read a book by yourself?"

Routine	Use	Benefit to English Language Learners
Morning sign in	A way of taking role and indicating lunch count	Students feel a part of the class and that their presence is valued
Set activity at the beginning of the school day	A way to engage students immediately. Such things as journal writing, reading library books, tasks such as watering plants, sharpening pencils are appropriate.	Students know what to do immediately. Have a chance to share their evening in writing, sign up to share journal entries, or chat briefly with peers and teacher.
Set place in the room where certain activities occur	Students move to certain areas for group lessons, review, sharing orally	Students know what to expect when moved to a certain area
A list of the day's activities and approximate times are posted in the same place each day	Helps students get their assignments in order and know which books to get out, when homework will be collected	Students have a visual reminder of the day's activities, less reliance on oral directions
Consistent use of modeling and contextualizing of oral directions	Helps students to follow directions	Students waste less energy wondering what to do next
Use of hand signals, light signals	Helps student to redirect their energies, know when activity changes are coming	Students alerted to upcoming events, drawing to a close of activities and events
Posting of assignments, page numbers, long-term assignments, homework	Helps students stay on task	Students are aware of expectations
Set place to submit assignments and get materials	Fosters reliability and self-reliance	Students are aware of expectations

Figure 1.1 Predictable Routines and Signals in the Classroom

- *Establishing routines*—Establish a set place for students to turn in assignments; pick up needed materials; and keep their bookbags, lunchboxes, and other personal belongings. Model putting these things in the established places.

- *Modeling routines*—Model each new routine as it is established and be careful to maintain the routines once they've been established. Anytime a student shows confusion about a classroom routine or expectation, determine if a set routine would lessen the student's confusion.

- *Contextualizing directions*—Be consistent about modeling as you give directions. For example, "Take out your math book," should be accompanied by you holding up the math book. "Open to page 21," should be modeled and *page 21* should be written on the board. Modeling, gestures, and demonstrations are all vital ways to contextualize instructions. **Be consistent!**

APPLICATIONS AND EXAMPLES

Mr. Castle's kindergarten students know exactly what to expect when he starts singing, "Time to clean up." They immediately begin to put their materials away. They seem to shift into high gear when they see their teacher pick up a book and go to sit in the rocking chair. They all know it's story time. They quickly clean up and go sit on the carpet. They love to hear Mr. Castle read stories.

Mr. Castle has a set of predictable routines and signals that he uses with his 5-year-olds. They know that when the light on the overhead projector comes on Mr. Castle wants them to quiet down. He has several songs that he sings to give them signals about changing activities and he always puts notices to go home on top of the bookshelf by the door. If Mr. Castle forgets to give out the notices, he hears from 20 youngsters, "You forgot to give us our notes!"

Ms. Newsome teaches high school economics. A number of her students are English language learners so she has set up study partners for them. Ms. Newsome uses a simple routine to signal to her students when an assignment can be done with the study partners. She writes the names of both partners on the top of the assignment page when she determines that the assignment can be done in collaboration. When she thinks that the assignment is one that her English language learners can handle on their own, she doesn't write the names on the assignment paper.

Ms. Newsome has established a set routine that also serves as a signal to her students as to when collaborative work is acceptable. She also has some lessons that she puts on tape and the English language learners are instructed to use the listening station to listen to the tape and follow the directions step by step. Her English language learners know when she wants them to move to the listening station because Ms. Newsome simply hands a tape to Joaquin, which signals that it is his job to go by and tap the others on the shoulder. Ms. Newsome doesn't have to say a word.

CONCLUSION

Predictable routines and signals save a lot of time in the classroom because a short signal or standard routine lets the students know what is expected of them. The signals and routines also serve to lower students' anxiety and help them feel that they are fully participating in the classroom community.

EXAMPLES OF APPROXIMATION BEHAVIORS RELATED TO THE TESOL STANDARDS

K–3 students will:

- restate information given.
- give or ask for permission.

4–8 students will:

- follow directions from modeling.
- associate labeled realia with vocabulary.

9–12 students will:

- ask for information and clarification.
- negotiate solutions to problems.

Reference

Krashen, S. (1982). *Principles and practice in second language acquisition.* Oxford: Pergamon Press.

Suggested Reading

Diaz-Rico, L., & Weed, K. (2002). *The crosscultural, language and academic development handbook.* (2nd ed.) Needham Heights, MA: Allyn & Bacon.

VISUAL SCAFFOLDING:
Providing Language Support Through Visual Images

2

This strategy addresses the following TESOL Standards:

Goal 1: To use English to communicate in social settings

Standard 3: Students will use learning strategies to extend their communicative competence.

Goal 2: To use English to achieve academically in all content areas

Standard 2: Students will use English to obtain, process, construct, and provide subject matter information in spoken and written form.

Standard 3: Students will use appropriate learning strategies to construct and apply academic knowledge.

Goal 3: To use English in socially and culturally appropriate ways

Standard 2: Students will use nonverbal communication appropriate to audience, purpose, and setting.

Visual scaffolding is an approach in which the language used in instruction is made more understandable by the display of drawings or photographs that allow students to hear English words and connect them to the visual images being displayed. To use this strategy, the teacher builds a file of visuals, such as photographs or drawings, that can be easily accessed for teaching. See Figure 2.1 for suggestions of resources for visuals.

STEP BY STEP

The steps in planning and implementing visual scaffolding are:

• **Identifying the vocabulary**—Identify the vocabulary in the lesson to be taught that can be scaffolded with visual images, such as drawings or photographs.

- Internet image resources—for example, *www.google.com* (select *images*) or *www.Altavista.com* (select *image*)
- Teacher-, student-, parent-taken photos
- Illustrations in old textbooks
- Line drawings from old black-line masters or workbooks
- Line drawings from children's coloring books
- Illustrations from big books
- Children's artwork

(all of the above can be converted to color transparencies)

- Vacation videos
- Commercial videos
- Class-made videos

To make color transparencies from photos or illustrations:
- Scan the picture into your computer using an inexpensive flatbed scanner and print it out. Most printers require special transparency film.
- Take photos using a digital camera, download them to your computer and print them out as hard copy or transparencies. The use of photo-quality printing paper will greatly enhance the quality of the hard copy.
- Download illustrations and photos from the Internet and print out as needed.
- Take standard photos and have them converted to picture CDs at your local photo shop or take them to a local copy and print center to have them converted to color transparencies, posters, calendars, and so on.

Storing transparencies
- A three-ring notebook with clear plastic sleeves can be used to store and organize transparencies. They can be projected without removing them from the sleeve.
- Small transparencies of individual pictures can be stored alphabetically in a shoebox (plastic or otherwise) and be kept near the overhead projector for quick access.
- Digital material may be stored on the hard drive of your classroom computer, on small floppy disks, or on picture CDs for quick, organized access.

Figure 2.1 Visual Scaffolding Resources

• *Collecting visuals*—Find (or make) photos or line drawings that can be used to visually support the vocabulary needed for the students to understand the lesson.

• *Reproducing and organizing visuals*—Reproduce the visuals on transparency film and organize them so that they can be easily used during teaching. Sequential order works well for a specific lesson, but you may want to organize your growing picture file alphabetically so that the pictures can be used easily for future lessons. Since pictures to be projected on an overhead projector need not be large, they can be stored in a shoe box on the overhead projector cart.

• *Engaging students*—Encourage students to use the transparency picture file in their presentations or as a way of asking and answering questions.

• *Building the file*—Continue to build your file on an ongoing basis.

APPLICATIONS AND EXAMPLES

Visual scaffolding can be used effectively at all grade levels and across curricular areas. In Mr. Chavez's second-grade class he is teaching a social studies unit on community. Because his students all walk to school and many of their parents use the city buses for transportation, many of the students have never been more than a few blocks away from the school. Mr. Chavez tries to plan the community unit to build the students' sense of pride in their community. Mr. Chavez takes digital photographs of local community helpers and institutions such as the local post office, postal workers, the neighborhood grocery store, the local grocer, the crossing guard at the corner, a local firefighter, and police officer. These are all places and people with whom his students are familiar. Mr. Chavez then downloads the photographs to his computer and prints them out on special ink jet transparency film from the local office supply store.

As he leads a discussion of community helpers, where they work, and what they do, Mr. Chavez uses the transparencies to connect the discussion to local places and people so that the vocabulary being used is identified with people and places the students know. Hard copies of the original photographs are printed and displayed in the room with written labels so that the students can begin to learn the written forms of the words.

Mr. Chavez and his students then take a field trip into the central part of town where the students are introduced to a supermarket. Mr. Chavez is busy taking pictures with his digital camera and the students join in the discussion back in their classroom as they compare the pictures of the supermarket with the ones of their little neighborhood grocery.

"So many food!" exclaims Mercedes as she looks at the photo of the supermarket produce aisle piled high with fruit and vegetables. "Mr. Santos have only some," she says as she points to the picture of Mr. Santos's small store.

Mercedes' observations are just the beginning of the conversations Mr. Chavez hears among his students during the next few days. He has placed the photos in the writing center and the students are writing about the sights they have seen on their bus trip to the supermarket. The photographs have provided support in the students' understanding of their community. They have also provided a source for verbal stimulation and comparison that lasts for many days.

In Ms. Hammond's high school history class, her students are studying ancient Egypt. Ms. Hammond has transferred her vacation pictures of Egypt onto a picture CD, which she downloads onto her classroom computer and shares with her students. The students are enthralled as she describes her feeling of being extremely small as she stood in front of the pyramids. The students are particularly interested in how the pyramids were built and they listen intently as Ms. Hammond displays transparencies she has scanned from photographs in David McCauley's book *Pyramid* (1976). The students begin a glossary of words they are learning as they study ancient Egypt. They illustrate their glossary using sketches they make of the pictures she displays to support their discussion. As a follow-up to their discussion of the pyramids, the students form groups to research various segments of daily life in ancient Egypt. They add to their glossaries, work together to give oral presentations, and prepare transparencies of their own to demonstrate the facts they are learning about their area of research.

As the students present their reports, Ms. Hammond finds they have followed her example. All of the groups have searched the Internet for pictures and illustrations of costumes, artifacts, and reproductions of Egyptian art to support their presentations. These have been downloaded and reproduced as hard copy or transparencies to share with others in the class.

CONCLUSION

Although visual scaffolding requires some planning, there is an abundance of resources for visuals. Photos can be copied or scanned from books, magazines, and the Internet, and transferred to transparency film to build the picture file for use in scaffolding vocabulary and concept understanding. Photos taken on vacation can often be used in classroom teaching and may even make part of your trip tax deductible. Parents can often contribute photographs that you can copy or scan for your growing file. Send out a request for photos of hard-to-find items to give the parents an opportunity to lend support.

Line drawings, photographs, maps, and realia are not the only visuals that can be used in scaffolding. Video is another visual support that is useful. It is often possible to film brief video clips in advance of a lesson so that students get a moving, real-life scaffold as a topic is discussed. Again, vacation video is a rich source of support.

EXAMPLES OF APPROXIMATION BEHAVIORS RELATED TO THE TESOL STANDARDS

Pre-K–3 students will:

- retell interesting events.
- ask questions to satisfy personal needs.

4–8 students will:

- work in cooperative groups and follow task roles.
- paraphrase directions given orally or in writing.

9–12 students will:

- use verbal communication to identify expectations for class assigments.
- assist in oral presentations as appropriate.

Reference

McCauley, D. (1976). *Pyramid*. Reading, MA: Addison-Wesley.

REALIA STRATEGIES:
Connecting Language Acquisition to the Real World

3

This strategy addresses the following TESOL Standards:

Goal 2: To use English to achieve academically in all content areas

Standard 2: Students will use English to obtain, process, construct, and provide subject matter information in spoken and written form.

Standard 3: Students will use appropriate learning strategies to construct and apply academic knowledge.

Realia is a term for real things—concrete objects—that are used in the classroom to build background knowledge and vocabulary. Realia is used to provide experiences on which to build and to provide students with opportunities to use all the senses in learning. While using realia in the classroom is not always possible, it is usually the best choice if the student is to learn all they can about a topic. Realia allows the student to see, feel, hear, and even smell the object being explored. If the real thing is not available, the teacher must move down the continuum from the concrete (real thing), to a replica such as a model, to a semiconcrete object such as a photograph or illustration. However, each move down the continuum causes the loss of some sensory information that could be helpful in comprehension. See Figure 3.1 for suggestions of classroom realia that are helpful in the presentation of powerful learning experiences.

STEP BY STEP

The steps in implementing the use of realia are:

- *Identifying opportunities to use realia*—Be aware of opportunities to include realia in lessons as you plan. Preread any stories to be read aloud or used for reading instruction to identify vocabulary that may be unfamiliar to the students and locate realia that will be helpful to their understanding.

- *Collecting realia*—Begin to collect items that can be stored in the classroom and organize them so that they can be easily accessed for instruction. Plastic tubs or large clear plastic bags are often used for this purpose. Some items will be used with only one theme or book and should be stored with the theme materials or book. Yard sales and end-of-season sales at craft stores are good sources of realia for classroom use. Parents can often be helpful in locating and supplying useful items.

Category	Realia	Uses
Household items	Eating utensils, kitchen appliances (from different cultures), miniatures such as household furniture, old-fashioned items no longer commonly seen	Active experiences, vocabulary development, role playing, story reenactment, prereading activities, oral language practice, story problems in math
Food	Fruit, vegetables, unusual items unfamiliar to children; many plastic food items are available for classroom use	Sensory experiences, vocabulary development, acting out stories, grammar activities (singular, plural)
Clothing	Different kinds of hats, gloves, sweaters, jackets, boots, any examples of ethnic clothing to support understanding	Vocabulary development, story reenactment, writing support, oral language practice
Literacy materials	Books, magazines, newspapers, encyclopedia, reference books, checkbooks, bank books	Role play, vocabulary development, easy access for research, exposure
Farm or occupational items	Rakes, plows, harnesses, tools, baskets, hay, nails, models of barns, silos, scarecrows, wagons, farm carts	Prereading activities, role playing, vocabulary development, knowledge of size and weight
Flowers and plants	Examples of flowers and plants being studied or read about; unusual plants such as large sunflowers, pumpkins	Vocabulary development, sensory experiences, size comparisons
Animals	Classroom pets, house pets, farm and zoo animals, birds	Sensory experiences, vocabulary development
Crafts	Knitting, crocheting, tatting, sculpting clay, potter's wheel, spinning wheel, loom	Vocabulary development, role playing, sensory experiences, prereading activities
Ethnic items	Piñatas, chopsticks, wok, tortilla press, tea sets, clothing	Vocabulary development, cross-cultural experiences

Figure 3.1   Realia for Powerful Learning

• *Building a library of realia*—Collaborate with other teachers at your school or grade level to build a library of realia that can be shared for major theme studies. Locate local merchants, farmers, and other resources for the loan of large items such as farm equipment or animals.

• *Using field trips as realia*—If it's too large to move and your students' learning would benefit by experiencing it, take a field trip. Give your students the opportunity to really understand what they are studying.

APPLICATIONS AND EXAMPLES

Ms. Castaño has found a beautiful little bilingual book, which she wants to use with her third graders. Many of her Hispanic students speak very good English now but the parents are concerned that they are losing their fluency in Spanish. Ms. Castaño is always looking for ways to encourage the use of their primary language. The book she has found, *My Mexico—México Mio* (Johnson, 1996) is a collection of poetry in English and Spanish. Many of her third graders will be able to read both the English and Spanish versions of the poems and there are many opportunities for active lessons and vocabulary development in both languages.

As Ms. Castaño prepares her lessons for the next week she also gathers realia to support the students' understanding. Her school is near a little park where she will be able to take the students on a walk to see an adobe wall like the one described in the poem "Adobe Brick." Maybe she can even talk her father into coming to school and demonstrating how to make adobe bricks.

Ms. Castaño has a broom in the classroom and she finds a huge plastic cockroach given to her as a joke years ago that she will use with the broom for the students to reenact the poem "I am Cucaracha." She's smiling to herself now as her preparations for the use of this lovely little poetry book begin to get exciting. Ms. Castaño knows of a market where she can buy some gourds to use in making maracas as described in the poem "Gourds." She knows that her friend Marcella will be glad to bring her loom to school so the children can practice weaving as they read "I Saw a Woman Weaving."

After that experience she can teach the children to weave paper place mats and maybe one of the mothers will come to school to make tortillas as a culminating activity on Friday. She picks up two ears of corn to take to school so the children will understand how the tortilla flour is made.

Ms. Castaño makes a list of new vocabulary that will be learned this week and is pleased to see many new Spanish and English words on the list. Her native English speakers will be learning a lot from this week's poetry unit, too.

Mr. Millar's sixth graders are exploring survival skills through a combined literature and science study based on several survival stories, *My Side of the Mountain* (George, 1959), *Island of the Blue Dolphins* (O'Dell, 1960), *River Rats, Inc.,* (George, 1979), and *Hatchet* (Paulsen, 1987). The students are working in groups to explore the realia they have found or had relatives send to them from the areas in which the stories took place. In some cases they have been able to actually taste the berries and boiled twigs that the characters in the books had to eat to survive.

Mr. Millar has contributed some of the realia used in the study, like some of the more primitive tools that are no longer readily available. In other cases the students have used some of the raw materials described in the books to actually construct the tools and cooking utensils made by the characters in the stories. Now that the students have all read one of the survival stories, they are comparing the survival strategies used in each of the books.

"Most of the tools they made in the stories depended a lot on the wood and stone and other materials that were available in the area," Johan observes.

"That is very true," Mr. Millar agrees. "What else was affected by the location of the story?"

"The problems they had," Susana replies. "Survival in the Canadian wilderness is very different from survival on a Pacific island."

"I thought it was interesting that they had different plants that they used for medicine," Teresa adds.

"The botany books we looked at listed a lot of plants that were edible or used for medicinal purposes," Jacob says. "I never knew that you could eat boiled twigs, either."

"They sure don't taste too great," Teresa says with a grin.

"What could you eat if you were stranded around this area?" Mr. Millar asks.

"Twinkies from the Minute Market," Susana jokes.

"No, seriously," Mr. Millar says. "Are there any local plants you could eat?"

"My grandmother says they used to eat dandelion salad," Johan says. "We could try that. We have a lot of dandelions growing in our yard."

"See whether you can get her recipe," Mr. Millar says with a smile. "We're going to take a survival hike in a few weeks so we need to research the plants that we may have to eat. Mr. Smithson, the botanist at the college, is coming along just to make sure we don't poison ourselves. We will also have to gather indigenous materials from the woods to use as tools and cooking utensils. We have some research to do before we go, though. All we will carry along is a supply of water and some very basic tools like the stone and wood hatchets and a first-aid kit. But first, let's go to the Internet and see if we can find out what kinds of plants are indigenous to our local area and decide if they can be safely eaten or not. Then we will be off to gather our survival feast!"

The students looked at Mr. Millar with a wide assortment of expressions, from excitement to apprehension.

CONCLUSION

The use of realia in the classroom supports student learning in a wide variety of ways. Introducing real objects that can be seen, felt, and manipulated is a powerful way to connect vocabulary to real life. The use of realia is motivating to students because they can actually use the real objects in the way in which they are intended to be used. Realia introduces an authentic hands-on nature to many lessons. The use of real objects conveys meaning in a way that no photograph or illustration can. There is no confusion over the size, weight, texture, or smell of an object, fruit, vegetable, or tool when the real thing is present. In some cases it becomes important to provide several objects in order to see the range of possibilities, such as several different kinds of apples or tiny sunflowers to be compared with the huge examples seen in certain parts of the world. The teacher can be extremely innovative in the use of realia as demonstrated in the applications and examples found in chapters 22 and 39 in this text.

EXAMPLES OF APPROXIMATION BEHAVIORS RELATED TO THE TESOL STANDARDS

Pre-K–3 students will:

- associate written symbols and realia.
- represent story sequence with realia.

4–8 students will:

- compare and contrast real objects.
- represent information through the use of realia.

9–12 students will:

- describe change and growth in real things.
- gather and organize realia appropriate for reports.

References

George, J. (1959). *My side of the mountain*. New York: Dutton.

George, J. (1979). *River rats, inc.* New York: Dutton.

Johnson, T. (1996). *My Mexico—México mio*. New York: G. P. Putnam's Sons.

O'Dell, S. (1960). *Island of the blue dolphins*. Houghton Mifflin.

Paulsen, G. (1987). *Hatchet*. New York: Aladdin Paperbacks/Simon & Schuster.

INTERACTIVE READ-ALOUD: Reading Designed to Support Understanding

4

21

This strategy addresses the following TESOL Standards:

Goal 1: To use English to communicate in social settings

Standard 2: Students will interact in, through, and with spoken and written English for personal expression and enjoyment.

Goal 2: To use English to achieve academically in all content areas

Standard 1: Students will use English to interact in the classroom.
Standard 2: Students will use English to obtain, process, construct, and provide subject matter information in spoken and written form.
Standard 3: Students will use appropriate learning strategies to construct and apply academic knowledge.

Goal 3: To use English in socially and culturally appropriate ways

Standard 1: Students will use the appropriate language variety, register, and genre according to audience, purpose, and setting.
Standard 2: Students will use nonverbal communication appropriate to audience, purpose, and setting.

Interactive read-aloud (Barrentine, 1996) is the reading of books out loud with the use of expression, different voices for different characters, gestures, and the active participation of the listener through predicting, discussion, and checking for understanding. It also involves the exploration of the structure of text and think-aloud strategies that demonstrate how the reader gains meaning from text. This form of read-aloud is a powerful teaching tool for use with English language learners because it produces a strong English language model and it reduces anxiety in the students since they can listen and comprehend due to the use of voices, illustrations, and gestures (Smallwood, 1992). Students see their teachers as role models and in interactive read-aloud the teachers demonstrate what good readers do (Tompkins, 1998).

Although read-aloud has traditionally been used extensively with young children, its effectiveness with older students has been documented many times (Krashen, 1993; Trelease, 1995). This research has led some administrators of high schools with low test scores in reading and comprehension to mandate the use of read-aloud schoolwide on a daily basis—with very positive results (Trelease, 1995).

Interactive read-aloud is motivational. When students observe a teacher reading fluently and with enthusiasm they often choose to read the same book, or another book by the same author for leisure reading (Wood, 1994). The discussion of characters, setting, and description that is involved in interactive read-aloud provides shared understanding and vocabulary that helps English language learners stretch their linguistic abilities (Swain, 1993). It's been documented that students who frequently hear books read aloud have a more extensive vocabulary than those who do not (Trelease, 1995).

STEP BY STEP

The steps in implementing interactive read-aloud are:

• ***Choosing an appropriate book***—Choose a book that is above the instructional reading level of the students that will give you an opportunity to provide a rich read-aloud experience through the use of different voices, excitement, and drama. Set aside a time each day when you will read aloud interactively with your students.

• ***Prereading and planning interactions***—Before beginning the read-aloud sessions, read the book you have chosen thoroughly. Use sticky notes to mark places for discussion, predicting, and connections to other books the students have read or personal experiences they can relate to the story.

• ***Stopping for interactions***—Select a 10–15 minute section of the text to read each time, stopping at logical places between readings. Read with enthusiasm, using gestures and voices, and review the events of each day's reading at the end of the session. Discuss predictions for the next day's reading and involve the stud nts in relating the events of the day to their own experiences or similar literary experiences. Use graphic devices like story mapping or daily illustrations of the events to keep the students interested. See Figure 4.1 for an example of a story map.

• ***Assessing student progress and understanding***—Students' abilities to paraphrase or retell events in a story are indicative of their understanding of the story. While English learners may understand the story and not have the vocabulary or confidence to retell or paraphrase, they can often

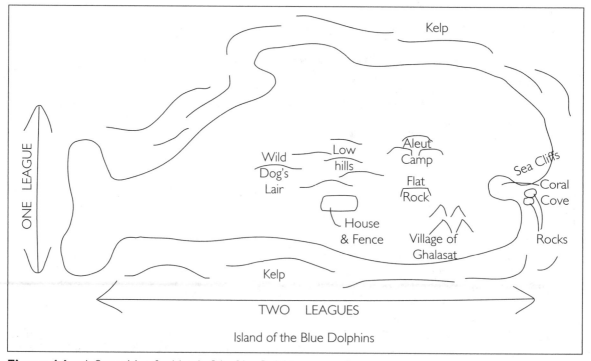

Figure 4.1   A Story Map for *Island of the Blue Dolphins*

draw illustrations or act out scenes to indicate their comprehension. To determine whether the strategy of interactive read-aloud is effective, pause occasionally to allow students to demonstrate their understanding by paraphrasing, illustrating, or acting scenes. Anecdotal records of these types of informal assessments can be kept in individual student portfolios.

APPLICATIONS AND EXAMPLES

In Mr. Castro's school district each grade level has been assigned five core books to be studied. Scott O'Dell's *Island of the Blue Dolphins* is one of the core books designated for fourth grade. Mr. Castro knows that many of his students will not be able to read and understand the book if they are required to read it independently. He decides to explore the book with his students using interactive read-aloud.

Mr. Castro reads the book to prepare for his lessons and identifies places where the students will need support in understanding the vocabulary and situations. He prepares the teaching points, vocabulary, and modeling that he wants to do as he reads and plans a half an hour a day for the read-aloud and follow-up discussion. Since the book has 29 chapters, Mr. Castro plans to read two chapters a day so he can complete the book in a three-week period. He marks the points in the book where he will stop for discussion, think-alouds, and vocabulary checks. He places sticky notes in the book to remind him of his plans to interact with the students and provide modeling of important comprehension processes. See Figure 4.2 for a sample of Mr. Castro's interactive read-aloud plan for *Island of the Blue Dolphins*.

After Mr. Castro reads each chapter he asks the students to tell him what happened in the chapter. The students dictate a sentence or two for each chapter and Mr. Castro writes the sentences on a large chart tablet. Later in the day the students may copy the sentences and illustrate them in their *Island of the Blue Dolphins* journal or write a different summary and illustrate it. Their journal also has a section reserved for the writing of new vocabulary learned each day. The students are given a

---

Chapter One
Preparing to Read
1. Look at the map and locate the Pacific Ocean and the Aleutian Islands.
2. Encourage discussion of times when the students have seen the ocean, sailboats, and tropical flora and fauna.
3. Look at the cover picture and predict what the story might be about.

During Reading
pg. 9 — Relate "Aleut Ship" to the Aleutian Islands on the map. Discuss the meaning of "it looked like a small shell afloat on the sea" and "it grew larger and was a gull with folded wings."
pg. 10 — Discuss the fact that neither of the children had ever seen a ship before. Think-aloud the possibilities and arrive at the inference that the island didn't have many visitors.
pg. 11 — Discuss the meaning of the first paragraph.
     Prediction Point —bottom of page 11.
pg. 12 — Discuss the meaning of *concealed, crouched,* and *ravine.*
pg. 13 — Discuss the meaning of the quote, "I come in peace and wish to parley."
     Discuss the explanation of the secret name and the belief that it has power.
pg. 14 — Show a picture of an otter. Discuss why the Aleuts were hunting them.
pg. 15 — Estimate the distance of 20 leagues and then look it up.

After Reading
1. Ask the students to tell what happened in this chapter and write their words on large chart paper.
2. Ask for predictions about what will happen in chapter two.
3. Review the means of *concealed, crouched, ravine,* and *mesa.*

Figure 4.2 Interactive Read-Aloud Plan for *Island of the Blue Dolphins*

challenge to find ways to use the new vocabulary in their writing and speaking each day so that they will "own the new words."

Mr. Castro has multiple copies of the book being studied because some of the students like to follow along while he reads aloud. There are also several copies in the listening center so the students can listen to a tape of the story if they want to hear the chapters read again. The students often use the listening center to review past chapters or to catch up with the story after an absence. Although there is no reason they can't listen ahead to coming chapters, they keep a strict code of silence about future chapters because "they don't want to spoil the story for the rest of the class."

Ms. Bosic is preparing her ninth-grade students to attend a performance of Hal Holbrook as Mark Twain. The students have read several short selections written by Mark Twain and want to hear *The Adventures of Huckleberry Finn*. Ms. Bosic knows that the students will benefit more from the theater excursion if they understand the stories they will hear and decides to expose the students to Huck Finn through interactive read-aloud.

After rereading the first few chapters of the book, Ms. Bosic decides to read the story in dialect and with a few props. She finds an old flannel shirt and decrepit straw hat and uses sticky notes to mark stopping points in the story. Because Ms. Bosic is interested in teaching the use of comprehension processes to her students, she plans to model the processes as a part of her read-aloud. See Figure 4.3 for an explanation of the comprehension processes.

Ms. Bosic introduces the reading of Huck Finn by showing the video of *The Adventures of Tom Sawyer*. She asks the students what they think might happen next with Huckleberry.

"I think he's going to run away," Ramon says. "He's never going to be able to live with the Widow Douglas."

"You may be right, Ramon," Ms. Bosic says with a smile. "We get to see in the next book, *The Adventures of Huckleberry Finn*.

Ms. Bosic opens the book and says, "Mark Twain begins this book with a warning and an explanation. Do you know what a warning is?"

"Do you mean a warning like, 'Be careful'?" Kelly asks.

"Yes, Kelly. It's something you say or read that tells you to be careful or that something is dangerous. Mark Twain starts this book with these words:"

Notice

Persons attempting to find a motive in this narrative will be prosecuted; persons attempting to find a moral in it will be banished; persons attempting to find a plot in it will be shot.

By order of the author, per G. G., Chief of Ordinance. (de Voto, 1984)

"What do you think Mark Twain is warning us about?" Ms. Bosic asks.

The students seemed very puzzled by the quote so Ms. Bosic decides to explore the word meanings. "Let's take the warnings one at a time. He says 'persons attempting to find a motive will be prosecuted.' What is a motive?"

"I've heard that word on television," Carlos says. "A person with a motive has a reason for murdering someone."

"That's right," Ms. Bosic says. "So Mark Twain says people who try to find a motive in this book will be prosecuted. What does that mean?"

"That's like the shoplifting signs in the stores," Katy says. "They say that anyone caught shoplifting will be prosecuted."

"And the lawyer who is trying to get the criminal put in jail is the prosecutor," Karim adds.

"That's right," Ms. Bosic says. "Mark Twain is saying if you try to find a reason for this story you'll be put in jail. Why would he say that?"

"I think it's a joke," Michael says. "He's saying not to take this story too seriously."

"I think you may be right," Ms. Bosic says. "Because he also says if you try to find a moral you'll be banished and if you try to find a plot you'll be shot.

"What is a moral?" Ms. Bosic asks.

"We studied that when we were reading *The Tortoise and the Hare*," Ramon says. "The moral of that story was, 'Slow and steady wins the race.' "

"Good for you!" Ms. Bosic says. "The moral is the lesson you learn from the story."

Process	Definition	Teaching Strategies
Microprocesses	Sentence level connections Making sense of elements within a sentence	Read-aloud, rereading for fluency, phrasing practice
Integrative processes	Connections between adjacent sentences within a selection	Finding cohesion links, referents, visualizing the connections between ideas
Elaborative processes	Making connections between personal experiences or other texts related to the text being read	Think-aloud referring to personal experiences or other texts that were similar to the one being read
Macroprocesses	Getting the main idea, the overarching meaning of a whole selection	Summarizing the text, stating the main idea, finding the topic sentences
Metacognitive	Monitoring your own understanding of what is being read	Stopping and taking stock and having strategies to use to support understanding Rereading, paraphrasing, looking up words, self-correcting and monitoring

Figure 4.3   Teaching Comprehension Processes

Adapted from: Irwin, J. (1991). *Teaching the comprehension processes*, and Tompkins, G. E. (1997). *Literacy for the 21st Century.*

"What does Mark Twain mean when he says you will be banished?" she asks next.

"That's when you are sent away and told never to come back," Carlos says.

"You are all too smart for me," Ms. Bosic says with a laugh. "You are doing a great job of making connections. You remember things from other stories or television that help you to understand the story. That's exactly what good readers do.

"Next Twain says if you attempt to find a plot, you'll be shot. Do you think he really intends to shoot people?" Ms. Bosic asks. "Or is he just joking again?"

"How can he write a book without a plot?" Karim asks. "This must really be a silly book."

"I think you've got the idea," Ms. Bosic agrees as she puts on her straw hat. "He also explains that the language he has written is the extremist form of backwoods Southwestern dialect. I'm going to try to read the story with that dialect."

The students are all smiling now. They love to hear Ms. Bosic read aloud. She always uses great voices and expression. They know they'll enjoy hearing the story of Huck Finn.

Because Ms. Bosic reads the story with the dialect of the people, she manages to set a tone that helps the students to relax and enjoy the story. She stops periodically to model comprehension processes like thinking aloud when something may be confusing or talking about something in the book that reminds her of the Tom Sawyer video. She stops every now and then and pretends to be confused by a pronoun, asking the students who is meant by the word *he* in that sentence or rereading a sentence to help the students make connections. She doesn't demonstrate these strategies constantly because she doesn't want to interrupt the flow of the story, but she gives the students a lot of ideas about how she is making meaning of the text by her short explanations and demonstrations.

At the end of each day's reading Ms. Bosic reviews some of the more difficult vocabulary and encourages the students to discuss the main events in the part of the story read that day. She asks questions that require the students to infer and she encourages them to predict about what might happen next. She is modeling fluent reading, obviously enjoying the story and using the storytelling mode with the addition of the simple costume and dialect.

CONCLUSION

Interactive read-aloud, while traditionally associated with primary classrooms, has been found to be highly effective in supporting comprehension and vocabulary development in older students. Even high school students benefit from hearing fluent, expressive reading of English text. By hearing literature read with the use of different voices, inflection, gestures, and body language, English language learners are supported in refining their reading and speaking skills.

EXAMPLES OF APPROXIMATION BEHAVIORS RELATED TO THE TESOL STANDARDS

Pre-K–3 students will:

- orally describe favorite storybook characters.
- orally describe personal experiences related to a text.

4–8 students will:

- describe a personal hero, orally or in writing.
- use words from books read in oral and/or written communications.

9–12 students will:

- respond to literature orally or in writing.
- participate in the performance of a scene from literature.

References

Barrentine, S. (1996). Engaging with reading through interactive read-alouds. *The Reading Teacher, 50,* 36–43.

de Voto, B. (Ed.). (1984). *The portable Mark Twain.* New York: Penguin Books.

Irwin, J. (1991). *Teaching reading comprehension processes* (2nd ed.). Needham Heights, MA: Allyn & Bacon.

Krashen, S. (1993). *The power of reading.* Englewood, CO: Libraries Unlimited.

O'Dell, S. (1960). *Island of the blue dolphins.* New York: Bantam Doubleday.

Smallwood, B. (1992). Children's literature for adult ESL literacy. Available online at www.cal.org/ncte/digests.

Swain, M. (1993). The output hypothesis: Just speaking and writing aren't enough. *The Canadian Modern Language Review, 50,* 158–164.

Tompkins, G. (1997). *Literacy for the 21st century.* Upper Saddle River, NJ: Merrill/Prentice Hall.

Tompkins, G. E. (1998). *Language arts: Content and teaching strategies.* Upper Saddle River, NJ: Merrill/Prentice Hall.

Trelease, J. (1995). Sustained silent reading. *California English, 1,* 8–9.

Wood, K. (1994). Hearing voices, telling tales: Finding the power of reading aloud. *Language Arts, 71,* 346–349.

ADVANCE ORGANIZERS:
Getting the Mind in Gear for Instruction

5

This strategy addresses the following TESOL Standards:

Goal 2: To use English to achieve academically in all content areas

Standard 2: Students will use English to obtain, process, construct, and provide subject matter information in spoken and written form.
Standard 3: Students will use appropriate learning strategies to construct and apply academic knowledge.

Advance organizers (Ausubel, 1963) are brief presentations of abstract concepts given before a lesson to help learners make connections between their existing knowledge and the new information to be presented. The form these organizers take should depend on the age, developmental level, and existing knowledge of the learner. Two forms of advance organizers can be used, depending on the nature of the material to be presented. An **expository organizer** is designed to present concepts and principles to the learner, which will help create a bridge between what is already known and the new material to be learned. This form of organizer is used when the new material is quite unfamiliar.

When the material to be learned is somewhat more familiar, a **comparative organizer** can be used. This form of organizer serves to integrate the new material with the similar material already understood by the learner and focuses on how the new and known material differ. This is particularly important when the new material may be confused with the previously known material (Newell, 1984).

Attention to the developmental levels and previous knowledge of the learners is very important when advance organizers are designed (Ausubel, 1963). The use of advance organizers with English language learners is particularly effective because their design depends on building on the past experiences of the learner and providing bridges to the new material to be taught. Because the developmental levels of the learners play an important part in the design of advance organizers, appropriate formats for organizers are shown in Figure 5.1.

Developmental Levels	Attributes of Learners & Suggested Formats for Advance Organizers
Preoperational preschool/ kindergarten	Need concrete experiences like field trips, hands-on activities, role plays, Venn diagrams with pictures, realia, photographs
Concrete-operational elementary grades	Depend less upon concrete props as they get older; ELL will still need some of the supports named for preoperational students for language development; activities like 20 questions, debate, oral readings, Venn diagrams with words can now be used
Abstract-logical middle and high school	Learners' dependence on concrete props decreases, they are able to go beyond the "here and now"; ELL will still need concrete props to demonstrate new vocabulary; activities like debates, use of biographies, current events, interviews are now appropriate

Figure 5.1 Appropriate Formats for Advance Organizers

STEP BY STEP

The steps in designing and using advance organizers are:

• ***Identifying the main concepts in a lesson***—Identify the main concepts or understandings the students must master in the lesson. Thinking about the previous knowledge and experiences of the students, develop a way to connect this previous knowledge to the new information.

• ***Designing a way to connect prior knowledge to the new concepts***—Design a visual, hands-on learning experience or discussion topic that will encourage the use of known vocabulary and relate new vocabulary to what is already understood. As you design the advance organizer, examine Figure 5.1 for suggestions as to appropriate formats for the developmental levels of your students.

• ***Presenting the advance organizer***—Present the organizer you have designed, encouraging discussion and questions. Relate the new vocabulary to known experiences and vocabulary using gestures, visuals, and restated explanations.

• ***Teaching the new information***—Teach the new information, relating it back to the advance organizer when appropriate.

• ***Assessing student progress and understanding***—It is vital to assess the connections made by the students. This can be done during the course of the presentation of the advance organizer and the teaching of the lesson through observations, anecdotal notes related to student interactions, responses, participation, and questions. It can also be done by asking the students to create a visual or graphic relating prior experiences explored in the first part of the lesson to those concepts introduced in the later part of the lesson. These graphics can then be examined for conceptual connections and placed in the individual student portfolios.

• ***Adding technology***—There are many ways in which technology is helpful in creating effective advance organizers. Videos related to the topic to be presented and PowerPoint presentations incorporating visuals downloaded from the Internet or scanned from book illustrations are very effective ways of integrating technology into advance organizers.

APPLICATIONS AND EXAMPLES

Ms. Flores has noticed that the only shape her kindergarten students recognize as triangles are isosceles triangles. To help them understand that all three-sided figures are triangles she designs an advance organizer to introduce a lesson on triangles. Because her students are only 5 and have limited English language ability, Ms. Flores knows that she must present the advance organizer in a concrete, hands-on form.

To build on the students' prior knowledge, Ms. Flores brings in five tomatoes she has selected because they all have different shapes.

She begins by showing the tomatoes and asking, "What are these?"

The students answer, "Tomatoes."

"How do you know they are tomatoes?" Ms. Flores asks. "What makes them tomatoes?"

"Red," Xiong answers.

"Round," Tina suggests.

"Yes," Ms. Flores agrees. "They are red and round. But they don't all look alike. How do you know they are tomatoes?"

"They smell like tomatoes," Nico says. "We could cut them open."

"Good suggestion," Ms. Flores says and she takes a knife and cuts two of the tomatoes in half.

"They have seeds inside," Michael says.

"Yes," Ms. Flores agrees. "We know they are tomatoes because they are red, they are round, they smell like tomatoes, and they have seeds inside."

Ms. Flores then takes out a green tomato, puts it on the table, and asks, "Is this a tomato?"

The students giggle and say, "Yes! But it's green."

"It will get red when it's ready," Nico says. "It's still a tomato, it's just not red yet."

"You are too smart for me," Ms. Flores says. "I want to show you something about triangles."

Ms. Flores takes out large cardboard examples of right-angle, isosceles, and obtuse triangles and places them on the chalk tray. "These are all triangles. They don't look exactly alike but they each have three sides." She runs her finger along the sides of each triangle as she counts, "One, two, three."

She then passes the cardboard triangles to the students and encourages them to run their fingers along the three sides of each example, counting the sides. She brings out enough examples for each student and they pass them around, touching the three sides and counting them. Ms. Flores then introduces a sorting game using the cardboard triangles and other cardboard shapes. The students place the shapes together, categorizing them as circles, squares, triangles, and rectangles even though the shapes within the categories are not all the same size. The students place the various types of triangles together and categorize them all as triangles.

Even though the students in Ms. Flores's kindergarten had previously recognized only isosceles triangles, they were able to use the advance organizer to help them understand that just as all tomatoes did not look exactly the same, there were different kinds of triangles.

Ms. Burton teaches ninth-grade social studies in a highly diverse neighborhood. She is planning a unit about pluralistic society in the United States and wants her students to recognize the value of diversity in society instead of focusing on rigid allegiance to their own cultural group. As she reads the information to present to the students, she decides to use an advance organizer to prepare the students to incorporate the new information with their existing knowledge.

Building on the old ideal of the United States as a "melting pot" of cultures and the pluralistic view of America as a "salad bowl" of cultures, Ms. Burton decides that an eating activity may help the students better understand the concept of valuing both differences and similarities in a pluralistic society.

Ms. Burton brings in a slow-cooking pot and a salad bowl to class. She takes some cheese, salsa, and chopped vegetables and combines them into the pot as she explains, "Years ago in America when people moved here from other countries, they were all expected to blend in together. America was called the melting pot of cultures. We're using this pot, or melting pot, today to demonstrate what happens when the cultures melt together."

After the ingredients melt together, Ms. Burton asks each student to take a tortilla chip and scoop some of the mixture onto their chip and taste it. After they have taken a taste, she asks them questions about the exact ingredients they had eaten.

"I think I got some peppers and salsa in my scoop," Angel says. "I definitely tasted something hot."

"Because the ingredients were all melted together, it was hard to identify exactly what you ate," Ms. Burton agrees. "This is exactly what happened to the new immigrants as they came to America. They learned to melt into American society and in many cases their languages and cultures were lost."

"My grandmother never lost her language," Jose says. "She stayed at home and took care of the children and only speaks Spanish to them."

"This is true," Ms. Burton says. "The older members of the families often stayed at home and did not melt into the American society."

"But now let's look at what happens in a society where the differences among people are appreciated," Ms. Burton says as she takes out the salad bowl and the salad ingredients. "In a salad bowl, which is the description of what happens in American society now, all the ingredients are mixed together. Instead of melting their flavors together as they did in the melting pot, each ingredient retains its own identity and flavor. The salad is better because of the variety of ingredients—lettuce, tomatoes, cucumbers, cheese, dressing, and even onions. As you eat the salad you can enjoy the unique flavors of each of the ingredients."

As the students enjoy small cups of salad, they talk about each of the ingredients they are tasting. "I like the tomatoes best because they taste sweet," Jesse says.

"I think tomatoes are best in a salad," Moua says. "I don't like tomatoes by themselves."

A bowl of salad is like American society today," Ms. Burton says. "America is strong because of all the different groups that have come here. The groups are trying to keep their identities and teach their children about their heritages."

Ms. Burton pauses to make this next important point, "In order for the different groups to keep their cultures and traditions and still be able to fit into American society and be accepted, we must learn to value and celebrate the contributions of each individual and group. This is called *pluralistic* society. It means that there is not just one right way to live, but that we can all participate in jobs and school and still celebrate our religions and cultures and even keep speaking our languages in business and within our family groups. For this to happen though, we must appreciate the ways people are different and the ways they are the same. Let's talk about these differences and similarities."

Ms. Burton then moves the students into a discussion of their cultures, languages, and traditions as the students help her make a list of these things on the board. She continues to use the terms *melting pot* and *salad bowl* to support the students' understanding of the importance of maintaining the value of diversity if a pluralistic society is to be peaceful.

CONCLUSION

Ms. Burton and Ms. Flores have found ways to help students build on their background knowledge by using advance organizers to help students understand unfamiliar concepts. By presenting an advance organizer before moving into instruction, teachers activate prior knowledge in their students, explore unfamiliar vocabulary, and support students in seeing similarities between familiar knowledge and new applications or concepts. The bridges formed by advance organizers are especially supportive of English language learners because they tend to reduce the students' anxiety levels and make English instruction more comprehensible.

EXAMPLES OF APPROXIMATION BEHAVIORS RELATED TO THE TESOL STANDARDS

Pre-K–3 students will:

- draw pictures representing their past experiences related to the topic being discussed.
- ask questions to make connections between their past experiences and the topic being discussed.

4–8 students will:

- verbalize relationships between new information and prior knowledge.
- Take notes about new information and relate it to prior knowledge.

9–12 students will:

- skim table of contents to determine key points related to the topic being studied.
- evaluate information and its relationship to prior knowledge.

References

Ausubel, D. (1963). *The psychology of meaningful verbal learning.* New York: Grune and Stratton.

Newell, J. (1984). *Advance organizers: Their construction and use in instructional development.* ERIC Document ED 298908.

PREVIEW/REVIEW:
Building Vocabulary and Concepts to Support Understanding

6

This strategy addresses the following TESOL Standards:

Goal 2: To use English to achieve academically in all content areas

Standard 1: Students will use English to interact in the classroom.

Standard 2: Students will use English to obtain, process, construct, and provide subject matter information in spoken and written form.

Standard 3: Students will use appropriate learning strategies to construct and apply academic knowledge.

Goal 3: To use English in socially and culturally appropriate ways

Standard 3: Students will use appropriate learning strategies to extend their sociolinguistic and cultural competence.

Preview/review (Lessow-Hurley, 1990) is a teaching strategy usually associated with bilingual classrooms where a teacher or instructional aide gives a preview of the lesson in the students' home language. The lesson is then taught in English and the material is reviewed in the home language to assure content understanding. This same strategy can be adapted to an English-only classroom by using realia, visuals, gestures, and vocabulary instruction as a part of the preview—making reference to the support materials during the actual lesson, and then reviewing and explaining the content of the lesson to the students using the support materials. Preview/review is especially effective in facilitating content knowledge acquisition because of the contextualization of the academic language through the use of realia and visuals. See Figure 6.1 for suggestions of appropriate support materials and activities for preview/review lessons. Also see Chapter 5, Advance Organizers, for additional suggestions.

STEP BY STEP

The steps in a preview/review lesson are:

- ***Planning and gathering materials***—Plan your lesson, identifying key concepts and vocabulary. Gather any realia, visuals, or support materials that will help the students to understand the concepts and vocabulary needed to comprehend the lesson.

- ***Introducing key vocabulary and concepts***—Introduce the important vocabulary and key concepts during the preview section of the lesson using support materials you have gathered. The

Realia	Visuals	Activities
Foods Household objects Animals Costumes of the period Music of the period	Transparencies made from photos Magazine pictures Line drawings Art prints Maps	Role playing Illustrating Sorting and labeling Lesson word walls Reader's theater Creating display boards Creating board games

Figure 6.1   Support Materials and Activities for Preview/Review Lessons

focus in this section of the lesson is NOT on actually teaching the lesson, but on making the students familiar with key vocabulary and concepts.

- *Teaching the lesson*—Teach the actual lesson, referring to the support materials and key vocabulary already introduced during the preview whenever possible.

- *Reviewing vocabulary and concepts*—Review the key vocabulary and concepts, encouraging the students to demonstrate understanding by referring to the support materials.

- *Providing additional practice*—Create a bulletin board or learning center that allows the students to practice the key concepts further through use of the support materials used in the lesson.

- *Assessing student progress and understanding*—Observe and document students' interactions with the materials and follow-up activities in the form of anecdotal records. Conduct individual conferences with students to give them an opportunity to demonstrate what they learned in the lesson. Anecdotal records can be included in individual student portfolios.

APPLICATIONS AND EXAMPLES

To prepare her second graders for a field trip to the zoo, Ms. Allen brings in photographs of zoo animals. She introduces the animals to the students using the photographs and creates a chart by displaying the photographs, listing key information about each animal, such as the names used for the baby animals, the type of food eaten by the animal, and the animal's natural habitat.

A map of the zoo is displayed in the classroom and Ms. Allen teaches a lesson on asking questions and gathering information during the zoo trip. Each student is given a clipboard with information sheets about each animal they will see. The class brainstorms questions they will ask the zoo guides about the animals and the students practice taking notes on their information sheets.

As a review of the lesson the students refer to the photographs of the animals and practice asking questions about them. The students are given individual zoo maps and they place the names of the animals they will see in the proper places on the maps. As they note the locations on the maps, they refer to the photographs and key information on the charts they have made.

The day of the zoo trip the students ask questions and note the answers on their information sheets. When they return to the classroom the next day they use their zoo maps and information sheets to add new information to the charts about the animals.

The students learned a lot about the zoo and the animals because they were prepared to ask questions during the field trip. By having the students practice asking questions, determining where they will locate the different animals at the zoo, and preparing them to take notes about the animals, Ms. Allen has given them an opportunity to fully benefit from their field trip. The students learned the vocabulary, language structures, and key concepts they would encounter on their trip.

Ms. Warren uses a preview/review approach to introduce vocabulary and historical settings to her high school English students prior to studying literary works. Prior to studying *The Great Gatsby* (Fitzgerald, 1925), Ms. Warren familiarizes her students with the music and art of the Roaring '20s. She uses transparencies of great art to familiarize her students with costumes of the period, plays music of the period, shows film clips from newsreels of the day, and engages the students in role playing to act out the vocabulary they will encounter in their reading.

During the reading of the literature, Ms. Warren stops whenever necessary to refer to the transparencies or role playing they did to make connections between the preview activities and the passage being read.

As a review, the students are asked to refer to the support materials or role playing to answer questions related to the literature being studied. The students are also asked to role play certain passages from the work to share their understanding of the motivations and emotions of the characters. Small groups of students are assigned short passages of the work to reenact and then that passage and key vocabulary are discussed.

CONCLUSION

Preview/review is an especially effective strategy because it helps motivate students to learn. The preview part of the lesson not only prepares them by introducing vocabulary but, when done well, creates an interest in the topic to be studied. The review section of the lesson gives the teacher an opportunity to make connections, correct misconceptions, and engage students in a celebration of their accomplishments.

EXAMPLES OF APPROXIMATION BEHAVIORS RELATED TO THE TESOL STANDARDS

Pre-K–3 students will:

- respond appropriately to gestures.
- rehearse appropriate language related to the formality of the setting.

4–8 students will:

- interact appropriately with adults in formal and informal settings.
- use English and L1 appropriately in a multilingual setting.

9–12 students will:

- preview assigned reading and ask questions appropriately.
- seek more knowledgeable peers or teachers who can answer questions related to assignments.

References

Fitzgerald, F. S. (1925). *The great Gatsby*. New York: Scribner/Simon & Schuster.
Lessow-Hurley, J. (1990). *The foundations of dual language instruction*. White Plains, NY: Longman.

LANGUAGE FOCUS LESSONS:
Planning Lessons to Support the Acquisition of English Vocabulary and Structures

7

This strategy addresses the following TESOL Standards:

Goal 1: To use English to communicate in social settings

Standard 2: Students will interact in, through, and with spoken and written English for personal expression and enjoyment.

Standard 3: Students will use learning strategies to extend their communicative competence.

Goal 2: To use English to achieve academically in all content areas

Standard 1: Students will use English to interact in the classroom.

Standard 2: Students will use English to obtain, process, construct, and provide subject matter information in spoken and written form.

Standard 3: Students will use appropriate learning strategies to construct and apply academic knowledge.

Goal 3: To use English in socially and culturally appropriate ways

Standard 1: Students will use the appropriate language variety, register, and genre according to audience, purpose, and setting.

Language focus lessons (Gibbons, 1993) are lessons in which the emphasis is on English vocabulary and usage, rather than the curricular content. These lessons may involve exploration of content such as math, science, or social studies, but the focus of the lesson is on the language being used rather than the content itself. The language selected for language focus lessons is based upon teacher observation and knowledge of the language forms and functions that give English language learners difficulty. Examples of appropriate language for language focus lessons are shown in Figure 7.1.

Language Form	Curricular Connections	Examples
Articles a, an, one, the, this, these	Words that indicate plurals, singular forms	Cloze activities, narratives with articles and numerical indicator left out, which might relate to any subject area
Prepositional phrases, position words in, on, under, beside, in back of	Language arts, science, social studies	Using literature that shows position, such as *Rosie's Walk* Math activities such as placing a certain number of things *beside* others or stacking things *on top of* others using number and position words
Degrees of obligation must, may, might, could, should	Predictions in science, literature, class rules	Discussion of class rules in which situations are discussed, and student choices compared with rules that *must* be followed Science experiments where hypotheses are being tested, students discuss what *might* happen Problem-solving activities in which things that *could* be tried are listed and compared with things that *must* be done
Comparison words smaller, larger, fewer, less, wider, narrower, taller, shorter, greater than, less than, equal to	Mathematics, describing in any subject area	Discussion of size of groups or objects, attributes of anything being compared
Content-related words	Mathematics, science, social studies, reading	Use of content words in context. Scientific terms such as experiment, liquid, solid, gas, presented with realia, multiple examples

Figure 7.1   Suggested Language Forms and Functions for Language Focus Lessons

▶ STEP BY STEP

The steps in teaching a language focus lesson are:

• ***Observing and noting language errors***—Observe your students and take notes on the types of language that they tend to misuse. Plan time to work with small groups of students who have the same needs for direct instruction in language usage.

• ***Gathering materials***—Gather realia, visuals, and ideas for hands-on demonstrations of the language usage to be taught.

- ***Explaining and modeling language usage***—Introduce the vocabulary and model its use, simultaneously using the language as you model. Give several examples for each term so that students can see when and how the language is used.

- ***Practicing in active mode***—Give the students an opportunity to actually perform or model a hands-on movement or activity as they use the focus language.

- ***Practicing for mastery***—Design an activity that allows you to observe the students' mastery of the focus language. If they do not connect the language to the actions correctly, repeat the third and fourth steps.

APPLICATIONS AND EXAMPLES

Mr. Lee is concerned because his second graders often leave off endings of words both orally and in writing. He observes and notes the students who are doing this and plans a language focus lesson for these students. During math the next day, Mr. Lee gathers six students to do an activity with joining sets and writing story problems. Each student is given a laminated picture of a lake with large lily pads and small frogs in green and brown. He instructs the students to pick out 15 green frogs and put them on the lily pads. He then says the following sentence, emphasizing the plural /s/ each time he says it, "There are 15 brown frogs on the lily pads in the lake. Six of them jump into the water to cool off. How many frogs are left on the lily pads?" As the students count out the six frogs he asks, "How many frogs jump into the water?"

The students answer, "Six."

"Yes," Mr. Lee says, "Six frogs jump into the water."

Mr. Lee then asks each student to repeat the words, "Six frogs," emphasizing the final /s/.

"When you add /s/ to the word *frog,* it lets you know there is more than one frog," Mr. Lee explains. "It is very important to pronounce the /s/. One thing you will notice is that when you add the /s/ to the end of the word *frog,* it sounds like a /z/. The 's' at the end of the words sometimes sounds like a /z/ but we still spell it with an 's'. We will make a chart of the words that sound like a /z/ at the end when we add 's' to them.

"We will put the word *frogs* in jail because the 's' doesn't follow the rules and sound like an 's' should sound," Mr. Lee says as he writes the word *frogs* on a 3-by-5 card and puts it on a bulletin board that has bars on it like a jail cell. "We will put other words in jail whenever we find that they are not following the rules. If you find any more words that are spelled with an 's' at the end but sound like /z/, be sure to tell me so we can put those words in jail."

Next, Mr. Lee has the students write the story problem about the frogs, emphasizing the writing of the "s" on the words *frogs* and *lily pads.*

"Mr. Lee, Mr. Lee!" calls Gustov. "We have to put *pads* in jail too! It sounds like a /z/, just like *frogs.*"

"Good for you, Gustov! You're a great word detective," Mr. Lee says as he hands Gustov a blank card and a marker. "Put that word in jail."

"Now, I want you to think of other word problems you can write using the frogs and the lily pads," Mr. Lee says.

After the students have a chance to write some problems, Mr. Lee has them read the problems aloud and the other students work them out using the frogs and the lily pad pictures. Once Mr. Lee sees that the students are adding the "s," both in speaking and in writing, he changes the focus of the lesson to the "ed" ending, using the same materials but emphasizing that the frogs already jumped into the water. Because the "ed" at the end of the word *jumped* sounds like a /t/ instead of /ed/, the children decide that *jumped* must also go to jail.

Jose says, "English is hard, Mr. Lee. There are a lot of rule breakers."

"This is very true," Mr. Lee says with a sigh. "But you are very smart and you will learn to speak English. Just look at the word jail if you need help with a rule breaker. Maybe we need to write the rule that each of the words breaks so we can remember. What should we say about *frogs* and *pads?*"

"They sound like /z/ when they should sound like /s/," Arturo suggests.

"What about *jumped?*" asks Mr. Lee.

"It sounds like /t/ when it should sound like /ed/," Tomas says.

"Let's put them in different cells!" Katey adds.

At the end of the lesson, Mr. Lee teaches the students a signal he will use to remind them when they are leaving off endings in their oral speech and in their written work. The signal he and the students agree on is a pinkie finger touched to the end of the nose. The students and Mr. Lee practice giving this signal to each other to help them to remember to carefully pronounce ending sounds.

Mr. Lee knows that one lesson will not solve the problem of the dropped endings on words, but he will use the pinkie to the nose signal to remind the students to clearly pronounce the /s/ and /ed/ when they are speaking, and to add them in writing. He also signals toward the word jail board to help the students remember how to pronounce the endings.

As the year progresses, Mr. Lee plans to teach more language focus lessons and add the other sounds for the "ed" ending as he sees the need. The children, in the meantime, are looking for more words to put in jail.

Ms. Karras plans to teach a language focus lesson with her sixth-grade English language learners who are having difficulty understanding words that describe the classroom rules. She plans a lesson in which they will review the rules and use examples to help the students understand the meanings of the words *must, may, might, should,* and *could.* To teach this lesson, Ms. Karras will refer to the rules and procedures chart shown in Figure 7.2.

Ms. Karras poses questions based on the statements printed on the chart. As Ms. Karras and the students discuss each item, they make a "requirement line" on the chalkboard, placing each of the "requirement words" from the chart along the line according to its strength. The students decide that *must* is a very strong word that means "every time, no question about it," and they place *must* at the far right of the "requirement line." They place *may* to the far left and discuss the word *could* in relation to *may.* They decide that *could* and *may* are about the same in strength. *Should* is discussed next. The students decide that *should* is not really as strong as *must* but in the classroom both words are often used to mean "It's required. You have to do it."

The lesson continues this way until all the words are placed along the line according to their strength. Ms. Karras then asks the students to think of laws and rules from home and the community that would be examples of each of the words on the chart. Cher suggests, "My dad got a ticket because he didn't stop at a stop sign. Stopping at stop signs goes under *must.*"

"Great example!" Ms. Karras says. "The laws are musts. Can you tell me why?"

"Because you can kill someone if you drive a car and don't follow the laws," Cher states solemnly.

"That's true, Cher," Ms. Karras says. "Can you think of an example for *might?*"

"If my mother has time after dinner, she *might* bake a cake," Tina suggests.

"Good example, Tina," Ms. Karras says. "She doesn't have to do it; it's just a possibility. Is there another word you can use in place of *might* in that same sentence?"

"If my mother has time after dinner, she *could* bake a cake," Tina replies.

"Does that mean the same thing?" Ms. Karras asks.

"Not really," Juan comments. "*Might* means she's thinking about it. *Could* means it's something she can do but maybe she's not even thinking about it."

"I think you've got it," Ms. Karras says. "Let's practice some more."

Ms. Karras gives the students cloze sentences written on sentence strips and asks them to take turns reading the sentences and decide which word from the chart completes the sentence best. After they decide on the best word, they have to explain their choice. When they finish this exercise, the chart looks like the one in Figure 7.3.

---

1. All students must respect the rights and space of others.
2. When finished with work, students may choose activities from the time management chart.
3. When choosing activities, students must consider any distractions their activities might cause and move away from students who are still completing work.
4. All work should be completed neatly and must be turned in on time.
5. Students must keep their voices low and respectful, being careful to avoid noise that could interfere with the activities of others in the class.

Figure 7.2 Classroom Rules and Procedures

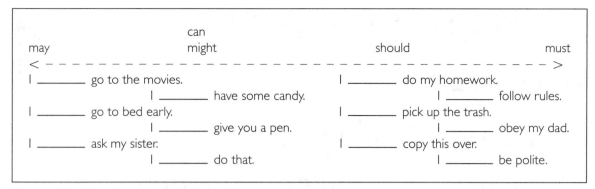

Figure 7.3 The Requirement Line and Sample Sentences

CONCLUSION

Language focus lessons are appropriate whenever the teacher identifies a mispronunciation or misuse of language that occurs consistently. The lessons can be used with individual students, small groups, or the whole class. However it is important with young students or those just beginning to risk oral communication, that the lesson not be allowed to interfere with communication. If a student mispronounces or misuses language but the message is clear, it is always important to respond to the request or message. The teacher should note the misuse and the speaker or speakers who misuse the language, and plan a language focus lesson to support the students in refining their use of English. Language focus lessons are most effective when they are presented in a positive way and the students are encouraged to practice the newly acquired skills in an authentic context.

EXAMPLES OF APPROXIMATION BEHAVIORS RELATED TO THE TESOL STANDARDS

Pre-K–3 students will:

- form and ask questions related to assignments.
- gather and organize materials needed to complete assigned work.

4–8 students will:

- find and use information from several sources to complete assignments.
- edit and revise written assignments.

9–12 students will:

- take and support a position on an assigned topic.
- prepare for and participate in an oral report or debate.

Reference

Gibbons, P. (1993). *Learning to learn in a second language.* Portsmouth, NH: Heinemann.

Suggested Readings

Chamot, A., & O'Malley, J. (1994). *The CALLA handbook.* Reading, MA: Addison-Wesley.

Diaz-Rico, L., & Weed, K. (2002). *The crosscultural, language, and academic development handbook* (2nd ed.). Needham Heights, MA: Allyn & Bacon.

ACADEMIC LANGUAGE SCAFFOLDING:

Supporting Student Use of Language in Academic Settings

This strategy addresses the following TESOL Standards:

Goal 2: To use English to achieve academically in all content areas

Standard 1: Students will use English to interact in the classroom.

Standard 2: Students will use English to obtain, process, construct, and provide subject matter information in spoken and written form.

Standard 3: Students will use appropriate learning strategies to construct and apply academic knowledge.

Academic language scaffolding supports students' successful participation in content-area instruction. Academic language is language associated with school subjects such as mathematics, science, and social studies. It places a higher cognitive demand on the listener or speaker. Jim Cummins (1986) identified two types of language that students acquire. The first, Basic Interpersonal Communications Skills (BICS)—or social language—is learned more quickly and easily than the second, Cognitive Academic Language Proficiency (CALP), or academic language. Academic language scaffolding supports the student in CALP, the language necessary for the student to participate successfully in classroom learning opportunities.

For students to participate successfully in academic lessons in the classroom, teachers use a series of scaffolding strategies that include modeling academic language; contextualizing academic language using visuals, gestures, and demonstrations; and supporting students in the use of academic language through active learning activities.

STEP BY STEP

The steps in an academic language scaffolding lesson are:

• ***Identifying academic vocabulary and language structures***—Identify the academic vocabulary and language functions necessary for the students to successfully participate in the lesson being taught. The vocabulary is selected from the reading assignments and explanations that are given as a part of the lesson. The language functions relate to the ways in which the student is expected to participate verbally. See Figure 8.1 for an explanation of academic language functions.

• ***Designing and teaching an introductory activity***—Provide an introductory activity that allows the scaffolding of both the academic vocabulary and language functions in a nonstressful way. If you start with a teacher explanation, support the students' understanding by using visuals for the main academic vocabulary. Then model the use of the language in the ways in which the students are expected to participate. If they are required to ask questions, model the use of the language in question form. If they are to take notes about a science experiment, provide a model of how the notes could be taken. If the academic language is complex and spelling is important, leave the words posted in the room and make it clear to the students that spelling is important and the words are posted for their use in spelling. If spelling is not vital, make that clear also.

• ***Practicing in pairs or small groups***—Include an activity that allows the students to work in pairs or small groups, interacting verbally so that they practice academic language in authentic ways.

• ***Guiding and monitoring the practice***—Move around the room during this active learning experience so that you can monitor and encourage the students' use of academic language. Provide scaffolding for the use of academic language by commenting on the work the students are doing, modeling the use of academic vocabulary, and describing the ways in which the students are solving the problems or working with the materials. When students are asked questions it enables them to demonstrate knowledge either by physically showing the teacher what was done or by explaining the process. Model the academic language as the student demonstrates the process used or restate the student's verbal explanation emphasizing the academic language.

• ***Reviewing the vocabulary and language structures***—Conclude the lesson with a review of the academic language. Offer the opportunity for the pairs or small groups to report back to the whole group again using the newly acquired academic language in context (see Chapter 28, Reporting Back).

▶ APPLICATIONS AND EXAMPLES

Miss Benninghoven's first graders are learning about things that are the same and different (see the third function in Figure 8.1). She introduces the lesson by showing pictures of the students' favorite foods they drew the day before. Displaying two drawings of pizza, Miss Benninghoven says, "Mia and Teng both drew pictures of pizza. They drew the same things. Their favorite food is the same—pizza. Maria drew a picture of a hamburger. Her favorite food is different. It is not pizza." Miss Benninghoven then displays commercial pictures of a variety of food. She chooses a picture of a hot dog and then goes through the students' drawings from the day before, modeling the sentence, "Moua drew a hamburger. A hamburger is different than a hot dog. It is not the same." When Miss Benninghoven finds a drawing of a hot dog she tapes it on the board next to the photo of the hot dog and says, "Jose drew a hot dog. His favorite food is the same as the picture. The picture of the hot dog is the same as Jose's favorite food."

For the next part of the lesson, Miss Benninghoven introduces the question, "Is it the same?" which requires the students to compare their pictures with an example. She displays a photo of an ice cream cone and goes through the students' drawings asking, "Is it the same as the picture?" If the students answer, "Yes!" she models the confirming sentence structure, "Yes, Hsi's picture is the same. Hsi drew an ice cream cone, too."

To give the students practice in using the academic language *same* and *different,* Miss Benninghoven divides the class into pairs of students and gives each pair a large sheet of paper on which she has photocopied a series of their drawings from the previous day. The pairs are instructed to work together, cut out the pictures of the favorite foods, and paste the ones that are the same together on a piece of construction paper. As the pairs complete their task they bring their paper to Miss Benninghoven and she asks them questions to encourage the use of the newly acquired words, *same* and *different.* See Chapter 28, Reporting Back, for a description of this strategy.

Tong and Moua bring their paper to Miss Benninghoven. She points to the group of hamburgers they have pasted near to each other on the paper and asks, "Why did you put these pictures together?"

Function	Definition	Examples
Analyze (mid-level)	Identify parts of whole, look for patterns and relationships	Using written materials or teacher explanations, the student is able to label parts and describe patterns and relationships among the parts
Classify (mid-level)	Sort or group by attributes	Describe the process used to classify Give examples and nonexamples
Compare (low-level)	Describe how objects or ideas are alike and how they are different	Explain how objects or ideas are the same and how they differ
Evaluate (high-level)	Determine the worth of objects, ideas	List criteria used, explain priorities, support judgments with facts
Infer (high-level)	Predict, hypothesize using information gathered from scholarly sources	Describe how inferences were made or hypothesize based on information read or observed
Inform (low-level)	Describe information or experiences	Recall and describe information obtained from another source or a personal experience
Justify and Persuade (high-level)	Describe reasons for decisions and convince others	Explain decisions and justify with evidence
Seek information (low-level)	Observe, explore, read to gain knowledge	Ask questions to gather information
Solve problems (high-level)	Identify a problem, determine a process, and follow steps to a solution	Identify the problem, describe the process used to solve it, relate it to real life
Synthesize (high-level)	Select, integrate information in new ways	Incorporate new knowledge into schema Summarize the processes used in integrating information from different sources

Figure 8.1   Academic Language Functions

Adapted from Chamot & O'Malley (1994)

Tong answers, "Hamburger!"

Miss Benninghoven models, "Yes, they are all hamburgers. They are the same." She points to each hamburger and says, "This is a hamburger." She concludes with, "They are all the same."

Miss Benninghoven points to the drawings of pizzas and asks, "Why did you put these together?"

Tong replies, "They all pizza. They same."

Miss Benninghoven smiles and confirms, "Yes, they are all pizza. They are the same." She then turns to Moua and repeats the process with her. The students were able to participate successfully in the activity because they were introduced to the academic language they needed, they were provided with visuals to support their understanding of the concepts, and they were supported in their authentic use of language to interact and to explain. The language was related to their experiences, and they were given opportunities to practice the use of the language in a nonstressful environment. By working in pairs, they were given support and more verbal practice. The teacher provided monitoring and encouragement. She also scaffolded and celebrated their success.

Scaffolding academic language can also take place at higher grade levels. In a middle-school classroom, Mr. Scott is introducing an integrated unit on living organisms. He starts by asking the students what they know about living organisms and makes a list on the overhead as they give him statements, such as:

They grow.

They die.

They need food and water.

Some are animals.

Some are plants.

Mr. Scott then reads a brief selection that explains how living organisms are categorized. After he has read the selection once, he lists the five categories on a chart and asks the students to copy the list onto a sheet of paper. He labels the list "The Five Kingdoms." Mr. Scott displays a poster of a castle and asks, "Are these kingdoms like kingdoms where kings rule and live in castles like this?" After discussing the difference in the king/castle type of kingdom and the living organisms kingdoms, the students agree that the living organisms kingdoms are divided into five because of the similarities between the living organisms in each kingdom.

Mr. Scott then rereads the original selection and instructs the students to list the living organisms that fall into each kingdom when they hear them discussed in the reading. After he completes the reading about each kingdom, he stops and the students tell him what to add to the lists on the chart. Figure 8.2 shows what this chart looks like at the conclusion of the second reading.

Mr. Scott displays enlarged photographs of the cells of the various organisms and discusses the academic language associated with cells (cell, nucleus, protean, and so on) as he points them out on the photographs.

The students are then divided into pairs to work with microscopes where they are given slides of members of each of the five kingdoms. They are to work together to draw and label the cells they see on transparency film and to compare their drawings with the enlarged photographs to determine which kingdom their slides represent.

Monerans	Protists	Fungus	Plants	Animals
• bacteria • blue-green algae	• protozoans • one-celled algae	• yeasts • molds • mushrooms	• mosses • ferns • seed plants	• birds • mammals • reptiles • insects

Figure 8.2 Categories of Living Organisms

As the students view and draw their cells, Mr. Scott circulates around the classroom, answering questions and encouraging the use of academic language.

After the microscope work, Mr. Scott displays the transparency cell drawings made by the students and they are discussed, focusing on the accuracy of the cell drawings and the labeling. The students' work is celebrated and they are ready to move onto independent reading using the academic language they have practiced.

The students in Mr. Scott's class are successful in their study of living organisms partly because of Mr. Scott's scaffolding of their academic language. He moves them through introductory steps in understanding vocabulary and the expectations of the tasks they will do. He encourages them to work together to provide verbal interactions and support for one another as they learn in an active mode. As he circulates around the room, he provides scaffolding by asking appropriate questions, while modeling the use of academic language and connecting the language being used to concrete examples of the concepts being studied. He also provides encouragement and celebrates the use of language by the students.

CONCLUSION

Academic language scaffolding is appropriate across curricular areas and at every grade level. While the words *same* and *different* may not seem difficult to adults, they are used in the classroom in a slightly different way than in social speech. Learning the multiple meaning of words, especially how they are used in different ways in content-area instruction, can be very confusing to new English speakers.

EXAMPLES OF APPROXIMATION BEHAVIORS RELATED TO THE TESOL STANDARDS

Pre-K–3 students will:

- identify and associate written symbols with words.
- use appropriate language when orally describing a school activity or lesson.

4–8 students will:

- use academic language in hypothesizing and predicting.
- use academic language to compare and contrast information.

9–12 students will:

- use logic and appropriate language to persuade or justify.
- use appropriate language to synthesize and apply knowledge.

References

Chamot, A., & O'Malley, J. (1994). *The CALLA handbook: Implementing the cognitive academic language learning approach*. Reading, MA: Addison-Wesley.

Cummins, J. (1986). Empowering minority students: A framework for interaction. *Harvard Review, 56,* 18–36.

Suggested Readings

Gibbons, P. (1993). *Learning to learn in a second language*. Portsmouth, NH: Heinemann.

Hernandez, H. (1997). *Teaching in multilingual classrooms*. Upper Saddle River, NJ: Merrill/Prentice Hall.

Hudelson, S. (1989). Teaching English through content-area activities. In P. Rigg and V. Allen (Eds.), *When they don't all speak English* (pp. 139–151). Urbana, IL: National Council of Teachers of English.

LANGUAGE FRAMEWORK PLANNING:

Creating a Framework for Language Success

9

Language framework planning (Gibbons, 1993) is a strategy in which the teacher identifies the language necessary for the students to be successful in a lesson and plans activities that support the use of the language in multiple functions. It is called language framework planning because the teacher creates a framework prior to the lesson that identifies the topic, activities, language functions, language structures, and vocabulary that will be a part of the lesson. In this way, language and content acquisition are both supported. The framework is shown in Figure 9.1.

Topic	Activities	Language Functions	Language Structures	Vocabulary
Shape	Sorting attribute blocks by shape	Classifying Describing	They are all (shape).	Triangle Circle Square Rectangle
Size	Sorting attribute blocks by size	Classifying Describing Comparing Contrasting	These (shape) are all (size). This one is (smaller, larger).	Large Small Medium Smaller Larger Bigger Littler

Figure 9.1   Language Framework Planning for a Kindergarten Sorting Lesson

STEP BY STEP

The steps in language framework planning are:

- ***Identifying language objectives***—Identify the language objectives of the lesson to be taught. These objectives should relate to the functions of language and the sentence patterns and structures to be practiced as a part of the lesson. To identify these objectives ask yourself these questions:

  - What are the language demands of this particular lesson?
  - What are the language levels of the students?

It is helpful to create a checklist on which you can record the functions the students use regularly so that you can structure lessons to give them practice in using new functions of language in a variety of content areas. A language function checklist is shown in Figure 9.2.

- ***Identifying and modeling problematic structures***—Identify the language structures that are likely to give the students problems and plan to model their use early in the lesson. If you are keeping regular samples of the students' language, these records are extremely helpful in planning language lessons as shown in Figure 9.3.

- ***Planning an instructional sequence***—Plan the sequence of the lesson by creating a chart like the one in Figure 9.1 in which the language functions, structures, and vocabulary are modeled and then practiced by the students as a part of the activity.

- ***Assessing and documenting student progress***—Plan a way to document the students' success in using the language in the context of the lesson and ways to build on this lesson to give them additional practice in the use of the language functions and structures gained. Anecdotal records and checklists are both helpful in documenting this type of learning.

Student's Name _____ School Year_____

Social Functions   Observed (date)

Asking permission									
Asking assistance									
Asking directions									
Denying									
Promising									
Requesting									
Suggesting									
Wishing/hoping									

Academic Functions

Classifying									
Comparing									
Giving/following directions									
Describing									
Questioning									
Evaluating									
Expressing position									
Explaining									
Hypothesizing									
Planning/predicting									
Reporting									
Sequencing									

Figure 9.2 Functions of Language in the Classroom

Adapted from Gibbons, 1993.

Roberto   January 23   Giving directions to Joey

Roberto and Joey are moving pieces around a game board. Roberto is telling Joey how to move his game piece. "No, put it by . . . put it by the tree." Joey places his piece beside the tree on the board. Roberto says, "No, not there . . . put it on the. . . ." He reaches over and moves the game piece under the tree. Joey says, "Oh, you meant UNDER the tree." Roberto nods.

Figure 9.3   Sample of an Anecdotal Record That Documents Language Needs

APPLICATIONS AND EXAMPLES

Language framework planning can be used at all grade levels and curricular areas to support language and content acquisition. For example, Mr. Gomez is planning a project using interviews to introduce his third-grade students to the ways information is gathered from primary sources or from people who experienced the events being studied. He wants his third graders to learn to conduct interviews, practice their oral language skills, and find ways to confirm information gathered in this format. He begins by reading several articles from the local paper concerning some recent decisions made by the city council, which will greatly restrict the amount of money being allocated to summer youth programs. The articles name the city council members who voted to lower the city's investment in summer programs. Mr. Gomez and the students list the names of the people who should be interviewed, including some of the people who lobbied for the continued allocation of funds for the summer programs. Mr. Gomez then begins to plan the language lessons that will help prepare his students to conduct worthwhile interviews. His language framework plan is shown in Figure 9.4.

Topic	Activities	Language Functions	Language Structures	Vocabulary
History	Read article from the newspaper	Describing Reporting Sequencing	First the council . . . then	Council sequence words
Research	Brainstorming	Following directions Questioning Planning Reporting	When did you . . . ? Why did you . . . ?	Prioritize Allocate
Visuals	Planning/ creating a visual	Expressing needs Expressing plans Asking for feedback	I will need . . . . I plan to . . . . Do you think . . . ?	Labels for materials
Oral reports	Presenting research	Explaining Summarizing Asking questions	First, I . . . . I found . . . . Do you . . . ?	Interviewed Documenting

Figure 9.4   Mr. Gomez' Language Framework Plan for Primary Source Projects

By planning ahead, Mr. Gomez is prepared to provide the support the students need to successfully participate in the primary source project. He knows that many of his students have difficulty coping with academic language, particularly in production. As a result of this their participation in class is severely restricted. To counter this, Mr. Gomez plans to model the language structures and allow the students to work together in small heterogeneous groups so that they can support each other in preparing their questions and interviews. Mr. Gomez also plans to encourage the students to work in pairs to conduct the interviews, requiring each of the students to ask some of the questions.

Mr. Gomez is aware that several of his English language learners are talented in art and he will encourage the other students to enlist their help in preparing visuals to accompany their reports. He has high hopes for the success of this project and his hopes are rewarded.

Language framework planning is especially helpful with older English language learners. Planning to provide language models for meeting needs specific to academic assignments supports the participation and success of all students.

Ms. Brock is preparing a lesson for her middle-school social science students to demonstrate how to prepare a project for History Day. Because her classes contain many English language learners she decides to prepare a language framework for the lesson. Her framework plan is shown in Figure 9.5.

As the students participate in planning their History Day presentations, Ms. Brock is able to observe and keep records of their use of the planning process and the language associated with the lesson. She can then plan subsequent lessons in which the students will have opportunities to use the history language that they are acquiring in connection with hands-on lessons.

Since Ms. Brock plans complete language framework lessons frequently, she decides that a simpler planning form is in order and adds a language planning section to her basic lesson plan format. She finds that this saves her time, but it also helps her to remember to consider vocabulary, language functions, and structures in all her lesson planning. Her basic lesson plan format is shown in Figure 9.6.

Topic	Activities	Language Functions	Language Structures	Vocabulary
History	Show video of last year's event	Describing Evaluating Explaining	This student is . . . . How could this be . . . ? How could you . . . ?	Simulate Display Research
Research	Demonstrate the planning process	Sequencing Describing Explaining Planning Reporting Sequencing	First, you . . . . Next, you . . . . You must plan and document	Sequence words Describe Reenact
Practice	Students walk through a simple simulation	Describing Explaining Enacting Reporting Sequencing	I think that . . . . This happened first. This happened because	Predict Confirm Cause/effect Document

Figure 9.5 Ms. Brock's Language Framework Plan

Lesson Title _____ Date _____

Objective:

Language Objective:
Vocabulary Focus:
Language Functions to Model:
Language Structures to Model:
Materials:
Motivation:

Procedure:

Closure:
Evaluation:
Provisions for Individual Differences:
Target Students: Needs:

Lesson Reflection:

Figure 9.6   Language Framework Planning Added to a Basic Lesson Plan Format

CONCLUSION

Although language framework planning is time consuming, it provides a vital link to the difficulties many English language learners experience in content-area classrooms. When teachers observe English language learners who are not participating fully in classroom activities or are finding little success in their classroom interactions, attention to the language framework of the lessons may provide valuable clues for ways to better support these students in the classroom.

EXAMPLES OF APPROXIMATION BEHAVIORS RELATED TO THE TESOL STANDARDS

Pre-K–3 students will:

- use appropriate language structures to ask and answer questions.
- imitate language and actions of others in interacting verbally.

4–8 students will:

- use context of reading materials to construct meaning.
- plan cognitive strategies to complete reading and writing assignments.

9–12 students will:

- use self-monitoring and self-correction to build a vocabulary .
- evaluate own success and set academic goals.

Reference

Gibbons, P. (1993). *Learning to learn in a second language.* Portsmouth, NH: Heinemann.

SKILLS GROUPING: Planning for More Individualized Instruction

10

This strategy addresses the following TESOL Standards:

Goal 1: To use English to communicate in social settings

Standard 1: Students will use English to participate in social interactions.

Goal 2: To use English to achieve academically in all content areas

Standard 1: Students will use English to interact in the classroom.

Standard 2: Students will use English to obtain, process, construct, and provide subject matter information in spoken and written form.

Standard 3: Students will use appropriate learning strategies to construct and apply academic knowledge.

Goal 3: To use English in socially and culturally appropriate ways

Standard 2: Students will use nonverbal communication appropriate to audience, purpose, and setting.

Skills grouping (Gibbons, 1993) is the act of arranging students in groups based on their need for instruction in a specific skill. Skills grouping is done for a short period of time, usually for only a few lessons, and is effective only when the groups are based on the teacher's knowledge of the language and skill levels of the students. The criterion for grouping is based on teacher observation of a specific instructional need. This greatly enhances the delivery of comprehensible input because the lessons are planned to scaffold learning at the students' present level of functioning (Krashen, 1985).

Skills groups tend to be heterogeneous as far as reading levels and overall academic functioning are concerned. A skills group might consist of students reading on a range of levels. Skills groups consist of students with a specific instructional need, for instance, a group of students who are not using quotation marks correctly or a group of students who need instruction in solving math problems involving fractions. Skills groups are used effectively in the teaching of language usage, reading, language arts, and mathematics skills.

STEP BY STEP

The steps in implementing skills grouping are:

• ***Observing and documenting language levels***—Set up a method for observing and documenting students' language levels, learning, and classroom performance. See the anecdotal records and performance sampling sections in this text for suggestions.

• ***Reviewing needs for instruction***—Frequently review the records you keep of the students' levels of functioning and needs for instruction and look for commonalities on which to base instruction. Form skills groups based on these commonalities.

• ***Designing and implementing lessons***—Design a lesson to teach the skill for which the group has a common need. Explain the skill, model it, and give the group opportunities to practice using the skill under your guidance. As a follow-up to the lesson give the students an authentic task that requires the use of the skill just taught. Observe the students' use of the skill in the assigned task. Celebrate with the students who are using the skill effectively and plan another lesson focusing on the same skill for the students who need more instruction. See Figure 10.1 for the cycle used in forming and teaching skills groups. Note that the skills groups are very flexible because future groups are formed on the basis of need. The students who achieve the objective of the lesson are not included in the next group of students reviewing the skill.

APPLICATIONS AND EXAMPLES

The fourth graders in Ms. Bersarian's class are writing simulation journals as they read their core literature books. They are taking the point of view of one of the characters in the book they are reading and writing in a journal each day as if they were the character. Their task is to write in the journal as if they had been a part of the action in the portion of the book that was read that day and "get in the head" of the character, telling about the events of the day and how they feel about what has happened. Although the students are reading a wide variety of books, Ms. Bersarian notices that there are several of the students who are simply summarizing the events in the stories without taking the point of view of one of the characters. She decides that a lesson on perspective-taking is needed.

Figure 10.1   The Cycle of Forming and Teaching Skills Groups

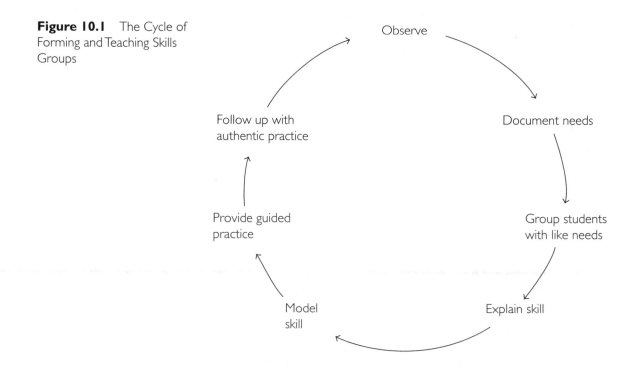

Fern	**Mr. Arable**	**Mrs. Arable**	**Avery**	**Wilbur**
8 years old	farmer	farmer's wife	10 years old	runt
passionate	practical	practical	heavily armed	white
outspoken	loves Fern	cooks breakfast	jealous of Fern	pink ears
fights for	willing to	helpful	sleeps late	good appetite
right	give Fern	supports husband's	wants a pig too	
	a chance	decisions		

Figure 10.2 Attributes of the Characters in Chapter 1 of *Charlotte's Web*

Because the students are all familiar with *Charlotte's Web,* Ms. Bersarian decides to use that book as an example in the perspective-taking lesson. She looks through the simulation journal and identifies the students who are not writing from the perspective of one of the characters and she calls the group together.

Ms. Bersarian begins by reading aloud the first chapter of *Charlotte's Web* to the students. She then asks the students to name the characters introduced in the chapter. As the students name the characters, Ms. Bersarian lists the character names across the top of the chalkboard. She then asks the students to tell what they know about the characters. See Figure 10.2 for the list of characteristics they created.

After the attributes of the characters are listed, Ms. Bersarian acts as the local television news reporter and asks each student to take the role of one of the five characters introduced in the chapter. Ms. Bersarian asks each character questions about the morning events on the Arable farm and the students pretend to be the character and answer the questions from the point of view of the character they are playing. The student playing Avery acts as though he were disgusted with his sister and the student playing Fern acts very excited that she saved the life of Wilbur, the runt pig. The student playing Wilbur, with the help of a pig puppet, tells the news reporter how grateful he is that Fern saved his life (Herrell & Fowler, 1997).

Ms. Bersarian has prepared five simulation journals, each one identified with the name of one of the five characters in the first chapter of *Charlotte's Web.* In Fern's journal, Ms. Bersarian and the students decide what Fern would write that day about her adventure. Ms. Bersarian and the students negotiate the sentences and she chooses one student to be the group scribe. Their entry says,

Dear Diary,

Today I saved a life. My dad was going to kill a runt pig just because he was too small. I grabbed his ax and held on tight. I said, "Would you have killed me if I had been small at birth?" I cried a lot and now I have charge of a tiny pig. Boy, is Avery mad! He wants a pig too. Dad says he only gives out pigs to early risers. Maybe Avery won't be so lazy after this. I'm really excited! I named the little pig Wilbur because it's such a pretty name.

Fern

After the group wrote the entry for Fern they did journal entries for each of the other four characters introduced in the chapter. Ms. Bersarian concluded the lesson by reminding the students that they are all writing simulation journals for the books they are reading in reading workshop.

"Today, I want you to do exactly what we have done with the characters from *Charlotte's Web.* Read your chapters and then tell the events in the chapter from your character's point of view. Pretend to be the character and explain how you feel and what happened to you," Ms. Bersarian says. "If you have trouble getting started, raise your hand. Or come back and look at the journal entries we made about the *Charlotte's Web* characters today."

As the students complete their simulation journals that day, Ms. Bersarian reviews them with the students. She finds that all but two of the students now understand what to do and with a little support those two students are able to take their character's perspective in the journal entries. Ms. Bersarian plans to monitor those two students' entries carefully for a few days to support their successful perspective taking. If the students are still experiencing difficulty, Ms. Bersarian will form a new skills group for the two struggling students and teach another lesson on perspective taking for those two students.

Mr. Tyler is reading his 11th-grade essays, and he notices that a number of the students are still having difficulty with the proper use of the homophones *there, their,* and *they're.* As he reads the essays he makes a list of the students who are still confusing these words. A little later he notices several students are confused about when to use an apostrophe in *it's.* Several of these same students are also using apostrophes inappropriately with nouns, sometimes creating possessives when they really need plurals. After Mr. Tyler completes the reading of the essays he has three skills group lists and decides that he will use some of the class time each day for the next week to work on these specific skills.

Mr. Tyler has identified the need for skills grouping in his classes. He has an additional problem because his classes meet for only 50 minutes and he must find time to teach skills groups while not wasting the time of the students in his classes who do not need this instruction. Although he is surprised that the students he has identified as misusing simple grammar and vocabulary in their essays are not all in his basic writing class, he realizes that he cannot ignore these errors in students nearing high school graduation.

Mr. Tyler designs a group assignment lesson that will enable him to teach the skills he has identified and still maintain the momentum for the rest of his class. Then he divides each class into cooperative groups. He calls students into a skills group to work with him on the skills he has identified. The rest of the class works in cooperative groups to identify a writing goal and design a presentation for the class using literature to demonstrate the ways in which different authors accomplish this goal. Mr. Tyler begins the class by conducting a brainstorming session in which the class identifies some of the writing goals they have. The list includes writing good dialogue, building tension in the plot development, using a rich vocabulary to make the writing interesting, developing interesting characters, understanding the use of metaphor and simile, determining approaches to creating and developing a problem and solution.

After the list is generated, Mr. Tyler divides the students into cooperative groups, placing one student from his skills group into each of the cooperative groups. The cooperative groups each identify a goal they want to research and begin to look at the literature they have been reading for good examples.

Mr. Tyler calls his skills group together and introduces the problem he has discovered in reading their essays, "I will be working with this small group for a short time each day for a while to help you to overcome a problem that I discovered in reading your essays," he begins. Mr. Tyler gives an explanation of the differences among the homophones *there, their,* and *they're* and how important it is that the words be used correctly. He sends the students back to their cooperative groups to begin to look for the examples needed for the group presentations on the way the professional writers approach the goals identified by the class. The skills group has one added task. They are to find sentences in the literature that demonstrate the correct usage of the homophones they are studying and copy at least one sentence that employs each of the homophones. For homework that night the skills group is assigned a paragraph to be written about an imaginary group of people. The skills group is to find a way to use all three forms of the homophone in their paragraph.

Mr. Tyler finds that the system he has set up works well. He identifies needs for skills groups and then provides time for cooperative group work, which can continue while he conducts quick skills instruction. He follows up with short assignments in which he monitors for understanding of the skills. He uses one additional technique to help the students in monitoring their own progress. He duplicates copies of the skill or vocabulary rules for the students to attach to the inside cover of their writing folders. Before they turn in any assignments they must work collaboratively with another student on editing, proofreading their writing for the types of errors that give them difficulty. Mr. Tyler finds that making the students aware of the errors they are committing helps them to self-monitor and self-correct. They are refining their use of the English language (Swain, 1993).

CONCLUSION

Skills grouping is a way to provide focused instruction for small groups of students with shared needs. Because skills groups are created to address a specific need, they are not long-standing groups. Instruction is given, skills are practiced and monitored, and the groups change. If some students require further instruction, that instruction is provided, but only for those who need it. This form of grouping is effective because students are receiving lessons tailored to their needs and the other students in the class are given assignments that allow them to practice their skills at appropriate levels without being bored by instruction they do not need.

EXAMPLES OF APPROXIMATION BEHAVIORS RELATED TO THE TESOL STANDARDS

Pre-K–3 students will:

- express needs and ideas.
- engage in verbal interaction in English.

4–8 students will:

- follow both implicit and explicit oral directions.
- elaborate on ideas of others.

9–12 students will:

- participate actively in small group interactions.
- listen to and expand on the verbal explanations of others.

References

Gibbons, P. (1993). *Learning to learn in a second language.* Portsmouth, NH: Heinemann.

Herrell, A., & Fowler, J. (1997). *Camcorder in the classroom: Using the video camera to enrich curriculum.* Upper Saddle River, NJ: Merrill/Prentice Hall.

Krashen, S. (1985). *The input hypothesis: Issues and implications.* New York: Longman.

Swain, M. (1993). The output hypothesis: Just speaking and writing aren't enough. *The Canadian Modern Language Review, 50,* 158–164.

White, E. B. (1952). *Charlotte's web.* New York: Harper & Row.

STRATEGIES FOR SUPPORTING STUDENT INVOLVEMENT

The 16 strategies included in this section provide ways for teachers to actively involve students in learning. The research in language acquisition and student motivation overwhelmingly support the importance of student engagement in facilitating student learning.

We begin the involvement strategies with a simple and almost remarkably effective one: Total Physical Response. This strategy has been the single most frequently used approach to transitioning students from their home languages to a second language.

All of the strategies in this section build heavily on language acquisition research which stresses the importance of providing English learners with multiple opportunities to interact in English in non-stressful settings.

All the strategies require teachers to observe students carefully to monitor their progress and successfully adapt lessons to meet their individual needs. Giving students opportunities to practice their growing English skills in partner- and small-group settings also gives teachers more opportunities to observe, document, and celebrate their progress.

Use of the sample progress indicators included in the national TESOL standards is especially appropriate in observing students in small-group settings. These progress indicators are listed standard by standard within each grade level range in the TESOL publication *ESL Standards for Pre-K-12 Students* (TESOL, 1997). These sample progress indicators are descriptive of student behaviors that document student growth. For example, the pre-K–3 standard, "Students will use English to participate in social interactions" includes the following progress indicators (among others):

- Elicit information and ask clarification questions.
- Clarify and restate information as needed.
- Indicate interests, opinions, or preferences related to class projects.

It is easy to use these progress indicators as benchmarks by which to focus anecdotal records of student observations by adding a description of the individual student's verbal interactions to the progress indicator. For example the indicator "elicit information and ask clarification questions" can be validated by the following anecdotal record: "Jose listened closely to the explanation of how to make a puppet and then asked, 'Use glue?' I answered, 'You can use glue, or staples will work.' He picked up the stapler and pretended to use it saying, 'Staple the puppet?' I then demonstrated how to use the stapler and he responded with a big grin."

The use of active-involvement activities in the classroom setting serves the English learners well. It gives them opportunities to practice and demonstrate their English skills and gives you, the teacher, many authentic situations in which you can observe, document, and celebrate student progress.

TOTAL PHYSICAL RESPONSE:
Integrating Movement Into Language Acquisition

11

This strategy addresses the following TESOL Standards:

Goal 1: To use English to communicate in social settings

Standard 3: Students will use learning strategies to extend their communicative competence.

Goal 3: To use English in socially and culturally appropriate ways

Standard 2: Students will use nonverbal communication appropriate to audience, purpose, and setting.

Standard 3: Students will use appropriate learning strategies to extend their sociolinguistic and cultural competence.

Total physical response (Asher, 1982) is an approach to second language acquisition based on first language acquisition research. In first language acquisition, children listen and acquire receptive language before they attempt to speak, they develop understanding through moving their bodies, and they are not forced to speak until they are ready. In total physical response, the teacher gradually introduces commands, acting them out as she says them. The students initially respond by performing the actions as the teacher demonstrates them. Gradually the teacher's demonstrations are removed and the students respond to the verbal commands only.

STEP BY STEP

The steps in teaching a total physical response lesson are:

• *Choosing vocabulary to physicalize*—Choose vocabulary that will be used in the class-room, such as verbal directions, colors, and parts of the body, and list the words the students will need to know. Think of simple commands that can be given using the target vocabulary and that require a movement response such as "Stand up," "Sit down," "Touch your head," or "Show me the red block."

• *Introducing vocabulary gradually*—Introduce two or three commands at first, giving the command while demonstrating physically. For example, "Stand up" is accompanied by standing up. Motion for the students to do it with you. Introduce the next command and demonstrate. After you have introduced three commands, randomly alternate them, still demonstrating and encouraging the students' responses.

• *Dropping the physical modeling*—After the students have practiced the commands as you demonstrate each time, and they appear to know what to do without waiting for your demonstration, drop the demonstration and encourage them to respond to the verbal commands.

• *Adding additional commands*—Add new commands, no more than three at a time. Always start with demonstrations as you introduce new commands, practice until the students appear to know what to do, and then drop the demonstrations.

• *Adding additional responses*—Find new ways for the students to demonstrate their understanding of the vocabulary being practiced—such as pointing to pictures, drawing pictures, taking turns demonstrating commands—just to add practice and variety while the students are gaining confidence.

• *Playing games for additional practice*—Play a game with a student volunteer giving the commands once the students gain confidence. Gradually encourage new student volunteers to give the commands as they become comfortable speaking the words. Never force students to speak the commands. Wait until they are confident enough to volunteer.

• *Assessing student progress and understanding*—Because students are responding to commands with physical movements it is easy to document their progress. Make a checklist of the commands you have taught and keep track of the commands that students know automatically, those which still require modeling, and be sure to document when students volunteer to be leaders in the games being played for practice. Share the things you have documented with the students and celebrate together.

APPLICATIONS AND EXAMPLES

Mr. Tong's kindergartners are learning the names of body parts. Because he has a number of English language learners in the class, Mr. Tong decides to use total physical response to support their understanding of the English names for the parts of the body. He begins the lesson by saying, "Point to your head," as he demonstrates. He motions for the students to join him in touching their heads, nods, and smiles as they follow his lead. He then introduces, "Touch your chin," as he demonstrates. He alternates the two commands for a few minutes and then adds, "Touch your nose."

Mr. Tong repeats these three commands several times before he drops the demonstrations and gives just the verbal commands. He watches the students carefully as he drops the demonstrations to make sure that the students are still able to follow along. He continues this game for a few days, until the students respond to commands to touch or point to their heads, chins, noses, ears, eyes, shoulders, feet, toes, knees, hands, arms, and elbows.

Mr. Tong changes games once he observes the students responding to verbal commands to identify each of the parts of the body. The second game he plays with the students involves their drawing body parts on a big chart. Mr. Tong begins by drawing a circle. He accompanies the drawing of the circle with the statement, "I am drawing a head."

He then asks for volunteers to draw each of the rest of the body parts on the chart. He follows the drawing of the body with requests for students to come up and point to body parts of the drawing.

Mr. Tong notices that several of the students are using the names of the body parts in their oral communications in the classroom, so he plans a game that will involve students giving directions in

English. Mr. Tong begins the game by demonstrating. He pairs the students and tells them to touch heads, and he demonstrates with his partner. Then he tells them to touch hands, demonstrating with his partner. He asks for a volunteer to give the directions and one child eagerly raises his hand. Mr. Tong gives up his partner to pair him with the volunteer child's partner and helps the volunteer to demonstrate the commands as the student gives the directions and the others follow them. This game is played for a few minutes a day for about a week to give additional volunteers a chance to be the leader. Even the native English speakers enjoy playing.

Ms. Lopez teaches seventh-grade science and she is concerned about safety with her students. Because she wants to make sure that everyone understands the safety procedures, she decides to teach them through a total physical response lesson. She introduces the terms *pitcher, beaker,* and *Bunsen burner,* and the directions "tip the beaker" and "pour carefully" at the beginning of the lesson with the burners turned off. She demonstrates exactly how to tip the beakers to make sure the liquid doesn't splash as she says, "Tip the beaker slowly toward the pitcher and pour carefully."

After she is sure that the students understand the terms and directions with the accompanying demonstration, she repeats the directions without demonstrating as she walks around the room.

Ms. Lopez observes the students as they practice transferring liquid from the pitcher to the beaker and placing the beaker into the holders, and she feels much more confident about their understanding of the safety precautions. The next day she plans to introduce the lighting of the burners and the procedures to be followed in case of an emergency. She will review today's lesson before she introduces a new one, however.

CONCLUSION

Although total physical responses are generally used with young children or English language learners with very little English knowledge, they can be used to introduce new procedures and vocabulary at almost any level. Figure 11.1 shows many ways in which this strategy is effective.

Total physical response is an active learning approach for supporting comprehension in a low-anxiety atmosphere (Krashen & Terrell, 1983). For this reason it is very popular with English language learners and teachers alike. Total physical response is also highly effective in teaching vocabulary associated with content-area knowledge. Teachers can introduce vocabulary and have students respond by drawing, pointing, putting pictures in order, or any other physical response that encourages active involvement and verifies understanding.

- Movement directions (stand up, sit down, line up, walk, run, kneel, skip, hop, etc.)
- Students' names
- Color words
- Number words
- Shapes
- Body parts
- Prepositional phrases
- Directions (up, down, left, right, high, low, etc.)
- Classroom procedures
- Content vocabulary/picture sorts

Figure 11.1 Applications for Total Physical Response

EXAMPLES OF APPROXIMATION BEHAVIORS RELATED TO THE TESOL STANDARDS

Pre-K–3 students will:

- observe and imitate motions of others.
- use practiced motion appropriately in class.

4–8 students will:

- use knowledge of the classroom setting to determine acceptable behavior.
- use observations to determine appropriate physical responses.

9–12 students will:

- observe and imitate the speech and actions appropriate in a particular given situation.
- vary oral responses according to social settings.

References

Asher, J. (1982). *Learning another language through actions: The complete teachers' guidebook.* Los Gatos, CA: Sky Oaks.

Krashen, S., & Terrell, T. (1983). *The natural approach: Language acquisition in the classroom.* Oxford: Pergamon Press.

SHARED READING:
Demonstrating How Reading Works

This strategy addresses the following TESOL Standards:

Goal 1: To use English to communicate in social settings

Standard 1: Students will use English to participate in social interactions.
Standard 2: Students will interact in, through, and with spoken and written English for personal expression and enjoyment.
Standard 3: Students will use learning strategies to extend their communicative competence.

Goal 2: To use English to achieve academically in all content areas

Standard 1: Students will use English to interact in the classroom.
Standard 2: Students will use English to obtain, process, construct, and provide subject matter information in spoken and written form.
Standard 3: Students will use appropriate learning strategies to construct and apply academic knowledge.

Shared reading (Holdaway, 1979) is a strategy that teachers use to read books, charts, and other texts with students when the text is too difficult for the students to read independently. Students and teacher read the text aloud together. Even when the students cannot read along with the teacher, they are hearing the words pronounced as their eyes follow the text. In the primary grades, large books with big print—called big books—are used with small groups of students so that everyone can see the illustrations and text (Depree & Iversen, 1996). Shared reading can also be done with multiple copies of small books, poetry charts, song lyrics, or any text as long as students and teacher can all see the words (Tompkins, 1997).

Using shared reading with English language learners is appropriate because the teacher has opportunities to use illustrations to support vocabulary development, to use think-aloud strategies to teach problem-solving approaches, and to integrate verbal interactions to support comprehension (Gibbons, 1993). When using shared reading with English language learners it becomes especially important to build background knowledge and experiences that help the students to understand the meaning of the text. The skills and strategies that can be taught through shared reading are shown in Figure 12.1.

Guided Reading Applications	Example
Word boundaries	"Frame the word *caps* in this sentence."
Left to right progression	"Point to the words with the pointer."
Punctuation uses	"How would you say this sentence?"
Word meaning	"Show me the dahlias in the picture."
Illustrations/story meaning	"How did you know he was scared?"
Cuing systems—visual, meaning, syntax	"How did you know the word was *monkeys?*" "Show me the picture that shows you what that word means." "Would we say, 'The boy went jeans'?"
Reading with expression	"How would he say that?"
Fix-it strategies	"How would it start if the word were lantern? Read it again."
Use of context for meaning	"Read the part that helps you understand what the word *flourish* means."
Reading for cohesion links	"Read the part that tells you that he heard the noise after he went to bed."
Reading to confirm	"Read the part that tells you why he was angry."

Figure 12.1   Skills and Strategies to Teach Through Shared Reading

STEP BY STEP

• ***Introducing the text***—Introduce the book or text. When using a book, examine the cover and predict from the illustrations on the cover. Encourage the students to talk about experiences they have had that relate to the topic of the book, chart, or poem.

• ***Reading the book and tracking the print***—Read the book or other text aloud, tracking the words as you read so the students can read along. Use a pointer to make sure the students are looking at and saying the word with you. They may not know all the words, but they will hear you pronounce them as you point to them.

• ***Stopping for discussion and prediction***—Stop at appropriate times to discuss what is happening or to predict what will happen next. Use the illustrations to help support understanding of vocabulary. Ask students to point to parts of the illustrations to show comprehension of words or events in the story. Involve the students in acting out movement words and story events to reinforce meaning.

- *Encouraging verbal interactions*—Encourage students to talk about the story. Go back through the book and ask them to talk about what happened on each page. This is a chance for the students to practice oral language and incorporate new vocabulary into their retelling of the story.

- *Rereading for additional practice and exposure*—Reread the book or text several times, tracking with a pointer. Encourage individual students to take turns reading a page or refrain aloud, use the pointer or turn the pages.

- *Practicing with small versions of the text*—After students have read the text several times, they can read small copies of the book or text independently or illustrate their favorite part of the story and write about it.

APPLICATIONS AND EXAMPLES

Ms. Baker and her kindergarten students are doing a shared reading of *Caps for Sale* (Slobodkina, 1968). Before they read the book, Ms. Baker shows the students some hats and caps. They talk about the difference between a hat and a cap. They examine the different caps and talk about the shape and color of each. Ms. Baker reminds the students of the *Curious George* stories (Rey, 1941) that they have read together and tells them that they will meet some more monkeys in the book they will read today.

When Ms. Baker reveals the cover of the book, Jana exclaims, "I see the monkeys!" and hops up to point to them.

"Yes," Ms. Baker says, "There are monkeys in this story. The title of the book is *Caps for Sale: A Tale of a Peddler, Some Monkeys, and Their Monkey Business.* That's a long title. What do you think it means?"

"The man in the tree is selling caps," Kevin suggests.

"You are right, Kevin!" Ms. Baker says. "He sells caps." She points to the peddler on the cover. "He is called a peddler. A peddler sells things."

"What do you think it means when it says a tale of a peddler, some monkeys, and their monkey business?" Ms. Baker asks.

"My dad says 'No monkey business!' " Curt says. "He says that when he wants us to be good."

"Yes, monkey business is being silly, like monkeys," Ms. Baker says. "We will see what monkey business is when we read the book." Ms. Baker opens the book and begins to read, pointing to the words as she reads them. When she gets to the refrain "Caps! Caps for sale!" she encourages the students to read with her. When she gets to the part where the monkeys imitate everything the peddler does, she has the students act out what the peddler and the monkeys do. She stops to have the students predict several times during the story, and she points to pictures as she says words that might be unfamiliar to the students. They are all very involved in the reading of the story.

After Ms. Baker and the students read the story several times, she gets the caps out again and shows the students how to stack them like the peddler in the story did. The caps and several copies of the book are placed in the dramatic play area, where the students are told that they can act out the story later. Ms. Baker suggests that one person can pretend to be the peddler and others can take the parts of the monkeys.

"If you forget what comes next in the story, the books will be there to help you," Ms. Baker says. "Just look at the pictures and the words in the book and you will remember what happens next."

Ms. Baker often uses big books in her kindergarten classroom. The large illustrations help her to teach new vocabulary. She finds that her English language learners follow along with the rest of the students as they read the books and enjoy using the language from the books to retell the stories.

Ms. Moua uses shared reading with the English language learners in her sixth-grade class as they read *Shiloh* (Naylor, 1991) together. The students each have an individual copy of the book. Ms. Moua introduces the new chapter by having the students review what has happened in the story so far.

The first day the students look at the cover of the book and predict what they think will happen. After they read the first chapter they act out the events of the day when Marty finds Shiloh. The second day they discuss the chapter from the previous day before they read the second chapter.

"I think Dad's going to find the owner of the dog," Josef predicts.

Marty found a dog.
He named him Shiloh
because he found him
near the Shiloh mountain.

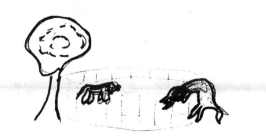

He found out that the dog
belonged to his neighbor on
the mountain, Judd. Judd
was mean to his dogs.

Marty hid the dog and
fed him part of his meals
each day. He built a pen
for him so he wouldn't
run away.

One night another dog
attacked Shiloh in his
pen. Marty's dad found
out about Shiloh that
night and took him to
the doctor's.

Judd found out that
Marty had the dog.
He came to Marty's
house and demanded that
he return the dog. Shiloh
was afraid of his owner.

Marty went to Judd's house
to tell him that he wouldn't
return the dog. He caught
Judd shooting deer out of
season and made a bargain
with him to work in return
for Shiloh. He worked very
hard, but Shiloh was his.

Figure 12.2 An Illustrated Retelling of a Shared Book

"No! There won't be a story if the dog doesn't stay," Manuel insists. "Marty will get to keep him."
"No! His dad said he thought the dog belongs to his neighbor," Graciel reminds Manuel.
"Let's read and find out," Ms. Moua suggests.

The students read the second chapter of the book—stopping to discuss the meanings of words—act out some words, and reread for fluency when they stumble over words. Ms. Moua models the fluent reading of passages and then has the students repeat the passage, reading along with her. When the group finishes reading the second chapter, Ms. Moua has them list the events in the story so far. Ms. Moua takes their dictation and writes the sentences on sentence strips, placing the sentence strips in order in the pocket chart. The students and Ms. Moua reread their dictated story together. After the shared reading the students copy the sentences onto pages of a blank booklet Ms. Moua supplies for each student and they illustrate each page. Ms. Moua knows these students have no books at home to read. After this activity they will each have a copy of their retelling of *Shiloh,* complete with their personal illustrations. One of their illustrated books is shown in Figure 12.2.

CONCLUSION

Shared reading is used across grade levels for many purposes. For emergent readers shared reading is a way to model concepts about print such as reading from left to right, starting on the left page before reading the right page, and the purpose of punctuation marks. For older readers, shared reading is a strategy used to support fluency, vocabulary, and comprehension. By reading books together students can see comprehension strategies modeled at the point in reading at which they are needed. Teachers have a chance to demonstrate what they do when they come to difficult words or concepts. Follow-up activities can include projects that strengthen involvement with the book, such as retellings, simulation journals, or illustration opportunities. It is with these shared readings and follow-up projects that teachers and students achieve a shared literary understanding.

EXAMPLES OF APPROXIMATION BEHAVIORS RELATED TO THE TESOL STANDARDS

Pre-K–3 students will:

- listen to and join in shared reading.
- imitate actions related to storybooks.

4–8 students will:

- explore alternative ways of saying things.
- make connections between stories and personal experiences.

9–12 students will:

- use comprehension strategies to make sense of text.
- connect new vocabulary to past experiences.

References

Depree, H., & Iversen, S. (1996). *Early literacy in the classroom: A new standard for young readers.* Bothell, WA: Wright Group.

Gibbons, P. (1993). *Learning to learn in a second language.* Portsmouth, NH: Heinemann.

Holdaway, D. (1979). *Foundations of literacy.* Auckland, New Zealand: Ashton Scholastic.

Naylor, P. R. (1991). *Shiloh.* New York: Bantam Doubleday.

Rey, H. A. (1941). *Curious George.* Boston: Houghton Mifflin.

Slobodkina, E. (1968). *Caps for sale: A tale of a peddler, some monkeys, and their monkey business.* New York: Harper Collins.

Tompkins, G. (1997). *Literacy for the 21st century.* Upper Saddle River, NJ: Merrill/Prentice Hall.

LEVELED QUESTIONS:

Adjusting Questioning Strategies to the Language Levels of Students

13

This strategy addresses the following TESOL Standards:

Goal 2: To use English to achieve academically in all content areas

Standard 1: Students will use English to interact in the classroom.

Standard 2: Students will use English to obtain, process, construct, and provide subject matter information in spoken and written form.

Standard 3: Students will use appropriate learning strategies to construct and apply academic knowledge.

Leveled questions are used when teachers adapt the way they ask questions so that students can respond to them according to their language acquisition stage (Krashen & Terrell, 1983). To level questions, the teacher must observe the students and note how they interact in English. Once the teacher knows the level at which the student interacts in English, the questions the teacher poses to the student can be adjusted to assure the student's success in answering. This may involve the teacher using gestures, visuals, or slowing the speech slightly while asking the question. The teacher asks the question in a way that encourages the student to answer by pointing to a visual, giving a one-word response or a complete sentence or explanation depending on the student's level of language acquisition. The teacher's role in using this strategy involves knowing the student's level of English acquisition and providing enough context in the question so that the student can respond, either verbally or nonverbally, with understanding and confidence.

▶ STEP BY STEP

The steps in using leveled questions are:

• **Observing and documenting students' language levels**—Observe your students to determine their current levels of interaction in English. On a class list, indicate whether each student is at the preproduction stage, early production stage, speech emergent stage, or intermediate fluency stage. See Figure 13.1 for a description of students' English proficiency at each of these stages. This list will need to be kept up to date as you work with the students and observe their responses.

Stage	Appropriate Expectations
Preproduction	Nodding, pointing, physically demonstrating
Early production	One- or two-word responses, making choices from given language samples (Is it a whale or a dolphin?)
Speech emergence	Phrase or short sentences (expect grammar errors)
Intermediate fluency	Longer sentences, fewer grammar errors

Figure 13.1   Appropriate Expectations for Students at Different Speech Stages

Adapted from Krashen & Terrell, 1983.

Stage	Question or Cue
Preproduction	"Show me . . . ." "Which of these . . . ?"
Early production	"Is it the _____ one or the _____ one?" Questions that can be answered with one or two words.
Speech emergence	"Did this happen at the beginning or at the end?" "What happened next?" "Where did you find the answer?"
Intermediate fluency	"How did you . . . ?" "What was the character trying to do?"

Figure 13.2   Appropriate Questions for Speech Stages

Adapted from Krashen & Terrell, 1983.

• *Choosing and gathering materials*—Determine which visuals, artifacts, or gestures you will need to make your meaning clear to the students whose understanding of English is limited. Gather these support materials to use during the presentation of the lesson and your questioning. Remember that English language learners feel more comfortable participating when they have ways to demonstrate their understanding with visuals and support materials.

• *Planning a hierarchy of questions*—Plan a series of questions that will help you involve your students and determine their levels of understanding of the material you will be teaching. In the beginning it is helpful to plan a series of questions at different levels so that you can move around the room and use levels of questions for appropriate students without too much hesitation or confusion. See Figure 13.2 for suggestions.

• *Involving all students*—Use the list of students and speech levels as a checklist to make sure that you are involving all the students in discussion and questioning and that you are adapting the levels of your questions to their changing language acquisition levels.

• *Assessing student progress and understanding*—Use the checklist you have created for observation purposes. Observe a few students each day until you have examples of the verbal responses typical for each student. Write these responses into an anecdotal record to include in the student's individual portfolio documenting periodic growth in their abilities to respond to questions in class. These documentation strategies apply to the students' progress in meeting TESOL standards related to classroom interactions and academic language (Goal 2 at the beginning of this chapter).

APPLICATIONS AND EXAMPLES

Leveled questions can be used at all grade levels and in all curricular areas. For example, in Ms. Chanis's first-grade class the children are using manipulatives to join sets and build number sentences. As Ms. Chanis moves around the room observing the students at work and asking questions, she varies the way she asks questions according to the language acquisition stages of her students. As she stops at Hnu's table she asks Hnu to show her a set of six objects. Because Hnu is functioning at the preproduction stage in English, Ms. Chanis asks, "Show me 6." Hnu quickly counts out six blocks and lines them up on her desk. Ms. Chanis says, "Yes! 1,2,3,4,5,6. You showed me 6." She points to the blocks as she counts them and smiles at Hnu.

By keeping her sentence short and using a sentence form that has been modeled during the lesson introduction Ms. Chanis is supporting Hnu's successful participation in the math lesson. As Ms. Chanis moves to other students she adjusts her questions to the language stages of the children. She is keeping track of the students with whom she interacts by checking their names off on a list, which also helps her to keep track of the students' language stages.

Ms. Chanis asks an early production student to tell her how many objects are in the set on his desk. A speech emergence student is asked to give the number sentence for the set of two red blocks added to the set of four green blocks. An intermediate fluency student is asked to tell a story about a picture of a group of two pigs joining a group of four pigs wallowing in the mud.

Each leveled question is followed by a brief modeling of language to help support the students in incorporating more English speech into their verbal interactions. A student responds with one word and then listens as Ms. Chanis models the use of that one word in a short sentence. A student who responds with a short phrase will hear a confirmation that the phrase is correct, but then Ms. Chanis will scaffold that student's response by extending the phrase into a full sentence. Even in math, Ms. Chanis is aware of the need to continually scaffold language for her English language learners.

Leveled questions are appropriate at any grade level as long as there are students who need them to successfully participate in class interactions. In Mr. Burrow's ninth-grade class there are a number of English language learners who need to have leveled questions to participate in class discussions and questioning periods.

As Mr. Burrows reviews the Cuban missile crisis with his students, he wants to discuss the reason for concern at the time. Mr. Burrows structures a series of questions to help his students locate Cuba on the map and recognize the geographic proximity to the United States, which was the reason for concern.

To encourage participation by a preproduction stage student, Mr. Burrows says, "Show me the country of Cuba on the map." The student then uses the map in the classroom to point to Cuba.

Mr. Burrows asks an early production student to go to the map and look at it carefully. He then asks, "What is the name of the ocean or sea in which Cuba is located? Show me where you found that information on the map."

For a speech emergence student he asks, "How far is Cuba from the United States?" He follows up that question with a request to "Show Cuba and Florida on the map."

For an intermediate fluency student, Mr. Burrows asks, "Why was President Kennedy so concerned about the build-up of missiles in Cuba in the early '60s?"

The discussion and questions continue, and the map is used to ensure that the students are able to understand the main points of the discussion. Mr. Burrows models English sentences as he points out the countries on the map and makes it clear that President Kennedy was concerned because the Soviet Union was building up missiles very close to U.S. shores. Mr. Burrows then uses small ship pictures placed on the map to illustrate how the United States blockaded the approaches to Cuba and caused the Soviet ships carrying missiles to return home. Mr. Burrows is aware of the need to provide visuals to support his English language learners' comprehension of English, but he is also aware that their understanding of spoken English is better than their ability to produce English sentences. He finds ways to make himself understood and to actively involve all his students.

CONCLUSION

The use of leveled questions in the classroom requires that the teacher know the stages of language development in which each student is functioning. It also requires that the teacher understand appropriate expectations of students in each stage of language development. Although this knowledge is vital, it is not difficult information to obtain if the teacher is willing to observe the students carefully.

After gathering this knowledge and establishing a method for updating the information regularly, the teacher is ready to use leveled questions to ensure that each student in the class is provided with opportunities to participate fully. The effectiveness of this strategy stems from several sources. The students become more fully engaged in the lessons when their anxiety levels are reduced, their participation supports their understanding, and their self-confidence and language use increases. All of these factors contribute to the reduction of classroom management challenges as well.

EXAMPLES OF APPROXIMATION BEHAVIORS RELATED TO THE TESOL STANDARDS

Pre-K–3 students will:

- respond to questions appropriate to their level of English language development.
- demonstrate understanding by physical and oral responses.

4–8 students will:

- ask clarification questions.
- demonstrate understanding through physical, verbal, and written replies.

9–12 students will:

- select, connect, and explain information.
- represent information visually and interpret the visual representation orally.

Reference

Krashen, S., & Terrell, T. (1983). *The natural approach: Language acquisition in the classroom.* Oxford: Pergamon Press.

Suggested Readings

Diaz-Rico, L. T., & Weed, K. Z. (2002). *The crosscultural, language, and academic development handbook* (2nd ed.). Needham Heights, MA: Allyn & Bacon.
Gibbons, P. (1993). *Learning to learn in a second language.* Portsmouth, NH: Heinemann.
TESOL, *ESL Standards for pre-K–12 Students.* Alexandria, VA: Author.

MANIPULATIVE STRATEGIES: 14
Using Objects to Connect Concepts

This strategy addresses the following TESOL Standards:

Goal 2: To use English to achieve academically in all content areas

Standard 1: Students will use English to interact in the classroom.

Standard 2: Students will use English to obtain, process, construct, and provide subject matter information in spoken and written form.

Standard 3: Students will use appropriate learning strategies to construct and apply academic knowledge.

Manipulatives are concrete devices that students can move and manipulate to support their thinking and learning. Although they are most often used in math and science, they can be very helpful in supporting language understanding in other subject areas. For manipulatives to be used effectively the teacher must demonstrate their use, while simultaneously modeling the connection to academic language. Manipulatives can be concrete representations of the concepts being taught as in models of the human body, which can be disassembled for study, or nonrepresentative manipulatives such as small wooden cubes used for counting and math calculations. The concrete representation manipulatives are often used to support the development of academic vocabulary, while the nonrepresentative manipulatives are used to manipulate an abstract concept such as number. See Figure 14.1 for suggestions for using manipulatives.

STEP BY STEP

The steps in the use of manipulatives are:

- *Identifying concepts to be taught and ways to represent them*—Identify the concept to be taught and the parts of the concept that could be represented by a concrete object of some kind. Design a teaching plan that allows the demonstration of the concept using the manipulatives as examples.

- *Demonstrating and explaining*—Demonstrate the use of the manipulatives as you explain the concept to the students. Use the demonstration to connect the manipulative, the concept, and any new vocabulary. Model the way you expect the students to use the manipulatives.

Subject Area	Suggested Manipulative Use
Vocabulary	• Miniatures or wooden cut-outs of objects • Colored blocks to teach colors, singular, plural forms • Attribute blocks to teach shapes, sizes, texture, color • Dolls to teach body parts
Mathematics	• Beans for counters • Small props for acting out word problems • Geometric shapes cut into fractional parts • Colored linking cubes for building patterns • Measuring cups and containers for studying measurement
Science	• Human body models • Realia for experiments • Styrofoam balls and toothpicks for construction • Magnets, batteries, iron filings

Figure 14.1 Manipulatives That Might Be Used in Various Subject Areas

• ***Providing guided practice***—Provide guided practice in the use of the manipulatives. Walk the students through the procedure to be used, demonstrating how to use the manipulatives and connecting the manipulatives to the vocabulary to be learned.

• ***Giving students time for additional practice***—Give the students time to use the manipulatives independently while you circulate around the classroom observing, giving feedback, and scaffolding language usage.

• ***Celebrating and reviewing***—Celebrate the students' demonstration of learning, again taking the opportunity to connect the manipulatives to the vocabulary and concepts learned.

APPLICATIONS AND EXAMPLES

Mr. Sanchez is using story props to teach his first graders the use of a Venn diagram. Two hula hoops are laid on the floor and the students sit around them. In front of each student are three or four props from one of the two versions of *Stone Soup* that the class has read together in the past few days.

"In the green hoop we will put the props from the newer version of *Stone Soup* (McGovern, 1968) that we read first," Mr. Sanchez says as he places the McGovern version of the book in the center of the green hoop. "In the red hoop we will put the props from the other version of the story," Mr. Sanchez says as he places the Brown (1947) version of the book in the center of the red hoop.

"Now watch what I am going to do," he says as he lifts one hoop and lays it so it overlaps the other one. "Now we have a section of the hoops that overlap. When you see two circles that overlap like this, it is called a Venn diagram. The part that overlaps is where we will put the props that show something that was the same in both versions of the story. Who has something that was in both versions of the story?"

Petra holds up a stone. Mr. Sanchez nods and smiles as he says, "Yes, Petra. There was a stone in each version. That's why it was called *Stone Soup*. Where should we put the stone?"

Petra smiles at Mr. Sanchez but makes no move to place the stone. Mr. Sanchez continues, "Put the stone in here, Petra," he says as he motions to the overlap in the hoops. "The stone was in the first story," he makes a circular motion to indicate the green hoop and points to the first book. "The stone was in the second story," he repeats the motion with the red hoop and the second book. "So we put the stone in here," he points to the overlap and Petra puts the stone in the correct place.

"Very good! The stone was in both stories," Mr. Sanchez smiles at Petra and points to both books.

The process is repeated with the students making decisions about the proper placement of each of the props in the Venn diagram. As they place the props the students talk about whether or not they were in both stories. When there is disagreement Mr. Sanchez urges them to look in the book. When all the props have been placed, Mr. Sanchez pairs the students to work together on another Venn diagram. He gives each pair of students a large laminated piece of construction paper with a Venn diagram drawn on it. He gives each pair a set of pictures of the same set of props they have just used. The partners are to reenact the sorting of the props and recreate the Venn diagram they have just done as a class. The only addition to the task is a set of word cards that identify each prop. The partners must read the words and put them into the Venn diagram along with the props. There is a lot of conversation among the pairs, in home languages and English, as the students make decisions about the placement of the props and words. Occasionally a student will come to get one of the versions of the story to prove a point. As the pairs complete their work they raise their hands and Mr. Sanchez comes to them so they can read the words they have placed on the diagram and explain their diagram. Mr. Sanchez uses this time to reinforce word identification skills, their pronunciation of the vocabulary, and their correct use of the Venn diagram.

In this use of manipulatives Mr. Sanchez has used concrete manipulatives, the props. He then moved to semiconcrete manipulatives, the pictures. Finally, he provided abstract manipulatives, the words. He also used partner work to facilitate the use of home languages to communicate and solve problems and supported the students as they reported their results in English.

Older students also benefit from the use of manipulatives in the classroom. As Ms. Yang's fifth graders study the human body, she provides a model of each of the systems of the body that contains removable parts so the students can take the model apart, closely examine the parts, and reassemble the model. They are completing a diagram of each system as a part of a human body notebook they are compiling.

Ms. Yang has put together groups of four students to work cooperatively to disassemble the model, use the parts of the model to help them label their diagrams, and then reassemble the model. The group works together to test each other on the names of the body parts and exactly where the parts fit into the system. Each group member must help the others to learn each of the body parts, where it fits in the model, how it is spelled, and where the label goes on the diagram in their notebooks.

Everyone knows that the diagrams must be completed again on Friday as a test. Each group that has every member pass the test with at least an 80 percent will get extra recess time on Friday afternoon, so everyone is anxious to help each other learn. No one wants to be sitting inside studying for a human body retest while everyone else is outside playing on Friday afternoon.

▶ CONCLUSION

The use of manipulatives, whether they are real objects that help students to relate language to concepts or representational objects such as blocks, counters, or beans are often supportive to students' understanding. Presenting new concepts in a concrete way, before moving to semiconcrete representations such as pictures, and finally to abstract symbols, helps students make the gradual switch from concrete to abstract thinking. Manipulatives can be used in many ways, but careful thought should be given to connecting the vocabulary, concepts, and thought processes through demonstration, in much the same way vocabulary is introduced to infants. For example, "This is a cup. We drink from a cup," as the cup is being shown and demonstrated.

EXAMPLES OF APPROXIMATION BEHAVIORS RELATED TO THE TESOL STANDARDS

Pre-K–3 students will:

- use manipulatives to represent real objects.
- manipulate objects to demonstrate concepts.

4–8 students will:

- use manipulatives to solve problems.
- use manipulatives and verbal explanations to demonstrate problem solutions.

9–12 students will:

- use manipulatives to represent complex interactions.
- use manipulatives to explain concepts to others.

References

Brown, M. (1947). *Stone Soup.* New York: Aladdin/Macmillan.
McGovern, A. (1968). *Stone Soup.* New York: Scholastic.

PARTNER WORK: Practicing Verbal Interaction

15

This strategy addresses the following TESOL Standards:

Goal 1: To use English to communicate in social settings

Standard 1: Students will use English to participate in social interactions.
Standard 2: Students will interact in, through, and with spoken and written English for personal expression and enjoyment.
Standard 3: Students will use learning strategies to extend their communicative competence.

Goal 2: To use English to achieve academically in all content areas

Standard 1: Students will use English to interact in the classroom.
Standard 2: Students will use English to obtain, process, construct, and provide subject matter information in spoken and written form.

Partner work (Meyers, 1993) is a form of cooperative learning that is particularly effective with English language learners because of the opportunities for verbal interaction and support it provides (Diaz-Rico & Weed, 2002). In partner work the teacher pairs two students to accomplish a learning task. They are given specific instructions and are expected to accomplish a process or product to share with the group or with other pairs. Suggested formats, learning tasks, and pairing schemes for partner work are shown in Figure 15.1.

STEP BY STEP

The steps in implementing partner work are:

• **Pairing the students**—Decide the purpose of the partner work to be done before you assign the pairs. If language development is one of the main purposes of the pairing, make sure one of the partners can provide a strong English model.

Format	Learning Tasks/Procedure	Pairing Scheme
Think-pair-share	Group discussions, literature studies, problem solving reviewing of content materials for tests. Teacher presents question or task. Students think about their responses and then share and discuss their responses with their partner.	One strong English model
Buddy read	Reading of content material, challenging text. One student reads, the other listens or takes notes. They stop periodically to discuss and create a graphic organizer for study.	One strong reader
Research interview	Content material in science, social studies, and any informational writing. Students do individual research on a topic or aspect of a topic. Partners interview each other to gain the knowledge obtained by their partner. When sharing with another pair or whole group, each partner reports the material learned from the partner. The original researcher has the responsibility of monitoring the report by the partner to guarantee its accuracy.	Equal partners or one strong reader
Conversation role play	Oral language development, adjusting to social situations, situational vocabulary. Partners role play certain social situations such as a birthday party, a job interview, meeting new people at a non-family party. Appropriate language is introduced by the teacher in advance and the partners pretend to be a part of the social situation. After a while pairs are combined into groups of four and the partners must introduce each other to the new pair, providing appropriate information they have gained by the initial conversations.	Equal partners
Convince me	Problem solving tasks in science or math. Teacher presents a problem to be solved. The students work independently to find innovative solutions to the problem. The students are then paired to try to convince each other of the viability of the two solutions or to combine their solutions to make a better solution. They then meet with another pair and the foursomes must decide on and present their best solution to the whole group.	One strong English model

Figure 15.1 Formats, Learning Tasks, and Pairing Schemes for Partner Work

- ***Modeling the task***—Model the task to be done. Choose one student to act as your partner for the demonstration and walk through the steps to be done. List the tasks on a chart or chalkboard to serve as a reminder of the steps in the process and the expectations of what will be accomplished.

- ***Providing support and practice***—Circulate among the pairs during the activity, giving them feedback on the way they are working together and communicating. Support pairs who are struggling by entering into their interactions, modeling strategies they can use to get the task done.

- ***Sharing progress***—Provide an opportunity for the pairs to share their process or product with another pair or the whole group. Celebrate their accomplishments and review the language they were able to use.

▶ APPLICATIONS AND EXAMPLES

Mr. Santiago's second graders are listening intently to his reading of *Wilfred Gordon McDonald Partridge* (Fox, 1985). When he finishes reading the book, he reviews the story by creating a flip book labeled *Beginning, Middle,* and *End.* He asks the students to tell the things that happen at the beginning of the story. As they mention the elements in the beginning of Mem Fox's wonderful book, he reviews them, "We meet the characters, Wilfred Gordon, Miss Nancy, and the other old folks at the home. We learn about the setting, that Wilfred Gordon lives next door to the old people's home. We learn about the problem, that Miss Nancy has lost her memory." As he talks about the elements, Mr. Santiago lists *Characters, Setting,* and *Problem introduced* under *Beginning* on the flip book. Mr. Santiago repeats the process for the *Middle* section of the flip book and writes, *Problem gets worse, Characters are developed.* Under *End* on the flip book, Mr. Santiago writes *Problem is solved.* His flip book now looks like the one shown in Figure 15.2.

Mr. Santiago asks each student to think about a memory they have that they could write about. He gives them time to think and jot some notes about their memories. Next, Mr. Santiago asks Erina to come up front and act as his partner so he can show the students what they will be doing next.

"I have written some notes about my memory. I will use my notes to tell you my story. As I tell you my story, I want you to take notes on this flip book labeled *Beginning, Middle,* and *End.* You are to take notes about my story because you will help me decide if I need to add anything to my story so that it will be more interesting. You will also be watching to see that I have included all the important parts of my story."

Mr. Santiago then tells his story and Erina writes the names of the characters by the word *Characters* on the *Beginning* section of the flip book. As he tells about the setting she writes a few words by *Setting* and writes a few words by *Problem introduced* as he tells about the problem. Erina continues to take notes as Mr. Santiago completes his story.

"Now that I have told my story to Erina, I want her to look at her notes to see if I have left out any important parts. Erina, what do you think?"

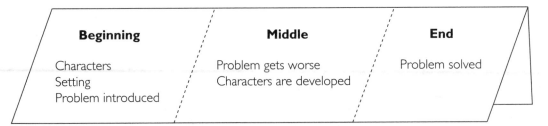

Figure 15.2 Mr. Santiago's Flip Book

"I don't have any notes in the *Middle* section under *Characters are developed*. I think you need to tell me some more about the characters in the middle of the story to make it more interesting."

"Good, I can do that when I actually write my story inside the flip book. That will be the next part. For now we need to work in pairs to tell our stories to our partners. Then they can take notes and help us to make sure we have all the parts to make our stories as interesting as Mem Fox's story about Wilfred Gordon."

Mr. Santiago gives the students time to think about their stories and jot some notes. Then he pairs the students up, making sure that there is a strong English speaker in each pair. The partners tell their stories to each other, creating the *Beginning, Middle,* and *End* notes on the cover of the flip books. Once everyone has told their stories and received feedback from their partners, they get to work actually writing the stories in the flip books. They know exactly what to write now that they've told the stories and received advice from their partners.

Partner work is a valuable strategy in many areas of the curriculum. It gives students confidence to tackle tough assignments by interacting and collaborating with another student.

Ms. Tucker's sixth graders are learning to use multiplication and division to solve real-life problems. She has brought in a diagram of a loft that she wants to build in the classroom and catalogues from a local hardware store that lists prices on building materials. She explains to the class that she would like to build the loft in the classroom so they will have a quiet place to read when they have finished their work each day. The students smile when they see the diagram of the loft with its comfortable beanbag seats and colorful posters.

"I want each of you to look through the catalogues and use the diagram to figure out how much money we need to raise to buy the materials to build the loft," Ms. Tucker explains. "There are several choices of materials that we can use. Some of the boards are more expensive than others. Some of the boards come in different lengths, so we need to figure out which length to buy so that we don't waste too much lumber."

"You will be working with a partner to determine your plan for buying materials and the total cost of materials if we follow your plan. After your planning time, you and your partner should work together to practice a presentation and make a picture of some kind to show the class so that the whole class can vote on which plan we will use."

"You will need to work closely with your partner to double check all your math. Also, make sure you haven't forgotten any materials like nails, paint, or paint brushes."

As Ms. Tucker is reviewing the steps in the partner work, she lists the steps the students must take to accomplish their task. Her list is shown in Figure 15.3.

As the partners begin to work, Ms. Tucker moves around the room listening to the active verbal interactions, making suggestions and giving encouragement. Some of the pairs have chosen some unusual materials for their loft. She can't wait to hear their presentations.

---

1. Look at the loft diagram.
2. Decide which materials you will need to build the loft and how much of each material will be needed.
3. Figure the cost of the materials using the price list in the catalogue. Try to find ways to save money and cut down on waste.
4. Double-check your math.
5. Prepare a presentation and diagram to show how you did your calculations.
6. Decide how to present your plan to the class.
7. Practice your presentation.

Figure 15.3   Steps in the Planning Process

CONCLUSION

Partner work can be used in many ways across the curriculum. By pairing students to support one another in the successful completion of the task or to review materials and prepare for an assignment, the students are given opportunities to interact verbally, practice relating facts and concepts, monitor each other's understanding, or provide home language support. English language learners can be paired in several ways depending on their stages in English acquisition. If a student needs home language explanations, then a perfect partner for that student is another student who shares the same home language and who is also more fluent in English.

If an English language learner is fairly fluent in English but needs more practice in speaking and writing English, then a good English speaking role model makes a good partner. Partners can also be used to create bilingual books and labels, versions of favorite literature in various languages, or illustrated books using partners with strengths in writing and illustration. Partners can be used in math and science by pairing students with strengths such as writing and science or art and science.

EXAMPLES OF APPROXIMATION BEHAVIORS RELATED TO THE TESOL STANDARDS

Pre-K–3 students will:

- use gestures to ascertain the location of items in the classroom.
- use simple questions to elicit information needed.

4–8 students will:

- ask who, what, where, when, why, how questions to obtain needed information.
- ask a series of questions to build knowledge.

9–12 students will:

- ask questions to generate descriptive terms.
- use verbal interaction to resolve conflict.

References

Diaz-Rico, L., & Weed, K. (2002). *The crosscultural language and academic development handbook* 2nd ed. Needham Heights, MA: Allyn & Bacon.

Fox, M. (1985). *Wilfred Gordon McDonald Partridge.* Brooklyn, NY: Kane/Miller Books.

Meyers, M. (1993). *Teaching to diversity: Teaching and learning in the multi-ethnic classroom.* Toronto, Canada: Irwin Publishing.

COMMUNICATION GAMES: Creating Opportunities for Verbal Interaction

This strategy addresses the following TESOL Standards:

Goal 1: To use English to communicate in social settings

Standard 1: Students will use English to participate in social interactions.
Standard 2: Students will interact in, through, and with spoken and written English for personal expression and enjoyment.

Goal 2: To use English to achieve academically in all content areas

Standard 1: Students will use English to interact in the classroom.
Standard 2: Students will use English to obtain, process, construct, and provide subject matter information in spoken and written form.
Standard 3: Students will use appropriate learning strategies to construct and apply academic knowledge.

Communication games (Gibbons, 1993) are activities set up in the classroom to create opportunities and purposes for verbal communication practice. Many times the purpose of the communication in these games is to convey information or cause something to occur as a result of the activity. Some of the games provide practice in the use of a particular language function such as giving directions or asking questions. Other games require students to work together and communicate to solve a problem. Suggested communication games are shown in Figure 16.1.

STEP BY STEP

The steps in teaching communication games are:

• ***Identifying a language need***—Identify a language function in which your students need practice. Following directions, asking questions, and conveying academic information are among some of the most commonly used in communication games. Choose a category of communication game from Figure 16.1.

Activity	Description	Example
Barrier games	Two students sit back-to-back or behind a screen (barrier). One student is given a complete set of instructions that must be conveyed verbally to the second student, who completes the task.	One student has a set of small colored blocks that must be arranged in a certain configuration. The other student, working from a diagram, gives oral directions to the student with the blocks so that the blocks end up in the proper configuration.
Information sharing	Each student has part of the information necessary to complete a task or solve a problem. They must share their information to accomplish the task.	Students are given materials to fold an origami flower. Each student has one section of the directions. Using the sequence words as a guide, the students take turns reading the directions silently and then conveying them orally so the members of the group can complete the folding task.
Inquiry & elimination	A small group of students works together. One student has a set of information that must be obtained by the others through questioning and elimination of irrelevant items. The group then decides the solution based upon their inquiry.	The class has been studying insects. The child designated as the expert in the group is given the name of an insect and a set of facts about that insect. By asking questions, the students must gather enough information about the insect so that they can determine which insect is described. When they have guessed the correct insect, they have also reviewed their knowledge of that insect.
Rank ordering	Students work together in a small group to suggest solutions to a problem and then reach consensus as to the rank order of the usefulness of each of the solutions.	The groups are asked to make a shopping list of important supplies to purchase for a camping trip. They are to brainstorm items, and then rank-order the importance of the items so that they could survive if they could take only the top five items. Food and water don't have to be listed; the groups are assured of having them.

Figure 16.1 Suggested Communication Games

Adapted from Gibbons, 1993.

- *Modeling the game*—Model the way the game is played by involving one or more students in demonstrating the game to be played. Review the rules carefully and post them in the room so the students can refer to them during the activity.

- *Organizing the pairs or groups*—Organize the students in pairs or small groups, making sure you have a fairly fluent English speaker in each pair or group. Give the pairs or groups their tasks and get them started.

- *Guiding the practice*—Move around the room providing support and encouragement.

- *Talking about the experience*—After the activity, ask the students to share their experiences, any problems they had, and the solutions they devised. Make a list of the vocabulary they found helpful and discuss how it was used.

▶ APPLICATIONS AND EXAMPLES

Ms. Darling's kindergartners are learning colors and shapes. She wants them to experience using the new vocabulary they are learning so she designs a barrier game using attribute blocks—blocks in various geometric shapes and colors. (Construction paper shapes in a variety of colors will also work.) She explains to the students that they will be playing a game. She asks Tony to help her teach the game. Tony comes to the front of the room and uses the shapes designed for the overhead projector to follow Ms. Darling's oral directions. Ms. Darling shows the class the drawing she is holding and tells them, "This is the design that I want Tony to make. I will give him directions. He can't see the design. I have to tell him how to make it.

"The design is in a straight line," she tells Tony. "I will tell you the shapes to put in the line. Start at the left and move across the glass from left to right, like you do when you read. First, find the large red circle and put it at the top of the projector."

Tony places the large red circle at the top of the glass, on the left side. Ms. Darling is standing with her back to him so she waits until he tells her he is ready for the next direction. "You will be sitting behind a screen so you won't be able to see what your partner is doing. You have to talk to each other in order to build the design," Ms. Darling reminds the students. "Next, find the small green circle and put it next to the large red circle," Ms. Darling says. Tony follows her directions.

Once the demonstration is complete, Ms. Darling arranges the students in pairs and puts up small science project boards between the pairs as barriers. She starts each pair with a simple design. They come to her for a new design when they finish one and they take turns giving instructions. Ms. Darling moves around the room giving encouragement and language scaffolding as needed. After the activity the class discusses the words that they used. Lara says, "It was hard. You had to remember a lot of things to say. The shape and the color and the size—a lot!"

Ms. Darling acknowledges Lara's comment. "Yes, it was hard. You had to use a lot of math language. You did a good job!"

Mr. Standford's 10th-grade English class is completing a study of *The Canterbury Tales* (Chaucer, 1365/1934). Because the language in the tales is so difficult, Mr. Standford reads the Geraldine McCaughrean (1984) version of the stories aloud, comparing the simplified, illustrated version with the language in the older, more traditional version. Occasionally, Mr. Standford even reads the Old English words to give the students a feel for the original. To provide a review of the work before the unit exam, Mr. Standford decides to give the students practice in discussing the tales and reviewing the information they have about each of them. He begins the lesson with an explanation, "Today we will be reviewing *The Canterbury Tales* so that you will all do well on the exam on Monday. You will be working in small groups to identify the main characters in the tales, their characteristics, and their stories. Let me show you how this will work."

Mr. Standford asks three students to come to the front of the class and ask him questions about the tales. He sets the stage for them. "You can ask me questions, which I must answer truthfully. You cannot ask me to name the character or tell you things directly about the character, but you can ask questions that can be answered by 'yes' or 'no.' " The person who is being questioned will have the character's name and the information about the character and tale so that the answers given will be accurate."

One student asks Mr. Standford if the character is a man. He answers, "No."

The next student asks if the character had animals. Mr. Standford answers, "No."

The third student asks if she was married several times. Mr. Standford answers, "Yes."

The first student then asks, "Is it the Wife of Bath?" Mr. Standford answers, "Yes."

The group then discusses how they eliminated characters as the questions were answered. They agreed that eliminating the men really narrowed the possibilities. They then reviewed the information about the Wife of Bath and her tale on the review sheet.

Mr. Standford divides the class into groups of four students and gives one student in each group a review sheet so that they are ready to field questions. He makes sure that there are strong students in each group. Each group has a copy of both the simplified, illustrated version and the more traditional version of the tales so they can check the accuracy of their answers.

Mr. Standford moves around the room as the questioning takes place. As each group reviews the characters, they take turns fielding questions. Mr. Standford saves the more easily recognizable characters for the English language learners and supports the students in returning to the texts whenever anyone needs help in answering questions. The students find they knew a lot about the characters and the tales.

CONCLUSION

Communication games can be used in many grade levels and across all curricular areas as shown by the vignettes. By providing students with authentic reasons to communicate in English, they are given opportunities to practice their English communication skills in a low-stress environment. Students are more likely to be successful because the situations are explained in advance, the vocabulary is practiced, and the context is built into the exercises. By lowering the stress, making the activities game-like, and providing examples of vocabulary and sentence structure, the teacher reduces the affective filter for all students involved in the activity.

EXAMPLES OF APPROXIMATION BEHAVIORS RELATED TO THE TESOL STANDARDS

Pre-K–3 students will:

- use listening skills in playing games.
- use verbal directions in playing games.

4–8 students will:

- use verbal descriptions to cause actions in others.
- follow a sequence of verbal directions to create a product.

9–12 students will:

- combine information in verbal directions to solve problems.
- give a sequence of directions and information to help another create a product.

References

Chaucer, G. (1934). *The Canterbury tales.* (J. Nicolson, Trans.). New York: Crown. (Original work published 1365)

Gibbons, P. (1993). *Learning to learn in a second language.* Portsmouth, NH: Heinemann.

McCaughrean, G. (1984). *The Canterbury tales.* Chicago: Rand McNally.

BILINGUAL BOOKS AND LABELS: Supporting Biliteracy Awareness

17

This strategy addresses the following TESOL Standards:

Goal 1: To use English to communicate in social settings

Standard 1: Students will use English to participate in social interactions.
Standard 2: Students will interact in, through, and with spoken and written English for personal expression and enjoyment.

Goal 2: To use English to achieve academically in all content areas

Standard 1: Students will use English to interact in the classroom.
Standard 2: Students will use English to obtain, process, construct, and provide subject matter information in spoken and written form.
Standard 3: Students will use appropriate learning strategies to construct and apply academic knowledge.

Goal 3: To use English in socially and culturally appropriate ways

Standard 1: Students will use the appropriate language variety, register, and genre according to audience, purpose, and setting.

Books and labels written in two or more languages, including English, are appropriate for use in bilingual or multilingual classes for several reasons. First, they validate the students' home languages and allow them to use their knowledge of the home language to support their understanding of the text. The books and labels written in the home languages of the students bring some of the students' native culture into the classroom. They also provide opportunities for all the students in the class to be exposed to multiple ways of expressing thoughts and value systems. In classrooms where students have learned to read and write in their first languages, labels and books in those languages provide access to information. Some of the books contain the entire text, written in two languages, and support the transfer of reading ability from the home language into English.

In classrooms where the students do not read and write in their native languages, the books and labels provide some exposure to the written systems of the native languages and to the customs and traditions of multiple cultures. Some may encourage parents to read and discuss the books with their children. There are now many books available in which the cultures are depicted by stories, in English, with some samples of common expressions in the first language added for a taste of the language. For example, in the poem "I Am Cucaracha" (Johnston, 1996) the Spanish words *señora, señor*, and *por favor* are integrated into the English version and serve to add a Spanish lilt to the rhyme and rhythm. Many of these books, while not truly bilingual books, are written by authors familiar with the cultures about which they are writing and are very helpful in supporting multicultural studies in the classroom (Tomlinson & Lynch-Brown, 1996). See Figure 17.1 for a listing of some of these books.

STEP BY STEP

The steps for implementing the use of bilingual books and labels are:

 • *Identifying the languages represented in the classroom*—Determine the home languages represented in your classroom and the stages of English development achieved by each student.

 • *Pronouncing and labeling common objects*—Provide opportunities for the students to verbalize the words for common items in the classroom using their home language. Involve the students in the writing and placing of labels within the classroom. For example, the words *door, la puerta; window, la ventana; chalk, la tiza* would be displayed in a Spanish/English first-grade classroom. In classrooms with older students the labels can be complete sentences such as *Pongan sus tareas de casa aquí.*

 • *Providing bilingual books*—Provide bilingual books, with the text written in both English and the home languages of the students, for use in read-aloud or independent reading according to the abilities of the students to read in their home language. If the students do not read in their home language, enlist the help of a bilingual parent or instructional assistant to read the text aloud in the home language(s) of the students before reading the English version. Take time to stop during the English reading to compare the words and sentences in the different languages. Draw attention to any similar words. Discuss the books and the similarities and differences in the customs and situations depicted in the books. Encourage the students to discuss how their experiences and family customs are similar to or different from the situations described in the books. Support the students in seeing that there is a range of customs and beliefs within any culture and that people from many cultures share similar customs and beliefs. See Chapter 12, "Shared Reading"; Chapter 19, "Culture Studies"; and Chapter 20, "Learning Centers" for additional ways to use bilingual books and labels.

 • *Providing translations*—Provide translations of important texts whenever possible. Students can often assist with these translations. These can be read aloud by bilingual parents or instructional assistants or put on tape for the students to use in the listening center.

 • *Exploring key vocabulary in several languages*—Periodically engage all students in the learning of key vocabulary in multiple languages. They can all learn the names of colors, counting, and asking basic questions in multiple languages. In addition, engage the students in discussions of the customs depicted in the multicultural literature that is being shared in the classroom.

APPLICATIONS AND EXAMPLES

Ms. Torres teaches a fifth-grade class in a border town in California. A number of her students move across the border to Mexico for a few months each year. Some of the students attend school regularly while they are in Mexico, but some do not. Ms. Torres is determined that the students will learn to read and write in English while they are in her class. She has decided to make the most of the students' reading and writing abilities in Spanish to move them toward more fluent literacy in English.

Books With Text in Two or More Languages

Spanish/English

Bofill, F. (1998). *Jack and the beanstalk—Juan y los frijoles magicos.* San Francisco: Chronicle Books.

Brothers Grimm (1999). *Little red riding hood—Caperucita roja.* San Francisco: Chronicle Books.

Cisneros, S. (1994). *Hairs—Pelitos.* New York: Dragonfly Books.

Johnston, T. (1996). *My Mexico—Mexico mío.* New York: G. P. Putnam's Sons.

Lachtman, O. (1998). *Big enough—Bastante grande.* Houston, TX: Piñata Books.

Mata, M. (1998). *Goldilocks and the three bears—Ricitas de oro y los tres osos.* San Francisco: Chronicle Books.

Moore, H. & Lucero, J. (1994). *25 Bilingual Mini-Books,* Scholastic.

Reisner, L. (1993). *Margaret and Margarita—Margarita y Margaret.* New York: Greenwillow Books.

Reisner, L. (1998). *Tortillas and Lullabies—Tortillas y cancioncitas.* New York: Greenwillow Books.

Hmong/English

Campbell, R. (1992). *I won't bite.* Union City, CA: Pan Asian Publications.

Thao, C. (1993). *Only a toad.* Green Bay, WI: Project Chong.

Vietnamese/English

Truyen, T. (1987). *The little weaver of Thai-yen Village—Co be tho-det lang thai-yen.* San Francisco, CA: Children's Book Press.

Books Available in More Than One Language

Spanish/English

Aliki, (1963). *Johnny Appleseed.* New York: Lectorum.

(1992). *La historia de Johnny Appleseed.* New York: Lectorum.

Brown, M.W. (1942). *The runaway bunny.* New York: Harper Collins.

(1995). *El conejito andarin.* New York: Harper Collins.

Brown, M.W. (1947). *Goodnight Moon.* New York: Harper Collins.

(1995). *Buenas noches, luna.* New York: Harper Collins.

Cooney, B. (1982). *Miss Rumphius.* New York: Puffin Books.

(1996). *La senorita Runfio.* New York: Puffin Books.

Galdone, P. (1973). *The little red hen.* Boston: Houghton Mifflin.

Lopez, E. (Trans.) (1987). *The Little Red Hen.* New York: Scholastic.

McQueen, L. (1987). *La gallinita roja.* New York: Scholastic. (Spanish version ISBN 0-590-44927-3)

Numeroff, L. (1985) *If you give a mouse a cookie.* New York: Harper Collins.

(1995). *Si le das una galletita a un raton.* New York: Harper Collins.

Numeroff, L. (1991). *If you give a moose a muffin.* New York: Harper Collins.

(1995). *Si le das un panecillo a un alce.* New York: Harper Collins.

Numeroff, L. (1998). *If you give a pig a pancake.* New York: Harper Collins.

(1999). *Si le das un panqueque a una cerdita.* New York: Harper Collins.

Numeroff, L. (2000). *If you take a mouse to the movies.* New York: Harper Collins.

(2001). *Si llevas un raton al cine.* New York: Harper Collins.

Walsh, E. S. (1989). *Mouse paint.* Orlando: Harcourt Brace.

(1992). *Pinta ratones.* Orlando: Harcourt Brace. (Spanish version ISBN 968-16-3768-2)

Walsh, E. S. (1991). *Mouse count.* Orlando: Harcourt Brace.

(1992). *Cuenta ratones.* Orlando: Harcourt Brace. (Spanish version ISBN 968-16-3766-6)

Williams, S. (1989). *I went walking.* Orlando: Harcourt Brace.

(1999). *Sali' de paseo.* Orlando: Harcourt Brace. (Spanish version ISBN 0-15-200288-X)

Wood, A. (1987). *Quick as a cricket.* New York: Child's Play.

(2000). *Veloz como el grillo.* New York: Child's Play.

Yolen, J. (1992) *Encounter.* Orlando, FL: Harcourt Brace.

(1996) *Encounter.* Orlando, FL: Libros Venjeros.

Figure 17.1 Bilingual Books

Hmong/Spanish/English
Coburn, J. R., & Lee, T. C. (1996). *Jouanah, a Hmong Cinderella*. Arcadia, CA: Shen's Books.

Books Written in English With Multicultural Themes
Cheltenham Elementary School Kindergartners (1991). *We are all alike . . . We are all different.* New York: Scholastic.
Dooley, N. (1991). *Everybody cooks rice.* Minneapolis, MN: Carolrhoda Books.
Dooley, N. (1996). *Everybody bakes bread.* Minneapolis, MN: Carolrhoda Books.
Hyun, P. (Ed.). (1995). *Korean children's songs and poems.* Elizabeth, NJ: Hollym.
Lessac. F. (1984). *My little island.* London: Macmillan.
Levine, E. (1989). *I hate English!* New York: Scholastic.
Morris, A. (1989). *Bread, bread, bread.* New York: Lothrop, Lee & Shepard Books.
Morris, A. (1989). *Hat, hats, hats.* New York: Lothrop, Lee & Shepard Books.
Morris, A. (1995). *Shoes, shoes, shoes.* New York: Mulberry Books.
Musgrove, M. (1977). *Ashanti to Zulu—African traditions.* New York: Dial Books.
Roland, D. (1986). *Grandfather's stories from Mexico.* El Cajon, CA: Open My World Publishing.
Steptoe, J. (1987). *Mufaro's beautiful daughters.* New York: Scholastic.
Trezise, P. (1988). *The cave painters.* Australia: Angus & Robertson.

Popular Series Books Available in Spanish and English
Arthur books by M. Brown, Little, Brown and Co.
Clifford books by N. Bridwell, Mariposa/Scholastic
Corduroy books by D. freeman, Puffin Books
Curious George books by H. A. Rey, Houghton Mifflin.
Frances books by R. Hoban, Harper Collins
Franklin books by P. Bourgeois, Lectorum Publishers.
Spot books by E. Hill, Puffin Books.

Simple Science Texts in Spanish, Illustrated with photographs, Published by Heinemann
Las flores—flowers
Las raices—roots
Las hojas—leaves
Las semillas—seeds
La langasa—lobsters
El cangrejo bayoneta—horseshoe crabs
La bellota de mar—barnacles
El caballito de mar—seahorse
El cangrejo ermtano—hermit crab
La medusa—jellyfish
El cangrejo de rio—crayfish
La anemone de mar—sea anemones
Animals acorozados 1 2 3—musty-crusty animals
La babosa—slugs
Animales rebaloses—ooey-gooey animals
La sanguijuela—leeches
La lombriz de tierra—earthworms
La salamandra—salamander

Chapter Books published in Spanish and English
Dahl, R. (1975). *Danny, the champion of the world.* New York: Scholastic.
    (1982). *Danny, campeon del mundo.* Madrid: Noguer. (Spanish version ISBN 84-279-31174)
Fleischman, S. (1963). *By the great horn spoon!* New York: Scholastic.
    (1994). *Por la gran cuchara de cuero!* New York: Lectorum. (Spanish version ISBN 1-880507-08-0.)

Figure 17.1   Continued

George, J. C. (1959). *My side of the mountain.* New York: E. P. Dutton.
  (1996). *Mi rincon en la Montana.* New York: Puffin Books.
O'Dell, S. (1960). *Island of the blue dolphins.* New York: Scholastic.
  (1964). *La isla de los delfines azules.* Madrid: NogueR. (Spanish version ISBN 84-279-3108-5)

Series Books Published in Spanish and English
Applegate, K. A. The Animorphs series, Scholastic.
Byars, B. The Midnight Fox series—La Zorra Negra. Spanish versions published by Nuevos
  Horizontes/Viking Press.
Cleary, B. The Henry Huggins and Ramona books. Spanish versions published by Beech Tree Paperbacks.

Figure 17.1 Continued

Ms. Torres and her students label everything in her classroom in both English and Spanish. They provide bulletin board captions in both languages and Ms. Torres encourages the children to write in the language with which they are most comfortable. If the students write in Spanish then she asks them to write a sentence or two in English giving the main gist of the page. By doing so, everyone in the class can read and enjoy the stories that have been written. She also encourages collaboration so that her students can publish bilingual books, with both English and Spanish texts.

Ms. Torres regularly reads picture books in English after her instructional assistant has read the same book in Spanish. After the book has been read in both languages, the students help her to add words to the word wall—matching the English and Spanish words and cross-listing them alphabetically. This encourages the Spanish-speaking students to build their English vocabularies—and the English-speaking students to build their Spanish vocabularies. With longer texts like chapter books, Ms. Torres reads one chapter in English and the next in Spanish. She then asks a student to summarize each chapter in the language that was not used. She finds that both her English and Spanish speakers are learning to listen carefully and are understanding both languages well.

One day, Juan, one of her Spanish speakers who regularly spends a few weeks in Mexico each year, comes to her with a special request. "My grandmother is very sick. I am afraid she is going to die. My mother would like for me to write the story of her life so that we will all remember her. Will you help me to translate it from Spanish to English so that my parents can read it and also my brothers and sisters?"

Ms. Torres is excited about the project and shares the idea with the whole class. "I think we all have relatives who have interesting stories. Why don't we each choose someone to interview? We can write biographies for our class library and learn more about our family history at the same time."

The students are interested in the idea of conducting interviews, although they are not sure about the writing part of the project until Ms. Torres suggests that they can publish their biographies using the word processing program on the computer.

The next step in the project is to formulate interview questions. The students work in small groups brainstorming the questions that will help them to learn more about the life stories of their relatives. The groups share their lists of questions and then the students go home to conduct their interviews.

Each day the students return with more of their questions answered and they begin to write the biographies. They work in pairs most of the time to help each other with vocabulary and sentence structure. Some of the more fluent Spanish writers finish their Spanish versions very quickly and then struggle over the English translations. Some of the English-speaking students are able to help with the translations because of the bilingual word wall and the number of Spanish/English dictionaries in the classroom. The English-speaking students use the same approach to writing in Spanish that Ms. Torres requires of the beginning English speakers. They write a sentence or two in Spanish to convey the gist of the story to the Spanish readers. The Spanish-speaking students assist the English speakers when they need help with this.

Toward the end of the school year all the biographies are complete, illustrated, and bound, and the class decides to have a celebration to share the books with their families. They sit in groups and read their favorite parts of the biographies to the visitors. Ms. Torres is touched by the attendance and the enthusiasm for the project. One of the grandmothers shares, "I never thought I would have a book written about me. And my relatives in Mexico can read it. So can my grandchildren who speak only English."

Students of all ages benefit from the use of bilingual literature, labeling, and sharing. Mr. Fong's 10th-grade class is preparing a Thanksgiving assembly for the nearby elementary school. They want to help the younger students understand the concept of the various groups of pilgrims who have come to America from all over the world. To begin their research they read books about emigrant groups that have come to America to escape war and oppression. The students decide to focus on several different pilgrim stories to illustrate how America is still receiving pilgrims today.

They begin with a brief reenactment of *Molly's Pilgrim* (Cohen, 1983) and then create a time-line of all the major immigrations to America. As they unroll the time line across the stage, each tenth grader reenacts a scene from the life of one of the pilgrims they have researched. They begin with Juan de Oñate, and the group of Mexican pilgrims who escaped to Texas 23 years before the Mayflower arrived, and continue the reenactments all the way to present-day Bosnian pilgrims. To make their presentations authentic, each student has researched the language of each of the pilgrim groups and learned to say, "Thank God! We have arrived in America and now we are free!" in the language appropriate to the group they represent.

Mr. Fong is so impressed with their research and dedication to the project that he makes a video-tape of their production to motivate the next year's social science group. When he interviews the students about the project he is surprised by some of their comments.

"I never knew there was more than one group of pilgrims."

"The hardest part of the research was learning to speak in Armenian—and it was only two sentences."

"I found out that my grandmother was a pilgrim. I never knew that."

"I never knew how hard the pilgrims had to work to survive."

CONCLUSION

The use of bilingual books and labels in the classroom encourages students to value other cultures and languages. English language learners are validated by the use of their home languages in the classroom and the study of their literature and culture. Native English speakers are given an opportunity to experience the challenge of remembering vocabulary in a second language. The comparison and celebration of a variety of approaches and beliefs helps to build a cohesive community in the classroom.

EXAMPLES OF APPROXIMATION BEHAVIORS RELATED TO THE TESOL STANDARDS

Pre-K–3 students will:

- respond appropriately to nonverbal cues.
- use acceptable tone, volume, and intonation in a variety of settings.

4–8 students will:

- use knowledge from L1 to inform L2 reading.
- use cultural knowledge to interpret literature.

9–12 students will:

- use L1 to enhance oral storytelling and writing.
- integrate cultural knowledge into oral and written reports.

References

Cohen, B. (1983). *Molly's pilgrim*. New York: Bantam Books,

Johnston, T. (1996). *My Mexico—Mexico mío*. New York: G. P. Putnam's Sons.

Tomlinson, C., & Lynch-Brown, C. (1996). *Essentials of children's literature* (2nd ed.). Needham Heights, MA: Allyn & Bacon.

COOPERATIVE LEARNING:
Group Interactions to Accomplish Goals

This strategy addresses the following TESOL Standards:

Goal 1: To use English to communicate in social settings

Standard 3: Students will use learning strategies to extend their communicative competence.

Goal 2: To use English to achieve academically in all content areas

Standard 1: Students will use English to interact in the classroom.
Standard 2: Students will use English to obtain, process, construct, and provide subject matter information in spoken and written form.
Standard 3: Students will use appropriate learning strategies to construct and apply academic knowledge.

Goal 3: To use English in socially and culturally appropriate ways

Standard 2: Students will use nonverbal communication appropriate to audience, purpose, and setting.
Standard 3: Students will use appropriate learning strategies to extend their sociolinguistic and cultural competence.

Cooperative learning (Johnson & Johnson, 1984) is a term used for a collection of strategies in which students work together to accomplish a group task.

K–12 researchers have concluded that, to succeed, group work must be carefully structured; the students must be thoroughly prepared through social skill-building activities; assignments must be open-ended rather than have preset answers; and the task

Activity	Rules
Arts project	Team members work together to create an artistic display of the team members' names.
Assembly line	Using an arts or crafts project, team members assemble a product in assembly-line fashion. One team member starts the project and passes it to the next member, who adds to it. Each member contributes to the final product.
Brainstorm	Teams work against the clock to try to find three commonalties among the team members. Following the rules for brainstorming accept all ideas, build on other people's ideas—teams try to find a category in which they can all agree—three favorite things that are common among the team, three things they all hate to do, or three movies they all liked, for example. One team member suggests a category, the others quickly give their favorites in that category until they are able to find an area of agreement.
Group task	Group works together to complete a puzzle, word search, or brain teaser.
Line up	Team members work quickly to line themselves up according to a given stipulation such as height, age, birthday, number of brothers and sisters, etc.
Team identity	Team works together to reach consensus on a team name, logo, and motto.

Figure 18.1 Common Team-Building Activities for Cooperative Learning Teams

Adapted from Meyers, 1993.

must be such that a group, rather than an individual, is required to accomplish it. (Leki, 2001, p. 41)

The group task is structured so that each member of the group is expected to perform an assigned task. Because of the embedded structure of the unique tasks assigned to each member of the group, cooperative learning is much more effective than ordinary group work usually done in classroom situations. Appropriate training and structure is introduced into the process. These approaches are especially effective for English language learners because the students have more opportunities for verbal interactions in small groups (Kagan, 1989). They are encouraged by the members of the group and can participate at the level at which they are able. English language learners working in cooperative groups must be given assignments according to their levels of English proficiency, which requires the teacher to be aware of their stages of language acquisition. (See chapter 13, Leveled Questions) and their levels of ability in English reading and writing.

Cooperative learning activities must be preceded by some team-building (see suggestions in Figure 18.1) for the members to understand the value of working together and get to know each other's strengths. In addition, teachers must make their expectations clear if cooperative learning activities are to be successful. Some of the principles of cooperative learning are explained in Figure 18.2.

Principle	Example	Benefit to English Language Learners
Cooperative tasks are designed so that individuals must work together for the task to be accomplished.	Jigsaw activities involve each member of the team being given a piece of the information so that they must work together or no one will have all the necessary data.	English language learners must be encouraged to participate in the tasks or the whole team will fail to accomplish their assignment.
Positive interactions are developed and encouraged.	The group's evaluation is based on individual and group marks. Group members are rewarded for peer tutoring and supporting weaker students.	Because peer tutoring and group support of individuals are encouraged and rewarded, all students are supported to succeed.
Students have opportunities to work in different teams.	A variety of plans are used for grouping, such as interest groups, random groups, heterogeneous groups, etc.	English language learners have an opportunity to get to know other students in meaningful ways and to demonstrate their competence in a variety of ways.
Social, language, and content skills are all learned in the process of interacting with the group.	Social and academic language interactions in cooperative groups help the students to learn pro-social behaviors as well as content knowledge.	English language learners benefit from the verbal interactions, learning social norms and content-related language.

Figure 18.2   Principles of Cooperative Learning

Adapted from Meyers, 1993.

STEP BY STEP

Steps in using cooperative learning strategies in the classroom are:

• *Assigning groups and building a team*—Divide the class into cooperative groups. Provide a team-building activity as "warm-up" for helping students to see the advantages of cooperation and getting to know each other. Each time a new team is formed, there should be a team-building activity to help members become familiar with each other's capabilities. Suggestions for team-building activities are given in Figure 18.1.

• *Assigning roles within the groups*—Give the team members cards that identify their assigned roles and list clear descriptions of their duties. Usually one member is designated as the leader, one as note-taker, one as reporter, one as timekeeper. It is also helpful to give each member a name tag which designates the role to be played so that all members of the group are aware of the roles of all the members. Tasks especially appropriate for English language learners include artist, visual creator (drawing or computer-generated), mime, or translator—providing a physical reenactment or second-language translation of key points for other second-language learners in the classroom.

• *Assigning the task*—Give each team a task to complete and remind each member of the roles they are expected to serve to assist the others in completing the task. The leader keeps everyone working and focused, the note-taker keeps records of the team activity, the reporter shares the information or results with the class at the completion of the activity, and the timekeeper makes sure they are on task and moving toward completion of the task within the time limit.

• *Intervening to ensure full participation*—The teacher's role is crucial in establishing the tone of cooperation and group interaction of its members. Without appropriate team-building, expectations, and validation of the contributions of all individuals within the group, cooperative learning exercises might actually be detrimental to the academic and linguistic development of English learners (Leki, 2001). Teachers must carefully monitor group participation and intervene whenever a student is being excluded from the group process or taking over the work of the group (Cohen, 1994). To monitor these behaviors, teachers must listen to make sure every member of the group is being given a chance to talk, watch for physical signs that students are being excluded from the group, and use a variety of strategies to assign status to nonparticipating or excluded members of the group. Teachers can do this by mentioning a personal skill or strength that excluded members can contribute to the task, or by asking questions such as "Is everyone having a chance to talk?" If the teacher's interventions don't correct the problem, a student should be assigned to tally the number of times that each student talks, and be responsible for asking each student his or her opinions in an organized way. If this continues to be a problem, the teacher should schedule more team-building activities before using cooperative learning again.

• *Reporting back to the class*—Provide an opportunity for the groups to report back to the class at the end of the assigned time. Each group should share their solutions.

• *Debriefing and examining the group process*—Give each group an opportunity to debrief, discussing the process and the roles each team member played in the success of the group. Have each group fill out a group report form that focuses on both product and process. A sample group report form is shown in Figure 18.3.

| **Group Name** _____ |
| **Task** _____ **Date** _____ |

Group Member	**Contributions**	**New skill practiced? (yes, no, or comment)**

Comments

_____
_____
_____
_____

_____
Group Member's Signature

Note: Each group member must fill out a form. The group must agree on the new skill to be practiced. Suggestions: taking turns, sharing materials, staying on task, asking questions, summarizing ideas, encouraging others, restating suggestions, etc.)

Figure 18.3 A Cooperative Learning Group Report Form

Adapted from Meyers, 1993.

APPLICATIONS AND EXAMPLES

Ms. Truit's fourth graders are working in cooperative groups to use their math and problem-solving skills to plan a party for the end of the year. Each group of four has been given a budget of $25 to spend and they are to decide on the refreshments, decorations, and games to be played. At the end of the planning period, each group will present its plan for the party, complete with a drawing of the decorations, a detailed refreshment list including costs figured from a grocery store price list and a presentation detailing the process the group used to solve the problems and make decisions. The group with the best plan will actually get to do the shopping, make the decorations, and be in charge of leading the games. The winning group will have a full school day without other assignments to complete their party preparations.

The groups work diligently to complete their calculations and draw their decorations. The group leaders are encouraging everyone to work together. The note-takers are in charge of preparing the detailed plans, while the reporters are working along with the others to practice what they will say in their oral presentations. The timekeepers are keeping a close eye on the clock. Motivation and cooperation is high. Everyone wants to have a chance to actually give their party.

Ms. Hill's math students at Mountain High are using their calculators to solve problems related to the state budget. One of the gubernatorial candidates is promising a 12 percent reduction in state income tax if he is elected. He is also promising an increase of 6 percent in state spending for education. Ms. Hill has formed cooperative groups for the purpose of figuring out the answers to some weighty questions.

Each group leader is given a list of line items on the state budget. The group comptroller has been given a detailed list of state income from income taxes, the state education budget, and anticipated revenues for the coming year. Each group secretary has been given a list of bills currently being considered by the state legislature and their anticipated cost. The group calculator has been given the task of making calculations as requested by other members of the group.

The groups have been given the following tasks:

1. Figure the effect of a 12 percent reduction in state income taxes.
2. Figure the effect of a 6 percent increase in state education funding.
3. Figure the cost of new legislation if all of the bills currently being considered are passed, or if only 50 percent of them are passed.
4. Figure by what percentage the state revenues must increase for it to be possible for the gubernatorial candidate to carry out his promises (listed in tasks 1 and 2).
5. Create a visual on transparency film showing your calculations and what combination of factors would make the candidate's promises possible. In this task you may decide which bills could be passed, what the increase in revenues would have to be, on any combination of factors.
6. Watch the clock to make sure the group will be able to complete the task within the time limit. You should be finished and ready to present in 45 minutes.
7. Group reporters will present the results at the end of the class period. They may enlist the help of any (or all) of the group members in making the presentation.

The groups are working hard to make professional presentation visuals, double-check their calculations, and make sure they haven't overlooked any bills that might make a big difference in their calculations. They are learning a lot about calculator math and state government, including vocabulary unfamiliar to a number of them. The teacher is circulating to monitor the group efforts, define unfamiliar words, or refer the students to resources within the room—including the computer online services.

CONCLUSION

Cooperative learning provides an opportunity for communication, planning, research, and oral and visual presentations in the classroom. Quality group cooperation does not occur overnight, however. Taking the time to build teams, monitoring the group interactions, and debriefing are all vital pieces of the cooperative learning process. The groups are not just learning content but valuable interpersonal interaction skills, as well. Videotaping the group interactions and having the group watch the video and examine their own behaviors, strengths, and weaknesses is a supportive activity when creating the learning community (Herrell & Fowler, 1997).

EXAMPLES OF APPROXIMATION BEHAVIORS RELATED TO THE TESOL STANDARDS

Pre-K–3 students will:

- use social language to request information.
- follow rules to interact in a small group setting.

4–8 students will:

- actively participate in assigned cooperative learning tasks.
- understand and perform a defined cooperative learning group role.

9–12 students will:

- select, connect, and explain information through cooperative group interaction.
- assume a role in the presentation of group outcomes.

References

Cohen, E. (1994). *Designing groupwork* (2nd ed.). New York: Teachers College Press.

Herrell, A., & Fowler, J. (1997). *Camcorder in the classroom: Using a video camera to enrich curriculum.* Upper Saddle River, NJ: Merrill/Prentice Hall.

Johnson, D. W., & Johnson, R. T. (1984). *Circles of learning: Cooperation in the classroom.* Alexandria, VA: Association for Supervision and Curriculum Development.

Kagan, S. (1989). *Cooperative learning: Resources for teachers.* San Juan Capistrano, CA: Resources for Teachers.

Leki, I. (2001). A narrow thinking system: Non-native English-speaking students in group projects across the curriculum. *TESOL Quarterly, 35*(1) 39–63.

Meyers, M. (1993). *Teaching to diversity.* Toronto, Canada: Irwin Publishing.

Suggested Reading

Chamot, A., & O'Malley, J. (1994). *The CALLA handbook.* Reading, MA: Addison-Wesley.

Lesson Planning

Ellis, S. S., & Whalen, S. F. (1990). *Cooperative learning: Getting started.* New York: Scholastic.

Johnson, D. W., & Johnson, R. T. (1985). *Structuring cooperative learning: Lesson plans for teachers.* Edina, MN: Interaction Book Company.

Video

Cooperative Learning. (1996). Alexandria, VA: Association for Supervision and Curriculum Development.

CULTURE STUDIES:
Learning Research Skills and Valuing Home Cultures in One Project

This strategy addresses the following TESOL Standards:

Goal 2: To use English to achieve academically in all content areas

Standard 1: Students will use English to interact in the classroom.
Standard 2: Students will use English to obtain, process, construct, and provide subject matter information in spoken and written form.
Standard 3: Students will use appropriate learning strategies to construct and apply academic knowledge.

Goal 3: To use English in socially and culturally appropriate ways

Standard 1: Students will use the appropriate language variety, register, and genre according to audience, purpose, and setting.
Standard 2: Students will use nonverbal communication appropriate to audience, purpose, and setting.
Standard 3: Students will use appropriate learning strategies to extend their sociolinguistic and cultural competence.

Culture studies (Freeman & Freeman, 1994) are studies in which the students research and share information about their own cultural history. These studies will vary greatly depending on the ages of the students in the class but generally fit well with the history or social science goals in most school districts.

Many different language arts skills can be supported by culture studies. Students are required to use reading, writing, speaking, listening, viewing, and visual representations of ideas to interview their parents, grandparents, and other members of their culture. The key to making this strategy work is the way the word *culture* is defined. Any culture study should begin with a discussion of culture and what makes up a culture. This can be done effectively by examining the culture of the classroom and what makes it unique. The use of time, the attitude toward learning, the expectations for participation, the rules about how to get along with each other, and the structure that is in place regarding the use of materials all contribute to the culture of the classroom.

Once the students understand the broad definition of *culture* that is to be investigated, they can begin to organize the study of their own culture. Some teachers have found it profitable to encourage students to work in pairs or small groups so that they can begin to compare and contrast cultural norms as an ongoing part of the study. For possible approaches to culture studies see Figure 19.1.

STEP BY STEP

The steps in implementing culture studies are:

• *Finding an age-appropriate project*—Decide on a project that is appropriate for the ages of your students and that supports the objectives for your grade level. Examine the objectives in both social sciences and language arts to determine ways to integrate both curricular areas. See Figure 19.1 for suggestions.

• *Setting up the goals and parameters*—Identify the purpose of the projects to be done and whether the research and activities should be done individually, in pairs, or in small groups. If a main goal is to get the students to interact and share the information they are gathering, then pairs or small groups should be used. Make a visual with the students that clearly identifies the steps they are to take in their research and the products they will be expected to create. For an example of this visual, see Figure 19.2.

• *Making expectations clear*—Encourage the students to identify the main elements of a good project and create a rubric or checklist based on their suggestions so that they know what is expected of them and how their report will be evaluated. See Figure 19.3 for a sample of a cultural study checklist.

• *Planning the culminating activity*—Plan a celebration involving school administrators and families so the students can share their research and results.

• *Assessing student growth and progress*—As students work in groups, the teacher has a unique opportunity to observe, take anecdotal records, and document their language interactions, social language skills, and research strategies. The self-evaluation checklist in Figure 19.3 provides a good format for individual conferences, the results of which make an informative anecdotal record. Anecdotal records and results of the culture study project should be included in individual student portfolios along with the student self-evaluation forms.

• *Adding technology*—Culture studies are a perfect format for the integration of technology. Students can complete a lot of their research using the Internet. Using the word processor to write the actual reports is very motivating for many students. Using other computer formats for creating charts and visuals makes the reports more interesting as does the creation of PowerPoint slide shows for the final presentations. Any use of technology in the process should be documented in the portfolio and celebrated as an additional format of effective communication.

APPLICATIONS AND EXAMPLES

Mr. Watanabe's fourth graders have been studying California history all year. They have explored the history of the state from the pre-Columbian settlements and people through modern day immigrations and rapid population growth. They have created a time line of the history of the state with major events prominently noted. As Mr. Watanabe introduces the final segment of the study of California history he shows some pictures of his family. "This is a picture of my family. This is my grandfather and my grandmother. This is my father and this is my mother. And this is me," He points to the small

Group	Projects	Activities
Kindergarten	Family portraits Working together	• Draw a picture of your family. • Tell about what your family likes to do together. • Draw a picture of some work that your family does together. • Tell about how the work is divided and who does each part. • Tell about the things each family member can do to help the work get done. • Is there anyone in your family who teaches other people in the family how to do things? What things?
Primary grades	People are different, people are the same The way we do things changes from generation to generation	• Group investigation of basic ways in which cultural groups are the same and different. Choosing one aspect at a time, have the students interview people of their own cultural groups about how the particular aspect is regarded. (For example, the use of time, the importance of education, the regard for animals, the significance of different colors, the role of food in celebrations, the division of work, etc.) • Individual students interview and research family photo albums for examples of how things have changed from generation to generation. Questions asked of family members should also examine how these changes have affected the use of time and the value system of the family.
Upper elementary grades	Our state and nation	Each student researches the impact of their own cultural group on the history of the state and nation. The child's own family history should be examined first to determine the reason for immigration, if any, or the family work history and how the occupations of generations fit in with the history of the state and nation. The changes in value systems, occupations, and places where the family moved should be compared to the general trends in the state, nation, and world history when applicable.
Middle school	Values and history	Students examine their family's values in relation to how time is spent, the priorities for the expenditure of money, the differences in expectations for male and female children, any inequalities in the past or present in the division of work or responsibilities within the family. The celebrations and rituals which have continued over time and the use of language and interactions in solving problems or disputes should also be examined.
High school	Nation-building	Students examine the movements in history which affect the building of nations and how their culture has followed or differed from the general trend. The contributions of women, minorities, the effect of world events are all considered in light of the building of nations across the world. The changes that have taken place in the students' own families and cultures as a result of or in response to these events should also be considered. The construction of time lines and personal family histories in relation to world events is appropriate.

Figure 19.1   Culture Studies Appropriate for Different Grade Levels

Please note that suggestions are given in relation to the broad themes recommended in the California History/Social Science Framework, 1988.

1. Introduce yourself to your group, telling your name and the cultural group with which you identify yourself. If you do not identify yourself with an ethnic group, try to identify your broad cultural affiliation such as Mexican-American, German-American, European-American, or White Anglo-Saxon Protestant. You may even have to identify the cultural group from your mother's side and your father's side.

2. As a group use your social studies book to research the history of the world from 1900 until today and create a time line of major events. Hint: Several of these time lines are included in your textbook. Each member of your group should make a copy of the general time line and place his/her own birth on the time line.

3. The group should brainstorm questions they will ask as they interview members of their family about the events on the time line that they remember. The purpose is to learn as much as you can about how the world events since 1900 affected your family. Did any members of your family fight in any of the wars? Did the family move to another city or country because of world or economic events? (See #5 for other ideas.)

4. Each member of the group should arrange to interview members of his/her own family or other members of their cultural group and report back each day to share the interviews that have been conducted and the information that has been revealed. Events shared by the interviewees should be charted on the time line and written in narrative form.

5. At the conclusion of the week groups should meet together to plan a presentation format for sharing the information they have gathered with the whole class. Be creative and include visuals or reenactments! Each member of the group should have a speaking part in the presentation. Information that should be highlighted in the presentation:
   - In what ways were the family events affected or family histories altered by world and economic events?
   - In what ways were the different cultural groups impacted by these events?
   - Which cultural groups seemed to be least affected by the world and economic events?
   - How did the world and economic events affect the basic values and priorities of the different cultural groups?

Figure 19.2 The Steps You Will Take to Create Your Family Time Line

Before you present your culture study, check to make sure you have all the following:
_____ I made a visual to help me show what I learned.
_____ My visual is large enough to see easily.
_____ I have checked the spelling and grammar.
_____ I have note cards prepared, which will help me remember the main points I want to make.
_____ I have included information in my report from interviews of people in my generation, my parents' generation, and my grandparents' generation.
_____ I have included information in my report about the main historical events that affected my family history.
_____ I have included information in my report about the changes in values and priorities from generation to generation.
_____ I have included interesting family stories in my report so that "the flavor" of my cultural heritage is evident.
_____ My visual and note cards will be submitted to my teacher at the conclusion of my report.

Figure 19.3 Checklist for Culture Study Reports

child in the picture. "I am going to tell you about how my family's history fits on the time line of California history we have created."

"My grandfather was a fisherman in the San Francisco area in the 1930s. When the Japanese bombed Pearl Harbor in 1941, the American people became very suspicious of all Japanese people. The American government moved all the Japanese families from the West Coast into camps so that they could not conspire with the Japanese government to attack the west coast of America. The picture I showed you was taken at the Manzanar War Relocation Camp here in California where my family lived for four years. I went to school there. My whole family lived behind barbed wire like criminals simply because we were of Japanese heritage.

"You would think that my mother and father would be very bitter about this part of history and how they were treated. My parents, however, see it as something that was natural. They say that people get frightened in time of war and do unreasonable things. Part of my Japanese culture is the value of serenity. I think that an important part of my culture is thinking serene thoughts so that the aggravations of life do not upset the higher thoughts of the mind. My father wrote some beautiful music while he was in the relocation camp. He used the time he was given to create something of beauty."

Mr. Watanabe placed a card along the class time line under January 1942 that said, "Mr. Watanabe's family goes to Manzanar War Relocation Camp." He then talks about what he wants each member of the class to do as a part of their final study of California history.

"As your final study of California history I want you to interview the members of your family, your clan elders, your priests, or older people you know who belong to your culture. I want you to find out how long your family or people have been in California, what caused them to come, and what part they played in any of the California events that we have been studying. If your parents do not know the answers to your questions, ask your grandparents or other elderly people in your families. What other ways can you think of to get information about this study?"

"We could look in old photograph albums," Juanita answers.

"My grandmother has a family Bible that has the whole history of our family in it!" Jerrod exclaims.

"That will be very helpful," Mr. Watanabe says with a smile. By the end of the week the time line is bulging with three-by-five cards noting events in the families of the students. Some of the students are amazed at how long some of the Mexican and Native American families have lived in California.

"I thought the Mexican families were all new immigrants," Melissa said. "My family only moved to California in 1980. Maria's family has been here for generations. Compared with her family, we are the new immigrants."

Ms. Jeffreys teaches 12th-grade English in a high school where most of the students are from white Protestant families. Her husband teaches the same grade level and subject in a highly multicultural school and they often discuss how different the students at the two schools are in their views of the world. One night, over dinner, Mr. and Ms. Jeffreys decide that they want to do a project that will help the students from the two schools get to know each other and their differing viewpoints. They decide that each of their students should write a cultural autobiography to be shared over the Internet with a student in the other's class. The Jeffreys decide to call the project "Cultural Conversations." They begin the study by identifying a piece of literature that they can explore with their classes.

Each student is asked to reflect on the incidents discussed in the book and how it relates to the customs, values, and interactions in their own families and cultural groups. The Jeffreys choose the book *Plain and Simple: A Woman's Journey to the Amish,* by Sue Bender (1989), because the book tells about one woman's visit to another culture and how the things she learns about another culture cause her to reflect on her own.

The Jeffreys assign conversation partners from their fourth-period classes. They intend to start small and see how well the project is accepted. They agree to read and discuss the first chapter of the book on Monday, having their students reflect on the chapter, talk to their families on Monday night, and post their first e-mail conversations on Tuesday.

The first chapter of the book talks about how the author falls in love with Amish quilts—their simple designs and bold colors—and begins to think about the Amish people. She compares her lifestyle and values with those of the Amish people and wants to create an area of calm peace in her life. As the Jeffreys read the first chapter they stop periodically and discuss their own lives, values, and cultures and how their family heritages contribute to their beliefs. They ask the students to think about the values Ms. Bender lists in the first chapter and how they equate their own personal and family's values to those the author discusses. The students are then given a list of things to discuss with their families that evening and told that they will be discussing their self-reflections and information gained from their families via e-mail with a student at the "other high school" the next day. The students all chuckle, knowing exactly how they are connected to the "other high school."

The next day in the computer lab, the students are all busily writing to their new conversation partners. The Jeffreys ask the students to save the correspondence each day so that the information they share and gather from their conversation partners can be used in the future. There is a lot of concern about spell-checking and proper English sentence structure because of the cross-town rivalry between the high schools, but the teachers and fellow students are all happy to give assistance.

On Wednesday, the discussion begins with what has been learned through the conversations. Many of the students are amazed to discover the differences in the use of time and the priorities expressed by their conversation partner.

"My partner has lessons every day after school. He's taking trumpet lessons, French lessons, and being tutored in calculus. He has no time for fun. He goes from school to lessons, to homework, to bed," says Mikel.

"What does that tell you about his values?" asks Mr. Jeffreys.

"I think it tells more about his family's values because he doesn't seem to want to take all those lessons," replies Mikel.

"That may be so—but he's doing it," says Mr. Jeffreys.

"Oh, I see your point," Mikel replies. "His values involve going along with his parents' expectations of him, improving himself in areas of music and languages. He did say he was expecting to go to college on a music scholarship."

After their discussion of the first day's conversations the Jeffreys read and discuss the second chapter of *Plain and Simple,* where Ms. Bender struggles with her interest in the Amish, her values, which seem to directly conflict with those of the Amish, and her desire to know more about the Amish culture. The chapter explores the value of the finished product in comparison with the value of the process of creating, the need to establish balance in life, and the impact of religion on the rules of the culture. The Jeffreys give the students their next assignment, which is to reflect on the chapter and their own family values related to these issues.

The study continues in this pattern over the next two weeks. After the book has been read and the conversation partners have discussed a number of issues related to culture, they are assigned a report to be written collaboratively and presented at a joint meeting of the two classes. The partners are to bring some artifacts from their cultures that represent the values they have discovered as they reflect on the book and exchange ideas. The partners are to share the things they discovered about their own cultures and how their belief systems were formed, including the influence of their families, their religion, their interests, their school, their friends. The Jeffreys plan a seminar where the two classes will get together for a Saturday morning to work on their presentations, eat lunch together, and then present their findings to their school administrators and families in the afternoon. Each student is invited to contribute a paper to a journal they will compile collaboratively, titled "Our Stories, Cultural Conversations." The Jeffreys are pleased to see that almost everyone contributes a story to the journal. The stories contributed show a respect for the students' own cultures and the new information they have gained about their partner's culture.

CONCLUSION

Culture studies provide a way for teachers to build the classroom community while engaging their students in an in-depth social studies project that requires research. Language arts skills such as interviewing, note-taking, using the steps in the writing process, and oral and visual presentations must be taught. The classroom community is greatly enhanced when the teacher shares his/her own culture study and discusses the multiple ways the study was conducted. Appreciation of the values, customs, and unique contributions of the different cultures is heightened through the process of investigating multiple cultures through first-hand accounts of personal experiences.

EXAMPLES OF APPROXIMATION BEHAVIORS RELATED TO THE TESOL STANDARDS

Pre-K–3 students will:

- represent family culture orally and in pictures.
- verbally explain ways that people are the same and different.

4–8 students will:

- explain the role of different cultures on U.S. and state histories.
- explore the values associated with different cultures.

9–12 students will:

- explain and explore the different roles and expectations of people from a perspective of gender in a variety of cultures.
- research and construct family histories and timelines in relation to world history.

References

Bender, S. (1989). *Plain and simple: A woman's journey to the Amish*. New York: Harper Collins.

California State Department of Education. (1988). History/social sequences framework. Sacramento, CA: California State Department of Education.

Freeman, D., & Freeman, Y. (1994). *Between worlds: Access to second language acquisition*. Portsmouth, NH: Heinemann.

LEARNING CENTERS:
Extending Learning Through Hands-On Practice

Learning centers are places set up in the classroom where the students can engage in hands-on activities that allow them to obtain additional experience in using new skills, expand skills usage to more closely match their individual needs, and work cooperatively with other students. Learning centers are thus especially effective for meeting the needs of English language learners and other students needing expanded verbal interaction or hands-on practice to enhance their learning. See Figure 20.1 for suggestions of ways in which learning centers can be used in the classroom.

STEP BY STEP

The steps in implementing learning centers in the classroom are:

• *Identifying skills to be practiced*—Identify skills that have already been taught in which the students need more practice. Set up places with materials that can be used for additional, authentic, and meaningful practice in the use of those skills.

• *Introducing the centers*—Introduce the centers to the students, making sure that you demonstrate how they are to use the materials, what your expectations are for the activities, and how their work will be assessed. Display the rules and expectations in the centers so that the students understand that center work is a part of their assigned job and will contribute toward their course grade. The rules for moving from one center to the next should also be discussed and modeled. Rules about cleaning up materials before moving to the next center should be made clear.

Grade	Center	Description
Kindergarten	Counting Center	Students count objects and match object groups with numerals.
	Sorting Center	Students sort objects by beginning sounds (vocabulary development).
	Listening Center	Students listen to stories read on a tape recorder while they look at the book.
	Language Master Center	Students hear the name of an object read as a card with a picture of the object and the printed word is fed through the Language Master machine.
	Story Retelling Center	Students retell a story they have heard using small props made out of baked dough (see Story Reenactment chapter of this text).
	Letter Work Center	Students match capital and lowercase letters, which can be expanded to include pictures or objects whose names begin with the letters.
Primary	Word Work Center	Students build high-frequency words with magnetic letters or letter stamps.
	Pocket Chart Center	Students build sentences with word cards and place the sentences in the pocket chart. Can also be used to build compound words, contractions, match synonyms, antonyms, and word families.
	Computer Center	Students work cooperatively to use word processing software to write collaborative stories, problem-solving software to practice math and science strategies, and simple programming software to create graphics (practicing language as they collaborate).
	Writing and Publishing Center	Students use materials at the center to write and publish stories, poetry, and informational books.
	Skills Center	After a skill (such as proofreading) has been taught, students practice the use of the skill in an authentic way. They can use proofreading marks to proof a story written by another student for the class newsletter, a letter written to be mailed, or stories written specifically to be edited.
	Literature Response	Students use this center to respond in double-entry journals, literature logs.
	Project Center	Students use materials in this center to create a project related to science (e.g., a model), social studies (e.g., a map), literature (e.g., a diorama), or math (e.g., props for a word problem), or any curricular area.
	Illustration center	Students use materials in this center to replicate the type of illustrations done by an illustrator they are studying such as Eric Carle (finger paint and collage materials) or Leslie Baker (watercolor).

Figure 20.1   Suggestions for Classroom Learning Centers

Grade	Center	Description
Upper elementary	Science Center	Students use materials in this center to replicate experiments demonstrated by the teacher.
	Observation Center	Students use this center to closely observe and write observations of nature, art, videotapes of performances in music, dance, and athletics.
	Theater Center	Students use this center to write scripts for scenes of their favorite books, enlist the help of peers to practice the scene, and then present it to the class.
	Editing Center	Students use this center to collaboratively edit student writing that is almost ready to be published. The center includes thesaurus, dictionaries, and English grammar texts.
Middle & high school	Logic Center	Student use this center to create "brainbenders," logic problems that can be solved by other students using props provided, or made by the students.
	Video Center	Videocamera, tripod, and tapes are available in this center so students can videotape scenes from literature, vocabulary role play, book commercials written by students, enactments of history, etc.
	Research Center	Encyclopedias, reference books, a computer with Internet access, are all available at this center to encourage student research on topics under study in the classroom.
	Multiple Intelligences Center	Seven different ways of studying a topic are presented in centers corresponding to Gardner's Seven Intelligences (soon to be expanded to nine). Students are encouraged to: • write a song about the topic in the Musical Intelligence Center. • write a poem about the topic in the Linguistic Intelligence Center. • debate the topic with a peer in the Interpersonal Intelligence Center. • write in a personal journal about the topic in the Intrapersonal Intelligence Center. • write a logic or word problem about the topic in the Logical/Mathematical Intelligence Center. • draw a poster about the topic in the Visual/Spatial Intelligence Center. • choreograph a dance or mime in the Bodily/Kinesthetic Intelligence Center.

Figure 20.1   Continued

- ***Documenting the center work***—Introduce a method for the students to use in documenting their participation in centers. This can be as simple as a list of names at the required centers, a contract form on which the students enter the names of the centers they will complete each day or a work folder in which they place all center work done each day. The students have to understand the requirements and the ways in which the center work will be assessed. Make your expectations very clear as to which centers are required and which are optional.

- ***Bringing students up to date***—Whenever centers are changed, repeat the explanation and modeling steps so that the students understand what is required. Centers should be changed regularly so that students are challenged and provided with opportunities to practice new skills as they are taught.

- ***Assessing student progress and understanding***—It is vital that teachers validate and evaluate the work students do in learning centers or the students will not take their center work seriously. Teachers should set up a method for collecting and assessing the quality of center work. Celebration circles are one way of gathering students together to share their accomplishments during center time and provide the teacher with an opportunity to encourage students who are using their center time productively. Center products are good additions to the individual student portfolios as well.

- ***Adding technology***—Computer centers are a powerful way of providing extra skill practice in a unique mode. Student-made PowerPoint presentations provide a good use of center time, as well. Some teachers have found the writing of video scripts and the making of class videos fascinating center activities.

APPLICATIONS AND EXAMPLES

The third graders in Mr. Martino's class are learning to write friendly letters. Mr. Martino decides that he will introduce a series of learning centers that will enable his students to practice writing letters as well as to produce a class newsletter, which will give them authentic practice in writing in several domains. The centers Mr. Martino sets up in his classroom will support the letter-writing project and expand it so that the students get practice in writing letters for different purposes.

Mr. Martino begins by creating a life-size mailbox out of a cardboard box that originally housed a washing machine. He sets up a Mail Processing Center in which the students must cancel the student-designed stamps on the incoming letters and place them in alphabetized letter cubbies labeled with the third-grade students' names. Mr. Martino also creates a mail cubby box for the kindergartners so his students can write to them also. The instructions in the mail processing center say, "Take the mail out of the mail collection box. Cancel the stamps using the mail cancellation rubber stamp. If anyone mailed a letter without putting a stamp on it, stamp it 'Return to sender' and place it in the mailbox of the person who sent it. Use the alphabetical sorting tray and sort the letters with canceled stamps alphabetically and then place them into the mail cubbies."

Mr. Martino has recently taught proofreading to his class and so he sets up a proofreading center and a class newsletter project that will be done on the computer. Students are encouraged to write articles for the class newsletter about class activities, activities with the kindergarten buddies, and any news about the students or families in the class. In addition to the news articles there will be a page of letters to the editor and letters to "Dear Anna," their class advice column, both of which will give authentic practice in writing friendly letters.

Mr. Martino sets up centers in which the news articles are to be written. In these News Article Centers, he displays photographs of recent school and classroom activities and field trips for the students to write about. The instructions in the news writing centers say, "Write an article for the class newsletter about a news event in our classroom or school. Be sure to include the who, what, when, and where information about the event. When the article is completed, take it to the proofreading center to be proofread."

In the Sports News Center he places photos of the latest kickball and softball games, as well as trophies some of the students have won in recent Little League games and swim-meet competitions and brought in to share with the class. The instructions in this center say, "Write an article about a sports event in which you participated. Be sure to include who scored, what the final score was, who was playing, and when the event took place. When you finish the article, take it to the proofreading center to be proofread."

In the Literary Review Center, Mr. Martino places copies of books that he has read aloud recently as well as several books that the students are reading and discussing in literature circles. The instructions in this center read, "Write a book review for the class newsletter. Be sure to write about the parts of the book that make it interesting or exciting without giving away the plot. Include the author's name, the name of the illustrator, and any quotes you can get from people who have read the book. When your article is complete, take it to the proofreading table to be proofread."

At the Letters to the Editor Center the instructions read, "Write a letter to the editor about something you would like to see changed in our classroom or school. Be sure to tell why you want something changed and exactly what needs to be changed and how. Write the letter in correct friendly letter format and sign it. When you have finished your letter, take it to the proofreading center for proofreading."

At the Dear Anna Center the students can either write a letter to Anna or answer letters that other students have left at the center. The instructions in this center read, "In this center you may write a letter to Dear Anna about a problem you have and leave it to be answered OR you can choose a letter from the box of letters and write a response to it. Remember that the writer of the letter is expecting a helpful response. You do not have to sign your name to the letters you leave to be answered but you must sign them in some way like, 'Someone in a hurry,' or 'A friend with a problem.' "

In the Cartoons Center the students are supplied with drawing materials and encouraged to draw cartoons to be included in the class newsletter. The instructions in this center read, "Draw a cartoon and submit it to the newsletter editor. Be sure to check your spelling before submitting it."

In the Proofreading Center Mr. Martino includes a poster showing the proofreading marks he has taught the class, some dictionaries, a thesaurus, and a grammar textbook. The instructions in this center say, "Work with a partner to proofread the articles. Use the dictionaries, thesaurus, or grammar books if you need them. Use the proofreading marks to show any changes that need to be made. Return the article to the author after it has been proofread."

In the Computer Center students type their article using a word processing program after the article has been proofread. The students work in pairs to help each other and once an article has been typed, it is saved on the newsletter file.

Mr. Martino takes his students through the centers, carefully modeling what is expected at each center. He shows the students how they cross their name off the list at each center as they work in the center and how they list their center work on the daily work schedule each day. See Figure 20.2

Name _____	Date _____	
Work I accomplished today:	Completed?	Self-Rating
News article on _____	Yes No	1 2 3 4 5
Sports article on _____	Yes No	1 2 3 4 5
Letter to the editor on _____	Yes No	1 2 3 4 5
Letter to Dear Anna on _____	Yes No	1 2 3 4 5
Cartoon on _____	Yes No	1 2 3 4 5
Proofread _____ articles on _____	Yes No	1 2 3 4 5
Typed articles on _____	Yes No	1 2 3 4 5
Processed mail on _____	Yes No	1 2 3 4 5
Other reading or writing: _____	Yes No	1 2 3 4 5
Conference with teacher on _____		
Teacher comments: _____		
Plans for tomorrow: _____		

Figure 20.2 Mr. Martino's Daily Work Schedule

for a sample of the daily work schedule Mr. Martino uses to keep track of the centers the students are using and the quality of the work they are accomplishing.

The students in Mr. Tanaka's eighth-grade humanities class are discussing *The House on Mango Street* by Sandra Cisneros (1984).

"I don't know why people think it's such a great book," says Kara. "It's just a jumble of little stories. Some of the chapters are only a page long."

"What do you think makes a book a good book?" Mr. Tanaka asks.

"I think books are good for different reasons," Franco replies.

"I like this book. What bothers Kara is just what I like about the book. It's like a whole lot of small pieces that tell you about her life—Sandra Cisneros's life. It's about people she knows and little stories about different people that are interesting."

"I guess that's what I don't like," Kara says. "The people are ordinary. They're talking about ordinary things. I like books that tell about things I don't see every day."

"I don't think they're ordinary," Franco says. "They're interesting. They have things to talk about."

"What do you write about when you write, Kara?" Mr. Tanaka asks. "Don't you write about the people you know and the things they do?" "I guess that's why I don't write much," Kara admits. "I never think I have anything interesting to write about."

"We need to do some thinking about where our writing ideas originate. Maybe we should write some letters to authors and find out where they get their ideas," Mr. Tanaka says.

During the next few weeks, Mr. Tanaka plans to teach a series of prewriting strategies to his students as they prepare to combine a personal writing study with a broad study of culture and its effect on the way people live, make decisions, and conduct their lives. Mr. Tanaka knows that most of his students identify with a certain ethnic group and define their culture in that way. He is hoping to help them see the many influences at home, at school, and in their communities that help the students to define themselves. The reading of *The House on Mango Street* is an introduction to this study.

In Sandra Cisneros's book one of the characters, Esperanza, writes poetry. She shares her poetry with an aunt who later dies, leaving Esperanza no one with whom to share her poetry. Mr. Tanaka discusses this character and her poetry with his class one day.

"How many of you have ever tried to write poetry?" he asks. No one raises a hand. "Well," Mr. Tanaka says slowly. "I think it's time we tried."

A soft moan is heard in the class. "I want to introduce you to some ways of writing poems," Mr. Tanaka says. "You might have noticed that the poems Esperanza writes don't rhyme. She tries to create a picture with words."

Mr. Tanaka begins the study of poetry forms by teaching the eighth graders how to write concrete poems where they write a sentence or two creating a visual image with words and then arrange the words on the page so they create a picture. He also teaches the class the formula for writing cinquain and diamonte poems. (See Figure 20.3.)

After he demonstrates and gives the class guided practice in writing poems in these three formats, Mr. Tanaka sets up a learning center where the students can gain extra experience in writing formula poems. He uses the word banks that the class has created in learning how to write formula poems and he places the words in pocket charts so that the students can rearrange them into cinquain and diamonte poems. Once the students have built poems in the center, Mr. Tanaka encourages them to recopy them on a single sheet of paper and leave them in the box at the learning center so that he can later bind the poems into a class poetry book. Mr. Tanaka reads the poems in the box each day and frequently asks permission to read them aloud in class. Sometimes the author asks him not to tell who wrote the poem and sometimes the poem is written in the student's home language. Mr. Tanaka shows appreciation for the students' efforts and gives them feedback on ways in which they can improve their poetry. He asks students to read and translate the poems for him if he can't read the language. See Figure 20.4 to see how Mr. Tanaka's poetry center is arranged.

As the study of writing and culture continues, Mr. Tanaka gradually teaches a number of skills and strategies to his students. As the lessons are taught, Mr. Tanaka sets up additional learning centers in the classroom to provide additional practice for the students. Before long, the students are all working in centers while Mr. Tanaka works with small groups of students on the projects they

A cinquain is a five-line poem with lines written in the following arrangement:

Line 1:   a one word subject with two syllables
Line 2:   four syllables describing the subject
Line 3:   six syllables of action words relating to the subject
Line 4:   eight syllables expressing a feeling or a thought about the subject
Line 5:   two syllables describing or renaming the subject

An example of a cinquain written by a second grader:

Sneakers

smelly, dirty

jumping, turning, squeaking

They are so comfortable now!

grungy

A diamonte is a seven-line poem that is written in the shape of a diamond. This poetic form helps students to demonstrate their understanding of opposites. A diamonte poem is written using this formula:

Line 1:   one noun as the subject
Line 2:   two adjectives describing the subject
Line 3:   three participles (ending in "ing") telling about the subject
Line 4:   four nouns, the first two tell about the subject, the second two tell about the opposite
Line 5:   three participles telling about the opposite
Line 6:   two adjectives describing the opposite
Line 7:   one noun that is the opposite of the subject

An example of a diamonte written by a seventh grader:

Winter

Cool and crisp

Rushing, reading, cramming

Books, papers, ball games, beaches

Sunning, swimming, playing

Hot and sweaty

Summer

Figure 20.3   Cinquain and Diamonte Formula Poetry

are creating. The centers he has created in the classroom provide Mr. Tanaka with time to give small-group instruction while his students are working on strengthening their writing and researching skills. The centers he has created in the classroom include:

- the Poetry Center where students create formula poems.
- an Internet Research Center where students can search for information related to the culture project on which they are working.
- a Webbing and Clustering Center where students create prewriting webs or clusters to get them started in writing.
- an Art Center for creating visuals to enhance the writing and presentations being prepared.
- an Unforgettable Character Center where a different character from *The House on Mango Street* is highlighted each day.

The students read the short chapter about a character and either create an illustration for the chapter read, or write a description of a character who is brought to mind by the Cisneros chacacter and create an illustration for the new character. This center was added after a lesson on characterization and the four ways in which authors create characters, what they say, what they do, what they think, and how they look (Tompkins, 1998).

- A Video Center where the students create a short video to be used as a part of their project presentation. This video should represent a part of their culture which is difficult to depict without a visual image, such as typical verbal interactions, body language, personal space, or important artifacts. The video created in this center may be a simulation or a series of video

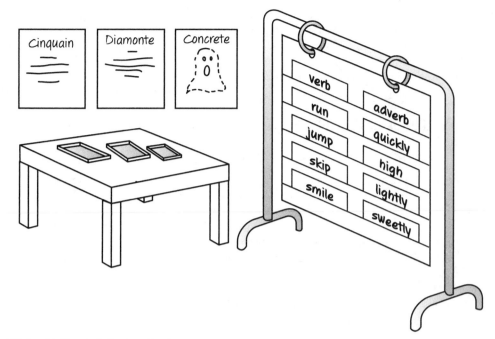

Figure 20.4   Mr. Tanaka's Poetry Center

clips made in the community or home, edited together using the simple editing equipment in the center.

- The Elements of Culture Center where Mr. Tanaka selects a quote from Edward T. Hall's book *Beyond Culture* (1981) and posts it each day. The students are instructed to read the quote and respond to it by talking into the tape recorder at the center. They may work alone or in pairs and they may respond in English or their home language. After they have reflected on the quote of the day they are to include the quote and their reflection in their culture report in some way, as a visual, a part of a video clip, or in writing. The quotes Mr. Tanaka uses include thoughts like:

> It (time) is also tangible; they speak of it as being saved, spent, wasted, lost, made up, accelerated, slowed down, crawling, and running out. (p. 19)
>
> Modern education has left us with the illusion that a lot is known about learning, that real learning goes on in the school, and that if it doesn't happen in a school or under the aegis of a school (like the year abroad), it has no validity. (p. 35)
>
> Each culture has its own characteristic manner of locomotion, sitting, standing, reclining, and gesturing. (p. 75)

At the end of the month-long study, Mr. Tanaka's students have a new vision of culture and its place in shaping their beliefs and priorities. They discuss differences in culture with peers of their same ethnic background and discover that their assumptions are not identical. The learning centers have given them opportunities to expand their skills with practice over time. The students have had extensive experience in using the Web for research and they have all read and discussed two pieces of literature that have helped them to broaden their understanding of literature, poetry and culture, *The House on Mango Street* and *Beyond Culture*.

CONCLUSION

The use of learning centers in the classroom is a powerful way to encourage students to practice the new skills they are gaining. Centers should be carefully explained to students so that they understand what is expected of them as they use the center. Both behavior and learning expectations must be made clear for the centers to support learning.

Well-planned centers enable students to refine their skills, expand their uses of newly acquired skills, and create new and different ways to demonstrate their learning. To harness the power of learning centers in the classroom, students must be encouraged to go beyond basic skill practice and find ways to be creative. Students should see their efforts recognized, valued, and celebrated if they are to expend maximum effort in learning center work.

EXAMPLES OF APPROXIMATION BEHAVIORS RELATED TO THE TESOL STANDARDS

Pre-K–3 students will:

- follow modeled oral directions to successfully participate in learning centers.
- ask for assistance from peers to succeed at the learning center task.

4–8 students will:

- use materials in a structured way to construct or discover a specific learning objective.
- extend skills through independent practice based on classroom instruction.

9–12 students will:

- build on skills and information taught in class to solve real-life problems.
- use writing skills to create an innovative composition.

References

Cisneros, S. (1984). *The house on Mango Street*. New York: Vintage Books (Random House).

Hall, E. (1981). *Beyond culture*. New York: Doubleday.

Tompkins, G. (1998). *Language arts: Content and teaching strategies* (4th ed.). Upper Saddle River, NJ: Merrill/Prentice Hall.

IMAGING:
Creating Visual Pictures to Support Understanding

This strategy addresses the following TESOL Standards:

Goal 2: To use English to achieve academically in all content areas

Standard 1: Students will use English to interact in the classroom.

Standard 2: Students will use English to obtain, process, construct, and provide subject matter information in spoken and written form.

Standard 3: Students will use appropriate learning strategies to construct and apply academic knowledge.

Goal 3: To use English in socially and culturally appropriate ways

Standard 2: Students will use nonverbal communication appropriate to audience, purpose, and setting.

Standard 3: Students will use appropriate learning strategies to extend their sociolinguistic and cultural competence.

Imaging (Chamot & O'Malley, 1994) is a strategy that encourages students to create an image in their minds to support the understanding of concepts or problems to be solved. The teacher is involved in supporting students to create mind-pictures that enable them to imagine the scene being described in the text being read or the problem to be solved. Once images are created in the students' minds, the teacher encourages the students to describe what they can see. This gives the teacher an opportunity to interact with the students to support their understanding. Research in reading comprehension (Irwin, 1991) has shown imaging as an attribute of effective readers, which is often not employed by poor readers. For this reason, it is an important strategy to teach. It is especially important to teach the strategy and discuss the images, or mind-pictures, with English language learners because they may form faulty images due to misconceptions related to language misunderstanding. Possible curricular uses of imaging are shown in Figure 21.1.

Curricular Area	Imaging Use
Vocabulary	Picture a _____ in your mind. Does it look like this? (Show an illustration or photograph.) What does yours look like?
Comprehension	Close your eyes and picture the scene in your mind. What do you see? (Question for details.)
Mathematics	Use with word problems. After the word problem is read, have the students close their eyes and picture the people, animals, and things involved in the problem. (Ask questions related to the relative size, number, and quantity in the problem.)
Summarizing	After a section of a text is read, have the students close their eyes and create a mind-picture of the text. Question about the overall scene they see and the important details pictured.
Art	Before having the students begin to create images in art media, have them close their eyes and picture what they want to create. Question them about the features of line, proportion, color, and movement that they see.
Music	As the students listen to music have them close their eyes and picture what the music is suggesting. Ask them to describe their mind-pictures.
Writing	Before the students write a passage, have them close their eyes and picture the image they want to create with words. Encourage them to verbalize the image they want to create before they write the words.

Figure 21.1 Curricular Uses of Imaging

STEP BY STEP

The steps in implementing imaging in the classroom are:

• ***Identifying a curricular connection***—Be aware of areas of the curriculum in which imaging would support your students' understanding. Are certain students having difficulty remembering or sequencing what they read? Are students having difficulty conceptualizing word problems in math? Are the sentences students write dull and uninteresting without much detail? These are all signs that students need instruction in imaging. Identify an area that would help students understand the power of imaging in supporting their academic understanding.

• ***Planning an introductory imaging activity***—Introduce imaging as a way of making students' academic work easier or a way of helping them to solve problems. You will need to start slowly and walk them through the first activity carefully. Not all students have experience in creating mental pictures. Some students will have to create actual drawings before they begin to understand the process.

- ***Creating mental pictures through verbalization***—Plan the words you will use to create the mental pictures carefully. Be prepared to use synonyms to make images clear with English learners. Because the purpose of this exercise is to support students in seeing the power of visual imaging, be prepared to integrate some words from the students' first languages in creating the images, when necessary.

- ***Assessing the students' understanding and progress***—Have the students describe or draw what they were able to picture in their minds. Encourage them to compare their images with the images of other students and discuss the sources of the differences. Sometimes this type of discussion brings out nuances of meaning in English vocabulary. Other times it helps make students aware of the need to listen carefully. Include periodic examples of products from imaging activities in the individual student portfolios to document growth. These products can be drawings with the descriptions attached or written descriptions based on verbal instructions given by the teacher. Make sure that enough information is included with the products so that anyone examining the portfolio will understand the purpose of the activity. It is often helpful to have students write a short paragraph to attach to portfolio entries in which they describe what they learned from the activity.

- ***Adding technology***—It is helpful in initial stages of imaging activities to have students draw their images on transparency film so that the images can be shared and discussed with the class. This also adds an element of interest for some students because of the use of unusual media. Imaging can also be done using drawing games such as Etch-a-Sketch or magic slates.

APPLICATIONS AND EXAMPLES

Mr. Fernandez's third graders are trying to figure out some difficult word problems in math. The first problem gives the following information:

Jan and Bob are cousins, Jan is 6 years old and Bob is 4 years older. Jan has a brother whose name is David. David is a year older than Jan but younger than Bob. Bob has a sister named Carol who is 2 years younger than Jan. Which of the cousins is the oldest? Who is the youngest? How old is each of the cousins?

Mr. Fernandez reads the problem aloud to the class and says, "This is a new kind of problem. There is a lot of information given but it's hard to keep track of it all. I find that it helps to create a picture to see if I have all the information I need to solve the problem. When I read the first sentence, I picture Jan as a little 6-year-old girl. I picture Bob as a tall 10-year-old boy. I know Bob is 10 because the problem says he is 4 years older than Jan. In my mind I see Jan and Bob. They look like this." Mr. Fernandez draws a stick figure of Jan and Bob.

"Now, the next part says that Jan has a brother named David who is a year older than she is. That makes him 7. In my mind I now see Jan, David, and Bob." Mr. Fernandez draws David and points to each of the stick figures as he says this. "So far I know that Jan is 6, David is 7, and Bob is 10. I can picture them in my mind. Now it says that Bob's sister Carol is two years younger than Jan. That makes her 4 years old. I can picture her in my mind." Mr. Fernandez adds Carol to the picture. See Figure 21.2 for Mr. Fernandez's picture.

"Now I have all the information I need to answer the questions," Mr. Fernandez smiles. "Now you try it. I'll read the next problem."

Ms. Garcia has three children, Jose, Maria, and Lidia. Each of them is exactly 2 years older than the next younger one. Jose is the eldest, and Lidia is the youngest. If Maria is 8 years old, how old are Jose and Lidia?

As Mr. Fernandez moves around the room, he notices that several of the children have their eyes closed and are talking to themselves. They begin to write down numbers and names as they see the pictures in their minds. Gabriella is drawing pictures on her paper. Mr. Fernandez stops to talk to Gabriella.

"I see you have Maria drawn on your paper." Mr. Fernandez says. "How old is she?"

"Eight," Gabriella says as she writes the number under the picture of Maria. "But that's the only one I know."

"OK," Mr. Fernandez says. "What else do you know?"

"Jose is the eldest," Gabriella says. "Does that mean the same as oldest?"

Figure 21.2 Mr. Fernandez's Picture

"Yes," Mr. Fernandez says as Gabriella draws Jose.

"Oh, now I see," Gabriella says as she draws Lidia and adds Jose's and Lidia's ages to the picture with a big smile.

The ninth graders in Ms. Patino's geography class are reading a passage in their text about the Louisiana bayou. As Ms. Patino shows the class a map of the Gulf Coast area, she talks about a trip that she made through the bayou on an airboat.

One of her students asks, "What is an airboat, Ms. Patino? I've never heard of one."

"It's a boat with a big fan mounted on the back," Ms. Patino explains as she draws a picture of an airboat on the chalkboard. "The bayou is an area of water that is not very deep. There are a lot of plants, trees, logs, and wildlife that live in the bayou. Regular boats can't move through the area because of the shallow water and all the roots that would interfere with the propeller. So, airboats are used. They skim across the top of the water propelled by the air that is blown through this huge fan. Of course, there is a big protective screen in front of the fan so no one in the boat gets hurt by the blades.

"Let's take a mind-trip through the bayou," Ms. Patino suggests. "Close your eyes and try to create mind-pictures as I describe my trip.

"It's a warm sunny day as I start my trip. I am wearing shorts, a sleeveless shirt, sneakers, and a big sun hat—but it is still very hot. It's also very humid. My clothes are sticking to my back as I walk across the landing platform to the airboat. The airboat is silver with a huge fan in the back. It seats about six people and has a very tall pole sticking up from the back of it with a red flag flying from the pole. I wonder what the flag is for.

"Are you picturing the day? Can you see the steam rising from the water and the airboat with the tall pole?" Ms. Patino asks. The students are sitting with their eyes closed but they all nod solemnly. Their faces are showing signs of concentration.

"As I get into the boat, it rocks slowly from side to side and I wonder if I really feel safe riding on this rocky vessel. As the boat fills up with people I begin to feel safer. I'm not the only one taking the risk. When the airboat pilot fires up the fan I am amazed at the noise it creates and I'm grateful for the earpieces that have been distributed so that we will be able to hear the guide's explanations of the bayou.

"I look around and see a wide expanse of water surrounded by strange trees with roots that seem to grow down from their branches. The airboat guide tells us that the trees are called banyan trees and that they grow in very wet terrain. As we continue through the main expanse of water we soon find out the reason for the tall pole and flag as we enter an area of tall brown grass that looks like tall hay. We are soon surrounded by the grass and feel as if we are traveling through a field of wheat that separates for us as the boat cuts through it. No one could see us coming if it weren't for the flag we fly. We are moving very quickly now and I hope the pilot and guide are watching for other airboats.

"We soon emerge into an area in which we are surrounded by banyan and cypress trees and small logs floating in the water. The guide soon points out that what looks like logs are actually small alligators sunning themselves. The guide also reminds us to keep our arms inside the boat. I am beginning to wish I had stayed behind on the dock.

"The movement of the boat produces a nice breeze and it isn't as hot as it was back on land. We are moving more slowly now. The pilot has turned off the engine and he and the guide are using long poles to move us slowly through the swamp so we can see the wildlife. I am amazed at the number of beautiful birds standing on tall legs in the water, the number of snakes we see swimming through the water, and the number of furry rodents and beavers we see busily building nests and chewing on trees. The guide calls our attention to a huge snake draped over a branch of a banyan tree, his tail almost dipping into the water. I slide a little farther down into my seat. The area is teeming with movement as we creep slowly through the tea-colored water. The water has a strong odor, not unpleasant but distinctive. The guide tells us the odor and the color of the water is called tannin and comes from the bark of the cypress trees. He also tells us that some of the natives use the bark of the cypress trees to make tea that they claim is very healthful.

"We enter another section of high grass and the pilot restarts the engine. We are soon flying back through the grass to the wide lakelike area where we began our trip. I feel very tired as I exit the airboat. My face is burning from the wind and sun, and I feel as if I've been on a journey to another world."

"Wow, Ms. Patino," Martino says as he opens his eyes. "I could really see the pictures in my mind."

"That's very good, Martino," Ms. Patino replies. "Being able to create pictures in your mind helps you understand what you read, too. Now that I've told you about my trip on the bayou, see if you can create pictures of it as you read about it in your geography book."

After the students have completed their reading, Ms. Patino goes back to the map to help them see the relationship between the scene she described, the passage they read, and the map. She wants to help them to make connections between the markings on the map and the visions they have in their heads.

CONCLUSION

Imaging can be used in a wide variety of classroom situations. It is helpful to students because often their inability to image or "picture in their minds" indicates that they don't really understand. Teachers cannot assume that students know how to image since research indicates that poor readers do not image (Irwin, 1991). It may be necessary for students to actually draw pictures on paper before they can paint pictures in their minds, but teaching imaging as a tool for understanding as well as a self-monitoring strategy can help students to become more responsible for their own learning.

EXAMPLES OF APPROXIMATION BEHAVIORS RELATED TO THE TESOL STANDARDS

Pre-K–3 students will:

- create a picture of a literary character.
- verbally describe a place they have visited.

4–8 students will:

- expand written sentences to include rich, descriptive language.
- illustrate literature based on their interpretation of the text.

9–12 students will:

- justify descriptions of characters and events from a text based on information found or inferred in the text or in real-life experiences.
- design costumes and/or sets for a dramatic presentation of a novel or historic event.

References

Chamot, A., & O'Malley, J. (1994). *The CALLA handbook: Implementing the cognitive academic language learning approach*. Reading, MA: Addison-Wesley.

Irwin, J. (1991). *Teaching reading comprehension processes* (2nd ed.). Needham Heights, MA: Allyn & Bacon.

INTEGRATED CURRICULUM PROJECTS:

Using Authentic Projects to Bring Knowledge Together

22

This strategy addresses the following TESOL Standards:

Goal 1: To use English to communicate in social settings

Standard 1: Students will use English to participate in social interactions.

Goal 2: To use English to achieve academically in all content areas

Standard 1: Students will use English to interact in the classroom.
Standard 2: Students will use English to obtain, process, construct, and provide subject matter information in spoken and written form.
Standard 3: Students will use appropriate learning strategies to construct and apply academic knowledge.

Goal 3: To use English in socially and culturally appropriate ways

Standard 1: Students will use the appropriate language variety, register, and genre according to audience, purpose, and setting.

The **integrated curriculum project** (Meyers, 1993) is an approach to planning curriculum in which knowledge and skills in several curricular areas are combined to accomplish an authentic task. The studies are integrated, usually around an active-learning project, so that the students are learning vocabulary and having experiences that demonstrate the need to use knowledge in multiple disciplines to complete real-life work. Integrated curriculum projects differ from thematic units in several ways. There is no attempt to bring all subject areas into the project. An authentic project is accomplished using only the curricular areas necessary to actually complete the objective.

This approach is appropriate for English language learners because of the use of vocabulary in multiple contexts and the focus on authentic projects, which embed the language in real tasks. In addition, the work that is done in an integrated curriculum project is almost always done with cooperative groups of students working together to create a project. This approach gives the English language learners many opportunities to interact verbally within a supportive, small-group setting, while engaging in activities that require communication.

124

STEP BY STEP

The steps in implementing integrated curriculum projects are:

• ***Identifying an authentic project opportunity***—Be alert to curriculum possibilities related to science and social studies curricula; national or local news events; and service project needs in the school, community, or your own classroom. If no ideas emerge from that approach, interview your students to determine their interests. Ask questions like, "If you could study anything at all, what would you like to learn about?" For further suggestions see Figure 22.1. Involve the students in the planning. This will enhance their intrinsic motivation. Present the project or possible projects and engage the students in brainstorming ideas about what might be accomplished. It is very important for the students to be enthusiastic about the project and see the opportunities to really accomplish things.

• ***Relating the project to grade-level and ESL standards***—While you plan the curricular connections, required vocabulary, and key lessons, keep in mind the concepts the students will need

Grade Level	Projects
Kindergarten	• Making our playground cleaner (prettier, safer) • Eating healthful food • Our families
Primary	• Making our neighborhood cleaner (prettier, safer, more friendly) • Making our school safer • Who are our neighbors? (neighborhood study) • Where does our food come from?
Upper elementary	• Our friends, our world (origins of the students and families) • Making our town (city, county) cleaner (safer, friendlier) • How our officials are elected • Lobbying for a cause • Manufacturing a product
Middle school	• Advocating for safe leisure activities • Adopting a group (peer tutoring, supporting old folks, etc.) • Beautifying a public area • Publishing a magazine or newspaper • Integrating photography, art, spokesmanship into school
Senior high school	• Uniting the community • Designing and implementing a homework center • Walking in their shoes (cross-cultural or studies of the physically challenged) • Advocating for changes in the school system
All levels	• Studies based on a good piece of literature

Figure 22.1   Suggestions for Integrated Curriculum Projects

to accomplish grade-level and ESL objectives. Focus on the multiple uses of vocabulary and skills they will need to successfully complete the project. List other groups, organizations, teachers, and administrators who can be enlisted to support the project.

• ***Identifying the class goals***—Conduct a class problem-solving session in which you and the students identify the most important products or accomplishments they want to achieve, the problems they will need to overcome, and the people who will need to be involved.

• ***Establishing working groups and their assignments***—Form cooperative groups, making sure that the English language learners are paired with strong language models, and divide the labor so that each group is responsible for designated tasks. Provide each group with a list of their responsibilities and roles and encourage them to work together to set a time line for accomplishments, as well as a checklist of tasks to be carried out.

• ***Integrating learning***—Plan ways to involve the cooperative groups in studying, planning, implementing, and celebrating each step of the way.

APPLICATIONS AND EXAMPLES

When Ms. Frangelica's first graders hear that they are getting a new student from the same Caribbean island where their teacher grew up, they are very excited.

"Do you know her, Ms. Frangelica?" Sandi asks.

"No, I don't know her but she is coming from a school not too far away from where I went to school," Ms. Frangelica replies with a smile.

"What is it like at that school?" Jerome asks.

"Why don't we wait until she gets here and we'll ask her to tell us about it," Ms. Frangelica suggests.

"We want you to tell us about what it was like when you went to school there," Sandi says.

Ms. Frangelica smiles and says, "Why don't we wait until Serieta gets here on Monday and we'll study all about the island. I'll even bring a book about the island and some of the music from there so we can all learn about it."

"Oh, good! A project!" reply the children, who like project studies.

As Ms. Frangelica begins to plan the study of her new student's native island she realizes that she can put together an integrated curriculum project based on her students' interest in the new student, and her native island. She plans to build the study on Frank Lessac's book, *My Little Island* (1984), which has always been a favorite of hers. The book is rich in vocabulary related to new foods, geography, and activities that will be fascinating to the first graders but familiar to the new student. Ms. Frangelica also plans a project in which her students will become pen pals to the students in Serieta's old class. Ms. Frangelica lists the curricular areas she can integrate:

Music: Caribbean music, dance, rhythm

Nutrition: new foods, food groups, diet

Geography: island, Caribbean

Social studies: the effect of climate and natural resources on housing, food supplies, activities, occupations; customs and celebrations and their origins; contrasting the use of time and resources with the way things are done in the United States.

Language arts: writing to pen pals, reading books about life and customs of the Caribbean

Vocabulary: a wall of Caribbean words with pictures and realia to illustrate them, native words and expressions

Parent involvement: bring other Caribbean parents in for interviews; demonstrations of music, dance, cooking

Because Ms. Frangelica knows how poor the schools are on her island, she plans a service learning project in which the children will become involved in sending something of educational value to Serieta's old school. She will involve the children in making this decision once Serieta has arrived and can tell them more about the needs of the school, but she envisions the students soliciting donations of or raising money for books for Serieta's old school. This will involve extensive research on her students' part, exchanges of letters between the schools, and decision-making in the selection of books to send. As she thinks about the integrated curriculum project that is growing in her mind, she realizes the children will learn a great deal because they will be involved in each step of the project. She immediately gets to work to choose the music that she will play as the students arrive on Monday morning and she gets out her old sun hat to wear to help set the mood. She gathers some artifacts from the island to label and place around in the classroom. As she looks around her apartment she finds a conch shell, photos of brightly painted houses on stilts, an artificial frangipani flower, a coconut, and a stuffed iguana. Her project is under way.

Ms. Boland teaches seventh-grade English in an inner-city middle school. Her students are from several cultural groups, some Hispanic, some Southeast Asian. They don't see much beauty as they walk to school each morning, but they usually come in smiling. One morning, Tia enters with an angry stomp. "I *hate* graffiti!" she states strongly. "My grandmother just painted her front fence yesterday, and it's already marked again."

Several of the other students join in the discussion but no one seems to have a solution to the problem. The discussion gets Ms. Boland thinking about the neighborhood in which her students live, however. Several of the school service groups have painted murals on the outside walls of the school. The murals do help. No graffiti is painted over them. But the walls without murals are still covered regularly, no matter how quickly they are painted. Ms. Boland is not convinced that graffiti is the main problem. She is more worried about the general feeling of despair and discouragement that she often recognizes as she confers with parents.

That evening, as she attends her photography class at the local community college, Ms. Boland has an idea. After class, she approaches her photography instructor. "I want to do a photography project with my seventh graders. Do you have students who would be available to help them learn how to take pictures?" she asks.

"Yes, I think we could do that," replies Mr. Stephens, the instructor. "Better than that, though, we have a service club on campus that I sponsor. We just happen to be looking for a project."

"Great!" Ms. Boland replies. "Here's my idea. I want my students to begin to see some beauty and hope in their neighborhood. I thought if they could look through the lens of a camera they could begin to see the beauty in their world and think about ways that they can contribute to their neighborhood. I plan to use the photography project to motivate their writing and their thinking about the control they have over their futures. Seventh graders are at such an important point in their education, I think maybe giving them some new interests might be helpful in inspiring them as readers, writers, and thinkers."

"Wow!" Mr. Stephens replies. "You're biting off a lot. I think I see where you are going, however. But, first things first. Do you have any cameras? Who will buy the film? Do they know how to take pictures?"

"No, I don't know, and no!" Ms. Boland says with a grin. "That's why I need help."

"Well, the service club meets Thursday night at the student union. Can you and a couple of your students come and present the idea?" Mr. Stephens asks.

"We can do that," Ms. Boland replies. "What time?"

The next day Ms. Boland presents her idea to her first-period class. She simply tells them that she thinks they will enjoy learning to take pictures as a prewriting strategy and asks if anyone is interested in the idea. Many hands go up. Tia's hand is one that is not raised.

"Tia, you don't want to learn to take pictures?" Ms. Boland asks.

"It's not that," Tia replies. "My grandmother still thinks that you steal people's souls when you take their pictures. She won't like this. And, also, I don't have a camera."

"What if we could get cameras to use and you can take pictures of scenery or buildings rather than people?" asks Ms. Boland.

"I think that will be all right," Tia replies slowly. "I'll have to ask."

"I'll be glad to talk to your grandmother, if that will help," Ms. Boland says.

The next few days are busy in Ms. Boland's class. She organizes cooperative groups to plan the photography projects. The groups plan their needs: cameras, film, release forms for people they will photograph, permission forms for walking field trips around the neighborhood. One group plans a presentation to the principal for his support. Another prepares for the presentation to the community college service club. On Thursday evening, Ms. Boland and her group attend the meeting of the community college service club and get support for disposable cameras for the class. They also get help from some of the photography students who agree to come and give lessons in basic photography. The next week is spent in planning their photography projects, looking for possible pictures to meet the criteria set by Ms. Boland. The pictures are to illustrate one of the following themes:

- My culture
- My neighborhood
- Beauty in unexpected places
- Intergenerational interactions

Ms. Boland teaches the use of photography as a prewriting strategy by asking the students to think of a picture they could take and then drafting a short essay that might accompany the picture. In the meantime, students from the community college come to the first-period class and teach basic principles of photography. The second week the students embark on a walking field trip and take pictures. Working as partners, the students each take six pictures. While one student is using the camera, the partner is writing a brief description of the picture that is taken, while jotting down any notes the photographer dictates. Once the photos are developed using funds donated by the community college service club, the students begin to work on their essays.

Ms. Boland is so impressed by the photos and the essays that she shares them with a professional photographer friend a few weeks later. "I would love to have a way to enlarge the photos, mount them, and display them," Ms. Boland says. "The students are very motivated by this project. They are learning a lot about photography and writing. But, more than that, they are developing a renewed interest in their neighborhood and the people who live there. I've created a monster. We simply do not have the money to continue this approach on an ongoing basis."

"Why don't you get the students involved in some problem solving?" her friend replies. "I'll work on some ideas through the local photo gallery group, but it would be wonderful if the students could help solve their own problem."

"I agree," Ms. Boland says.

The next morning Ms. Boland presents the problem to her class. She reconvenes the cooperative groups for a brainstorming session and the groups quickly formulate a list of ideas. By the end of the period the groups each have a project they are willing to pursue to raise funds to continue their photography project. One group is going to approach the local newspaper to do an article about the project with the hope of identifying possible donors. One group is going to approach the principal for help. One group is going to talk to the cafeteria manager to see if they can sell ice cream or snacks at the end of each lunch period to raise funds. One group is going to call the photography and education departments at the local university to see if there are any funds available to support university/college partnerships. Each group has a plan of action.

Six months later Ms. Boland can hardly believe how many of the plans have produced results. As she watches the parents circulating around the room looking at the beautifully mounted photos and essays, she notices the local television station filming the event for the evening news. The article and full-color spread that appeared in the local newspaper is displayed prominently on one wall. The university professors, community college instructor, and students who were all a part of the project are beaming their approval. The students are getting many opportunities for oral language practice explaining how they got their ideas and how exciting the project has become. Ms. Boland is thinking about all the knowledge of grants and budgets and advocacy that the students have gained through this endeavor and she is already planning her next integrated curriculum project.

CONCLUSION

Integrated curriculum projects are powerful because they go a step beyond the traditional thematic unit to complete an authentic task. Whether the task is providing books for students in a poor community, using photography to improve writing skills and community pride, or using math and science skills to design a reading loft for the classroom, students begin to see the practical applications of school subjects through integrated curriculum projects. They also gain multiple opportunities to practice their spoken and written English as they gather information, make presentations to possible supporters of the project, and participate in the planning and implementation of the project.

EXAMPLES OF APPROXIMATION BEHAVIORS RELATED TO THE TESOL STANDARDS:

Pre-K–3 students will:

- verbally describe a classroom or school problem to solve.
- use appropriate language to suggest solutions.

4–8 students will:

- use beginning research skills to find solutions to real problems.
- use language skills to persuade others to support a project.

9–12 students will:

- verbally describe neighborhood, city, or state problems that need a solution.
- participate in planning and implementing problem solving projects.

References

Lessac, F. (1984). *My little island*. London: Harper Trophy (Macmillan).

Meyers, M. (1993). *Teaching to diversity: Teaching and learning in the multi-ethnic classroom*. Toronto, Canada: Irwin Publishing.

SORTING ACTIVITIES: Organizing Information into Categories

23

This strategy addresses the following TESOL Standards:

Goal 2: To use English to achieve academically in all content areas

Standard 1: Students will use English to interact in the classroom.

Standard 2: Students will use English to obtain, process, construct, and provide subject matter information in spoken and written form.

Standard 3: Students will use appropriate learning strategies to construct and apply academic knowledge.

Sorting activities (Bear, Invernizzi, Templeton, & Johnston, 1996) are activities that require the students to sort objects, words, phrases, and sentences according to set parameters. Sorting activities are appropriate for use with English language learners because they provide a way for students to manipulate objects and written symbols to show their understanding of concepts, while acquiring the vocabulary and structures needed for verbal interaction.

Sorting activities can be used in a wide range of curricular areas and are appropriate from kindergarten through 12th grade with careful planning and adaptations. See Figure 23.1 for suggestions in the use of sorting activities.

STEP BY STEP

The steps in implementing sorting activities are:

• *Identifying skills to practice in sorting mode*—Identify a skill that can be practiced or demonstrated using sorting. See Figure 23.1 for suggestions. Prepare the materials to be sorted, including containers or pocket charts in which to place the sorts.

• *Explaining the activity*—Explain the activity, model what the students will do, and provide some guided practice before asking the students to sort independently. Decide whether you want the students to sort individually, in pairs, or small groups. If practice of the concept is the purpose of the sort, individual sorts are effective. If you want the sort to include practice in using English vocabulary and communication, paired or small-group sorts are more effective.

130

Grade Level	Curricular Area	Description of Sorting Activity
Kindergarten	Phonemic awareness	Using small objects or pictures, students sort by matching sounds.
	Phonics	Using small objects or pictures, students sort by initial sound/letter representation.
	Math	Using small objects or math manipulatives, students sort by size, shape, or number.
	Science	Using animal pictures, children sort by attributes such as fur, feathers, and scales.
	Social studies	Using pictures depicting weather conditions, students sort by season.
Primary	Phonics	Using small objects, pictures, or words, students sort by ending sound, vowel sounds.
	Math	Using number sentences, students sort by sum or difference.
	Writing	Using short sentences written on sentence strips, students sort by type of sentence (declarative, question, exclamation).
	English	Using word cards, students sort by parts of speech (nouns, verbs, adjectives, etc.)
	Science	Using leaves, students sort by leaf shape. Using animal pictures, students sort by classification (mammal, reptile, amphibian, bird).
Upper Elementary	Reading	Using sentence strips with sentences written on them, students sequence them to form a topic sentence and supporting details.
	Math	Using cards with word problems written on them, students sort them into stacks representing the four operations (addition, subtraction, multiplication, and division).
		Using cards with word problems written on them, students sort them into stacks estimating their correct solutions (1–5, 6–10, 11–15, 16–20, etc.)
	Vocabulary	Using word cards, students sort words into categories such as synonyms, antonyms, etc.
Secondary	Science	Students sort rock samples into classifications.
		Students match description cards with scientific samples, slides, experiments.
	Literature	Students sort plot summaries into genre classifications.
		Students match main character description with literature titles.
	Learning strategies	Students sequence cards with learning strategy step descriptions.
	Life skills	Students sequence cards with job application procedure descriptions.
		Students sort descriptions of job application and interview behaviors into piles marked *Positive Behavior* and *Negative Behavior.*
	Social studies	Students sequence the steps in the legislative process.
		Students match attributes of nations to the names of the nations.

Figure 23.1   Suggestions for Using Sorting Activities

- ***Setting up the routine and requirements***—Establish a routine for the students to use when they complete their sort. Some teachers encourage the students to take a Polaroid picture of the sort and turn the picture in, others require a written response that explains the sort, and others simply have a peer check the sort.

- ***Assessing the students' progress and understanding***—Any independent activity is only as powerful as the value given to it by the teacher. Take the time to have students explain their sorts and how they made their choices. This doesn't have to be done daily but students must believe that the teacher values their efforts. These individual conferences also give the teacher an additional opportunity for verbal interactions and a chance to document growth in both the student's sorting skills but also in verbal English communication.

APPLICATIONS AND EXAMPLES

The students in Mr. Avedesian's kindergarten class are learning how to sort objects by listening to the beginning sounds of the words. Each student has an empty milk carton with the top cut off. On the table in the sorting center is a tray full of small objects such as balls, pencils, erasers, bracelets, hearts, apples, baby bottles, crayons, and markers. The students are looking for objects that begin with the same sound as their names. Mr. Avedesian reminds them to say their names and then say the name of the object to see if the sound matches.

Michael says, "Michael, ball," then shakes his head and returns the ball to the table and picks up the marker.

"Michael, marker," he says and smiles as he places the marker into his milk carton.

After the students have found the items that begin with the same sound as their names, they bring their milk cartons to Mr. Avedesian and show him the items they have found. Mr. Avedesian asks them to say the names of the items and then return the items to the table. Mr. Avedesian keeps a list of the students who are successful with this initial sort and pairs them the next day to search for items for their partners' names. He plans to match Michael and Simon for the second day. Michael will be looking for items that begin like Simon's name and Simon will be looking for things that match Michael's name.

Gradually through the year, Mr. Avedesian will move through the initial consonants and begin to have the students sort for items that match the letters of the alphabet.

The 12th graders in Ms. Tan's pre-employment class are getting ready for practice job interviews. She has designed a series of picture and description sorts to help them make good decisions as they practice interviewing and begin to apply for jobs. The first sort involves pictures of people in various forms of dress. The students sort the pictures into piles according to the job interviews for which the dress is appropriate.

This first sort is a picture to picture sort. The students simply match the pictures of the people to pictures of places of employment. After the students complete the sort they fill out a form, which lists the places of employment, and the students enter the number of a picture of a person next to the place of employment. After all the students have completed the sort, the class discusses the responses and why certain dress is appropriate for certain jobs.

The second sort involves reading a series of employment advertisements and matching pictures of people with their education and experience listed on the back with the jobs for which they are most qualified. Again, the students fill out a brief form which matches the letters that identify the job ads and the numbers that identify the applicants. The class discusses the meanings of the ads and the qualifications that would be needed for each.

The third sort involves placing a series of job application forms into piles marked *Definite NO, File, Interview,* and *Top Candidate.* The students place the names of the applicants on a list with the same indicators at the top. For the list marked *Definite NO* they are asked to state why they placed the application on this list. They are asked the same question for the names on the *Top Candidate* list. The class discussed the sort after everyone has completed the "paper screen."

"You mean you would get placed on the *Definite NO* list just because of a few misspelled words on the application?" Jerome asks with indignation in his voice.

"For this particular job, spelling is a major requirement," Karen replies. "You are painting signs and decorating windows for sales. Besides, why would you hire someone who isn't careful enough to double check his spelling on something as important as a job application?"

"Exactly," Ms. Tan confirms. "Remember, you are probably not the only applicant for the job. The employers are looking for the best candidates. They don't want to waste time interviewing people who are probably not qualified to do a good job."

CONCLUSION

Sorting activities provide hands-on experiences with the manipulation of pictures, letters, words, and longer texts. Sorting activities provide practice in making decisions and differentiating among concepts but also illustrate a technique for studying and organizing materials. Although sorting activities have a wide range of applications, they are highly effective for use with English language learners because they provide the students with an opportunity to demonstrate their understanding with re-

EXAMPLES OF APPROXIMATION BEHAVIORS RELATED TO THE TESOL STANDARDS

Pre-K–3 students will:

- sort pictures into categories.
- use phonic knowledge to sort words and pictures.

4–8 students will:

- sort words into categories, such as parts of speech, tenses, number of syllables, and so on.
- sort curricular knowledge into appropriate categories.

9–12 students will:

- use categories to organize curricular materials.
- sort information and materials and verbally explain the rules used for the sorting.

duced reliance on language skills. Asking the students to justify their sorts creates an opportunity for verbal interaction based on visual cues, which is supportive of emergent English speakers.

Reference

Bear, D. R., Invernizzi, M., Templeton, S., & Johnston, F. (1996). *Words their way: Word study for phonics, vocabulary, and spelling instruction*. Upper Saddle River, NJ: Merrill/Prentice Hall.

COLLABORATIVE READING: What To Do When They Can't Read the Textbook

This strategy addresses the following TESOL Standards:

Goal 2: To use English to achieve academically in all content areas

Standard 1: Students will use English to interact in the classroom.

Standard 2: Students will use English to obtain, process, construct, and provide subject matter information in spoken and written form.

Standard 3: Students will use appropriate learning strategies to construct and apply academic knowledge.

Collaborative reading (Gibbons, 1993) is a strategy that is helpful to English language learners when they are reading for information. This strategy also allows a teacher to support readers of various abilities to work collaboratively as they study a specific topic. Students use a variety of library and/or textbooks with information on the topic being studied. These books are selected to provide a wide range of reading levels to meet the needs within the class. The group has the advantage of reviewing information from four or five different sources, depending on the number of students in each group. Members of the group then discuss the information gathered so that everyone becomes an expert on the topic. Collaborative reading provides a method for all students—regardless of reading ability—to participate in a group research activity (Tompkins, 1997). Because the teacher selects books appropriate for the reading levels within the group of students, each student can make a significant contribution to the collaborative task. English language learners are supported because, if necessary, they have texts with simpler language and illustrations. Each member of the group can contribute in unique ways. English language learners may contribute by drawing a visual to represent the main points of the collaborative research. This allows them to provide a translation of the information by reporting orally to the group if there are other students who share the same home language, or providing information related to the difference in use of the concept being studied in the students' home cultures.

STEP BY STEP

The steps in a collaborative reading lesson are:

- *Gathering a range of books on a topic*—Gather books on the topics to be studied, making sure to include books at various reading levels so that all students will be successful in finding information.

- ***Organizing heterogeneous groups***—Carefully considering the strengths and needs of the students, organize your students into groups of four or five to explore topics. Make sure that each group contains a student with strong reading and writing skills. Have each group explore either a different topic or a different aspect of one topic. Instruct the groups to brainstorm questions they want to answer about their topic. These questions can be included on a KWL chart, a chart on which the students note the things they KNOW about the topic, the things they WANT to know about the topic and, after the collaborative reading, the things they LEARNED about the topic. They may just simply brainstorm their questions on a list. Depending on the topics, it sometimes works to have the whole class brainstorm questions and then have each group answer the same group of questions on their topic. Provide each member of the group with a book on the group's topic. Be careful to match the books with the students' reading levels. Each member of the group researches the group's questions using a different book on the topic.

- ***Providing research instruction***—Instruct the members of the groups to find the answers to the group's questions in their books and take notes about the information they will share with their group. You may have to teach a minilesson on how to read and take notes, jotting down important facts.

- ***Creating a data chart***—After group members have completed their note-taking, have them discuss their findings, create a data chart—a form of information matrix—or other visual, and plan how they will share their research with the whole class. A data chart form is shown in Figure 24.1.

- ***Practicing and sharing information***—Have the groups work on their group presentation and then share their research and visuals with the whole class.

- ***Documenting the group process***—Document the group's success in working together, following instructions, gathering information, and presenting their information to the group. You can do this documentation through anecdotal records, checklists, or rubrics. See the section in the theoretical overview for suggestions.

APPLICATIONS AND EXAMPLES

Ms. Frederick's third graders are studying insects. Because the students' reading abilities vary greatly and the science textbooks are too difficult for many of the students, Ms. Frederick decides to gather a number of library books for them to use in researching insects. The media specialist at her school is extremely helpful in locating books at varying reading levels and Ms. Frederick locates four or five books or chapters in books for each of the insects the students have identified as interesting. Ms. Frederick arranges the books by topic: bees, ants, beetles, grasshoppers, and roaches. She labels the books with correction tape so that she will be able to give students books at their reading levels. The easiest books are marked 5, next easiest 4, and so on, with the most difficult labeled with the number 1.

The students sign up for groups depending on their interests, but Ms. Frederick makes sure that there are some able readers in each group. Before she lets them start their research, Ms. Frederick does a lesson on note-taking. Using an informational book on spiders, she reads aloud and models note-taking on the overhead projector. She stops after a few examples and involves the students in deciding what notes she should add. Before she has finished, the students understand how to select important information for their notes and they also have learned why spiders were not included on their list of insects to be researched. The next part of the minilesson involves finding research questions. Ms. Frederick leads the class to ask basic questions, which she writes on the transparency of the data chart. This enables the students to discover how to look for information, answer the research questions, and note the information in the proper box on the chart. She models the use of several books on spiders to demonstrate that the students will not find the answers to all the questions in the same book. She also points out some conflicting information in several of the books.

Ms. Frederick moves the students into their interest groups and they begin to read their books and take notes. Toward the end of the period, she instructs the students to add their information to the group data chart. The students are then given a few minutes to discuss their findings within the group.

Group Members _____

Topic _____

	Questions				
	How does it look?	**What does it eat?**	**Where does it live?**	**What are its natural enemies?**	**Other important information?**
Sources and Readers					
Book: Reader:					
Book: Reader:					
Book: Reader:					
Book: Reader:					
Book: Reader:					

Figure 24.1   Data Chart Form

Adapted from McKenzie, 1979.

During science period the next day, the students get back into their groups and discuss how they will present their findings to the class. One group decides to make a fact book about bees and read it aloud to the class. One group decides to make a poster about grasshoppers with a large labeled picture of a grasshopper and small posters surrounding the large one with facts about grasshoppers. The ant group wants to make a model of an ant with paper mache. They will write facts about the ant on large green paper shaped like blades of grass and place the ant in the grass. The beetle group decides to put their data chart on poster board and give an oral presentation using the data chart. Each group is busy preparing their visual and their presentation.

Ms. Frederick's class was able to learn many things through their collaborative reading projects. Every student contributed information to the group reports. All the students learned much more about the topics than they could have learned reading independently. They felt like researchers and were successful in presenting information orally.

Ms. Stacy is a fifth-grade teacher with a multicultural class ranging in reading ability from first-grade level to eighth-grade level. She decides to do a collaborative reading project on the human body. Ms. Stacy follows much the same procedure as Ms. Frederick did but with one interesting twist. The day of the presentations Ms. Stacy moves all the desks in her classroom to one side. She sets the chairs up in a large semicircle, three chairs deep. At the door of the classroom that morning, Ms. Stacy has each child sign in and get a name tag, a folder with a yellow pad and pencil, and a paper robe that she purchased at a medical supply house. Her students are all presenters at a mock medical conference. She has invited the local television station to come and tape the conference, and she has set up a lectern, microphone and sound system—transforming the students into medical professionals at a conference. They present their reports and visuals solemnly, smiling for the camera only when they're finished with their reports. After their reports, the groups must field questions. They handle the questions well. They have obviously done their research thoroughly. Each group seems to know which member of the group is likely to know the answer to the question. One student, when stumped for an answer, replies, "I'll have to get back to you on that one."

CONCLUSION

Collaborative reading can be used to provide students with knowledge from a variety of sources. It supports the formation and strengthening of a classroom community by providing students with an activity in which their unique gifts (such as speaking more than one language, drawing, or using a computer or other technology to create visuals) supply a valuable component to the group presentation. In the process of creating, practicing, and presenting the group report the students are given several opportunities to acquire new vocabulary, to write and reread English and home language summaries of the material read and written, and to communicate in English for a meaningful purpose.

EXAMPLES OF APPROXIMATION BEHAVIORS RELATED TO THE TESOL STANDARDS

Pre-K–3 students will:

- verbally explain information gained from book illustrations.
- use the table of contents to locate information in nonfiction books at appropriate reading levels.

4–8 students will:

- use indices to locate information in nonfiction books.
- contribute to a group topic study by reading and sharing information.

9–12 students will:

- participate in group studies by reading and organizing data in a useable way.
- verbally explain facts and connections between information read in nonfiction books.

References

Gibbons, P. (1993). *Learning to learn in a second language.* Portsmouth, NH: Heinemann.

McKenzie, G. (1979). Data charts: A crutch for helping pupils organize reports. *Language Arts, 56,* 784–788.

Tompkins, G. (1997). *Literacy for the 21st century.* Upper Saddle River, NJ: Merrill/Prentice Hall.

MULTIMEDIA PRESENTATIONS:
Oral Reports for the New Millennium

25

This strategy addresses the following TESOL Standards:

Goal 2: To use English to achieve academically in all content areas

Standard 1: Students will use English to interact in the classroom.

Standard 2: Students will use English to obtain, process, construct, and provide subject matter information in spoken and written form.

Standard 3: Students will use appropriate learning strategies to construct and apply academic knowledge.

Goal 3: To use English in socially and culturally appropriate ways

Standard 2: Students will use nonverbal communication appropriate to audience, purpose, and setting.

Standard 3: Students will use appropriate learning strategies to extend their sociolinguistic and cultural competence.

Multimedia presentations (Diaz-Rico & Weed, 1995) involve the use of media such as audio and video equipment (VCRs, video disk players, video cameras), computers and related software and Internet sources to do research, publish, and make classroom presentations. In recent years the availability of computer multimedia technology, Internet access, and materials in multiple languages has greatly improved, making the use of these resources in the classroom more practical. The use of multimedia presentations with English language learners is especially important because of the flexibility the approach lends in both teaching and learning. Students benefit when teachers use multimedia in presenting lessons because the media usage adds context to the language and the lessons. Students using multimedia to gain access to information in multiple languages are supported in their learning. When students use multimedia to present their research, writings, and projects, they can document and present their growing capabilities without the constraints encountered when making oral reports.

In the use of multimedia it is not just the finished product—the report or presentation—but also the processes of exploring, synthesizing, and summarizing that with technology creates opportunities for meaningful learning to take place.

The use of multimedia in the classroom presents some challenges for both teachers and students. In fact, a teacher without experience in this approach is sometimes overwhelmed with both the possibilities and the potential barriers. However, there are many resources available to teachers in the use of multimedia in the classroom. See Figure 25.1 for a partial list of resources for more information.

STEP BY STEP

The steps in implementing multimedia presentations are:

- *Modeling media use*—Model the use of multimedia by incorporating video clips, overhead projector, audiotapes, and other media as you teach. Emphasize how the use of the media allows you to visually or auditorally demonstrate as you teach. Before you ask students to use multimedia approaches give them experience in seeing the effectiveness of different media in the support of learning.

- *Introducing media slowly*—Introduce the different media slowly. Begin with one piece of equipment and encourage students to use it as they demonstrate learning. You might choose to begin with the overhead projector and transparency film by having cooperative groups work together to create a transparency that documents the work of the group. Have the students practice standing in front of the class using the overhead to show their work. Give instructions as to where to stand and how to turn the projector on and off. Demonstrate how they can reveal one portion of the transparency at a time to show new information as it is discussed and how two or three transparencies can be placed on top of each other to create a graph or a more detailed visual.

- *Adding new media as appropriate*—Repeat the demonstration and use of different media as it is appropriate. Always review the reasons that equipment is used so students can begin to make wise choices about the media they may want to use to support their presentations, determining whether the use of media actually enhances the quality of the demonstration.

- *Allowing time for practice*—Allow yourself and the students time to practice with the equipment before using it for more formal presentations. When computers are introduced, new users need time to explore them, their functions, and possibilities. When introducing the Internet system, new users, teachers, and students alike will need to see the procedures for gaining access and the Website addresses clearly displayed so they can practice logging on, gaining access, and searching for information until they are comfortable with the sequences.

- *Creating working partners*—Pair computer users by experience, with a more experienced user supporting a new user. Don't overlook the more experienced user as a classroom resource. Often students have a lot of expertise to share with teachers and other students. Be sure to include training for the more experienced users so that they are aware of the importance of "talking the new user through the procedure" and NOT jumping in to do it for him or her.

- *Making a media assignment*—Assign a presentation that requires a multimedia element and support the students in developing their presentations. Gradually require more sophisticated media use. Start by using media with which the students are comfortable and gradually add different possibilities as the students become more familiar with equipment, software, and usage. Encourage partner work in the beginning so that more experienced users of technology can provide support for new users. See Figure 25.2 for suggestions of multimedia projects.

Books

Herrell, A., & Fowler, J. (1997). *Camcorder in the classroom: Using the videocamera to enrich curriculum.* Upper Saddle River, NJ: Macmillan/Prentice Hall.

International Society for Technology in Education. (2000). *National educational technology standards for students: Connecting curriculum and technology.* Washington, DC: Author.

Lewis, C. (1997). *Exploring multimedia.* New York: DK Publishing.

Serim, F., & Koch, M. (1996). *NetLearning: Why teachers use the Internet.* Sebastopol, CA: Songline Publications.

Articles

Harris, J. (series of articles). Mining the Internet. *The Computing Teacher.* www.ed.uiuc.edu/Mining/Overview.html

Rogers, A., Andres, Y., Jacks, M., & Clauset, T. (1990). Telecommunicating in the classroom: Keys to successful telecommunicating. *The Computing Teacher, 17,* 25–28. (Online: www.gsn.org)

Educational Websites

The Internet Public Library www.ipl.org
Content Literacy Information Consortium curry. edschool.virginia.edu/centers/clic
International Reading Association www.reading.org/publications
Busy Teacher's Website www.ceismc.gatech.edu/ceismc/programs/edtech/busyt.htm
Scholastic Network www.scholasticnetwork.com
Ed's & Edie's Oasis www.edsoasis.org/
Kathy Schrock's Guide for Educators http://school.discovery.com/schrockguide/
Teacher/Pathfinder teacherpathfinder.org/
The Learning Space www.learningspace.org
BLUE WEB'N www.kn.pacbell.com/wired/bluewebn/

Bilingual and Multicultural Education
Culture Pages www.hut.fi/-rvilmi/Project/Culture/
CyberSpanish Website www.actlab.utexas.edu/-seagull/spanglist.html
International E-Mail Classroom Connections www.stolaf.edu/network/iecc/

Space Exploration
http://spacelink.msfc.nasa.gov/

High School Literature Studies
www.romeoandjuliet.com
web.uvic.ca/shakespeare/index.html

Graphic Organizers
Teacher Vision www.teachervision.com/lesson-plans/lesson-6293.html?s2
WriteDesign www.writedesignonline.com/organizers/
Reading Strategies www.sarasota.k12.fl.us/sarasota/matrix.htm
Index of Graphic Organizers www.graphic.org/goindex.html
Sample Web www.graphic.org/squirrel.html
NCREL www.ncrel.org
Rubric Creation rubistar.4teachers.org/index.shtml
Technology Connections www.ncrel.org/tplan/guide.pdf
Semantic Mapping www.owu.edu/~mggrote/pp/child_lit/c_semantic.html
Graphic Organizers www.ncrel.org/sdrs/areas/issues/students/learning/lr1grorg.htm.
Education Place www.eduplace.com/graphicorganizer/

Figure 25.1 Resources for Teachers Interested in Multimedia in the Classroom

Grade Level	Project	Equipment/Access
Kindergarten	Story retelling	Overhead projector Transparency pictures
	Math presentations	Math manipulatives Overhead projector
Primary	Book talks (video book reports)	Video Camera, VCR, monitor
	Publishing books	Computer with software for word processing & illustrating (Children's Writing & Publishing Center)
	Research on the Internet	Computer with Internet access, listing of websites that the teacher has previewed
Above Third	The sky's the limit!	Computer with Internet access Writing and publishing software Hyperstudio Video productions Computer programmed presentations using professional presentation packages such as PowerPoint
	Classroom connections projects	Internet projects connecting classrooms across the nation (www.gsn.org)
	Space exploration projects	Internet projects related to space travel & exploration http://spacelink.msfc.nasa.gov/

Figure 25.2   Suggestions for Multimedia Projects

APPLICATIONS AND EXAMPLES

Ms. Grundbrecher's second graders are busily engaged in a project titled *Farm to Market*. Because their school is in an agricultural area, the district encourages the study of the production of food; how it is harvested and transported to market; and the interdependence of farmers, food processors, and distributors.

The students are familiar with the Macintosh computer because they use it regularly to publish their writing. For this project Ms. Grundbrecher introduces them to Kid Pix, a computer program that allows them to create graphs and illustrate their research. The students are using a "stamp" option, which has a large library of pictures, to illustrate their reports.

For this introductory unit using computer technology, the students will use the library and a few Websites already selected by the teacher to gather their information. They start with the area of the country where they live and the foods they see growing in the fields. They widen their search to determine the different foods that are grown in the rest of the state and finally research agriculture in other states. They then create a graph using the stamps from the Kid Pix program to illustrate the variety of foods grown in the United States. After identifying the wide range of food grown across the country, the class begins to look at transporting the food from place to place. Again using the Kid Pix stamps, the students create a map that visually represents the journey of the crop and the many different people employed to make it possible for the food to be available.

Ms. Grundbrecher is lucky enough to live in an area where she can take the students to visit the fields, a processing plant, and a distribution center. After all the research the second graders have done they are very knowledgeable visitors. They ask important questions about the types of transportation used to deliver the food, where it goes, and how long it takes to get there. The foreman at the processing center is impressed and asks one of the students how they know so much about the processing and distribution of food.

"We researched it on the Internet," the smiling 7-year-old replies.

Mr. Bateman's 10th-grade chemistry class is discussing possible ·uses for chemistry in real life. Yolanda is interested in becoming an astronaut and asks, "Why do I need to study chemistry if I want to be an astronaut. I can't see any use for it in space."

"That's an interesting question, Yolanda," Mr. Bateman replies. "I was just reading about a service provided by NASA where students can read articles about the space program and even have their questions answered by astronauts and engineers associated with the program. Let's start a list of questions that we would like to have answered."

Mr. Bateman creates a KWL chart on a large sheet of butcher paper. "Let's first talk about what we know about the space program and then we'll generate some questions we want to have answered. We'll use the textbooks and online resources to try to find answers first, and then create a list of questions for the engineers and astronauts at NASA."

The students list all the information they have about the space program and when they are finished they realize that what they know is mostly related to the launch procedures that they view on television. They really have little knowledge about the actual experiments that are being done in space or what scientific knowledge is being gained through the launches.

Mr. Bateman has contacted NASA online and has received a copy of the teacher's guide that accompanies the NASA "Live from . . . " series. Through this introduction to the NASA programs the students interact with scientists through the NASA question/answer repository, where a number of their questions are answered. The students find that by reading information about research goals, viewing photos online, and searching for actual data gathered from shuttle flights and other NASA projects they are gaining a much broader understanding of all the different types of research being conducted through the space programs.

As it becomes obvious that the NASA research connection will be an ongoing study, Mr. Bateman realizes that several of his students are spending a lot of time in the chemistry labs and computer stations working on projects that stem from the NASA teaching materials and the Internet connections. Yolanda is no longer the only student interested in the space program.

"Mr. Bateman, did you know that the space program uses engineers, chemists, biologists, data analyzers, doctors, veterinarians, and a whole lot of other types of scientists?" Joseph asks. "I never knew that so many different jobs were involved in the space industry."

"It's an exciting program," Mr. Bateman replies. "The American public knows very little about all the inventions and medical benefits we have gained from the research."

"Well, if they'd just get on the Internet they'd know," Joseph says. "It's all on there."

CONCLUSION

Multimedia presentations in the classroom support students in conveying information to their peers. The use of visuals of many types helps students and teachers to connect vocabulary and meaning, making their reports more interesting. The use of the computer, VCR, camcorder, and other technology in the classroom is appealing to students and motivates them to be more innovative in completing assignments. The use of the Internet in the classroom introduces some challenges, however. Just as in researching from more traditional materials, students will need instruction in giving credit and citing sources. They may be tempted to simply download reports from the Internet, therefore, specific guidelines will need to be set and monitored in the classroom setting.

NASA Web Page:
http://quest.arc.nasa.gov/interactive.html

To send an e-mail message for information about future projects use:
listmanager@quest.arc.nasa.gov
Leave the subject line blank and in the message body write: subscribe sharing-nasa

EXAMPLES OF APPROXIMATION BEHAVIORS RELATED TO THE TESOL STANDARDS

Pre-K–3 students will:

- use a drawing to illustrate a story read, told, or written.
- use classroom computer and Internet to locate answers to questions.

4–8 students will:

- conduct research using a variety of resources (books and technology).
- orally present information aided by computer created visuals.

9–12 students will:

- use multimedia software to enhance oral presentations.
- create innovative projects combining media.

References

Diaz-Rico, L., & Weed, K. (2002). *The crosscultural, language, and academic development handbook* (2nd ed.) Needham Heights, MA: Allyn & Bacon.
Kid Pix Deluxe (version 4.1). Novato, CA: Broderbund (www.broderbund.com).
PowerPoint, (version 7.0). Redmond, WA: Microsoft (www.microsoft.com).

Other sources of pictures online

www.google.com (click on images).
www.altavista.com (click on image).

RECIPROCAL TEACHING: Group Work with an Interactive Structure

26

This strategy addresses the following TESOL Standards:

Goal 2: To use English to achieve academically in all content areas

Standard 1: Students will use English to interact in the classroom.

Standard 2: Students will use English to obtain, process, construct, and provide subject matter information in spoken and written form.

Standard 3: Students will use appropriate learning strategies to construct and apply academic knowledge.

Goal 3: To use English in socially and culturally appropriate ways

Standard 1: Students will use the appropriate language variety, register, and genre according to audience, purpose, and setting.

Reciprocal teaching (Palincsar & Brown, 1986) is a reading strategy in which students take turns teaching small sections of text. It is usually done in small groups. All students initially read a section of the text. One student begins by summarizing a section of the text and questioning the others about the meaning of the section. Any difficult parts are identified and discussed and then predictions are made about the next section to be read. The students take turns summarizing, clarifying, and questioning until all sections of the text have been read, summarized, and discussed.

This strategy is recommended for use with English language learners because of the potential for supporting comprehension in small-group interactions and the active use of learning strategies. Support from the group in explaining and discussing in the student's first language is a positive factor that can be added by making sure that students with the same home language are put in groups together. It is important, also, to make sure that each group contains at least one student who is a strong speaker and reader of English.

STEP BY STEP

The steps in implementing reciprocal teaching are:

* ***Identifying tough text***—Identify a section of text that has some difficult vocabulary or concepts. Plan a lesson where you model the steps in reciprocal teaching and relate them to learning

strategies that support comprehension of the text. (See Chapter 44, Learning Strategy Instruction, for more information.)

- ***Explaining the process and purpose***—Explain to the students that they will work in small groups helping each other make sense of the information they will be reading. Form a small group of students to work with you in demonstrating the approach. Start by giving everyone in the group a paragraph of text that contains some difficult vocabulary or concepts and ask them to read it silently.

- ***Walking through the process***—After the group has finished reading silently, briefly summarize the content of the material and pose questions to students in the group. Model and identify literal questions (simple recall), inferential questions (finding unstated meaning), and critical questions (calling for higher-level thinking). See Figure 26.1 for a chart of questioning examples that can be used with your students.

- ***Clarifying difficult concepts***—Identify any difficulties in understanding the text that you or any member of the group experience and relate the identification and exploration of those difficulties as "comprehension monitoring." (See Chapter 4, Interactive Read-Aloud.) Ask the group to suggest ways in which they overcame the difficulties as they were reading. As they suggest possibilities,

Type of Questions	Examples
Literal (Knowledge) Identification and recall	Who . . . ? What . . . ? When . . .? Where . . . ? How . . . ?
Comprehension Selection of facts and ideas	Tell in your own words. What is the main idea . . . ?
Application Use of facts, rules	How is _____ an example of _____? Why is _____ important?
Analysis Separating the whole into parts	What are the main elements of _____? How does _____ compare or contrast with _____?
Synthesis Combination of ideas into a new whole	How could you design a _____? What might happen if you combined _____ and _____?
Evaluation Developing opinions, judgments, decisions	Do you agree with _____? How would you decide to _____?

Figure 26.1 Levels of Questions and Examples

Adapted from Chamot & O'Malley (1993).

Step	What to Do	Learning Strategy
Group formation	Form a group of students to read cooperatively. Choose the sequence of reciprocal teachers (students).	Cooperation
Read	Each member of the group reads the first section of the text to him/herself.	Silent reading
Summarize	The first student summarizes the section just read.	Summarizing
Question	The first student questions other members of the group moving from low-level to high-level questions.	Literal Inferential Critical Questioning
Identify	The first student identifies any area of text that presented difficulty to any member of the group.	Comprehension monitoring
Problem solving	The group discusses possible solutions or strategies that could be used.	Cooperation
Prediction	The first student makes a prediction about what is likely to happen in the next section of text.	Predicting Inferring
Read	The group reads the next section silently.	Silent reading

Figure 26.2   Steps in Reciprocal Teaching

The whole procedure is repeated with the second student in the group leading.

remind the group that they are using cooperative learning strategies when they share solutions in groups like this.

• **Anticipating the next section to be read**—Make a prediction about what you think will happen in the next section of text, identify the strategy as "predicting," and relate it to making inferences. Give the group the next paragraph to read silently and encourage a student to be the next reciprocal teacher.

• **Using a chart to keep on track**—Post a chart that reviews the steps to be taken. Divide the class into groups and encourage them to take turns teaching the materials to one another. See Figure 26.2 for an example of the steps to be listed on a reciprocal teaching chart.

APPLICATIONS AND EXAMPLES

The fifth graders in Ms. Tobias' class are moving from their study of Australia into the exploration of the Aborigine tribes and their ways of communicating. Ms. Tobias wants them to read *The Cave Painters* by Percy Trezise (1988) for its comprehensive look at the wide variety of terrain in Australia and the different cultures represented by the Aborigine peoples. She knows the text is challenging, not because of the content, but because of the unusual proper names and so she decides to do two things. First, she will preteach some of the proper names and second, she will encourage the students to work in cooperative groups and do reciprocal teaching to support one another in the reading of this "tough text."

Ms. Tobias divides the students into cooperative groups of five students each and gives each student a number. She reminds the groups of their experiences with reciprocal teaching and quickly reviews the steps on the chart in the room (see Fig. 26.2). Each student is given a copy of the book and each group is given a large map of Australia with instructions to plot the locations of the various tribes described in the book. As the groups get started, Ms. Tobias wanders around the room listening to the discussion. Because she has tried to put the less fluent English speakers into a group with another student who has the same home language, there are a lot of side discussions in Spanish and Punjabi in the groups. The students seem to be doing a lot of group problem solving, and she hears some references to the videos of Australia, which she has shown in the past few days.

After the groups have finished reading and discussing the book, Ms. Tobias calls everyone together to review the process and talk about the history of the people that was recorded in the caves. The group also adds a number of new words to the Australian word wall. The students were especially fascinated by the different foods described in the book.

"They talked about poison yams, Ms. Tobias," Richie says. "I never knew yams could be poisonous."

"That was a surprise to me too," Ms. Tobias exclaims. "I knew mushrooms could be poisonous. I'd never heard of poisonous yams."

"You never tasted the ones my mother makes," Sammy quips.

Ms. Tobias smiles, "I'm going to tell her you said that."

"Can we make some cave paintings like the ones in the book, Ms. Tobias?" Jennifer asks. "I think they would look nice on the walls for Parent's Night."

"Good idea, Jennifer," Ms. Tobias replies. "Maybe some of you could write a script about the travels of the Aborigines. I think there is a lot to learn about Australia. There were a number of new animals, plants, and foods mentioned in this book that we need to research."

"I'll get on the Internet and see what I can find," Simon offers.

"Great idea!" Ms. Tobias says with a smile. "The rest of you look things up in the books we checked out from the library. Let Simon know if there's anything you can't find and maybe he can locate the information online. Let's make a list of the things we want to research."

Mr. Wishon's eighth graders are studying the U.S. Constitution. They are trying to understand the process the Constitutional Congress went through in writing the Constitution and the nature of the government that it created. Mr. Wishon has divided the class into cooperative groups and they are getting ready to read the Constitution for the purpose of understanding two things: (a) how the constitution has changed over the years, and (b) what was built into the original document that has allowed it to remain in place for more than 200 years with all of the changes that have taken place in U.S. society.

Mr. Wishon walks the groups through the first round of reciprocal teaching with the preamble and Article I. Since Article I includes 10 sections, Mr. Wishon has an opportunity to model a number of different levels of questions. He lists them with examples of questions he asks at each level.

First the class walks through Article I with Mr. Wishon asking the questions and the small groups discussing them. Then the groups begin the reciprocal teaching process on their own, with students taking turns summarizing, questioning, and clarifying.

Once the reciprocal teaching groups have explored all seven articles, Mr. Wishon conducts a group discussion where the class reviews the things they know about the original Constitution and its contents. They note the date of the signing, then Mr. Wishon has the groups open their social science books and use reciprocal teaching to read what the book has to say about the Constitution.

"It's sure a short description for such a long document," Martina observes.

"Yes, it is," Mr. Wishon agrees. "That's why I wanted you to read it thoroughly. I'm sure there are a number of citizens in this country who have never read it as thoroughly as you have today. Now what I want to do is look at the amendments and the history of why they were added. Who notices something about the dates of the amendments?"

"They started amending it almost right away," Brian notes.

"Yes, it was only three years later," Mr. Wishon says. "Why do you think that happened?"

The discussion continues with the students actively involved in thinking, reading their textbook, and discussing the amendments and what they change in the original document. The group seems to have a good understanding of the process involved in amending the constitution and the discussion shows that they comprehend the importance of each of the amendments. Sometimes Mr. Wishon asks one of the students to translate for others when the language gets complicated. Everyone seems to be very interested in the lesson.

CONCLUSION

Reciprocal teaching supports student learning in several ways. It encourages students to self-monitor for understanding. It requires the use of key vocabulary in explaining concepts. It encourages collaboration and group support in making sure that each member of the group fully understands the lesson.

Reciprocal teaching may require some adaptations for English language learners depending on their levels of English development. Some English language learners may not be ready to take a role as teacher but can serve in another capacity, perhaps as monitor of understanding, translator for other English language learners, or lister of key vocabulary words. Members of the group may have to adjust the questioning procedures so that the English language learners can draw pictures, point, or read aloud from the text to answer questions. These strategies should be modeled for the groups and students should be aware that they are responsible for supporting each member of their group in understanding the text.

EXAMPLES OF APPROXIMATION BEHAVIORS RELATED TO THE TESOL STANDARDS

Pre-K–3 students will:

- rephrase oral questions to elicit more specific information.
- ask questions for clarifying purposes.

4–8 students will:

- skim chapter headings to locate key points in a text.
- listen and respond to questions from peers.

9–12 students will:

- integrate and verbalize the connections between new information and previously known information.
- ask questions to check for understanding.

References

Chamot, A., & O'Malley, J. (1993). *The CALLA Handbook: Implementing the cognitive academic language learning approach*. Reading, MA: Addison-Wesley.

Palincsar, A. S., & Brown, A. L. (1986). Interactive teaching to promote independent learning from text. *The Reading Teacher, 39,* 771–777.

Trezise, P. (1988). *The cave painters*. Auckland, NZ: Harper Collins.

STRATEGIES FOR BUILDING VOCABULARY AND FLUENCY

The nine strategies contained in this section provide teachers with active-involvement activities for building two vital skills—vocabulary and fluency. Vocabulary knowledge is essential in all areas of learning. Students learn through verbal explanations in all areas of curriculum. To gain information through reading, students must understand the meanings of words.

The research on vocabulary identifies levels of vocabulary knowledge. **Fast mapping** is the level of word knowledge that allows students to understand words in a superficial way. The student may be able to read the word and understand its application within the context of a certain sentence. To develop **extended mapping,** however, students must encounter words in a number of contexts over time.

Developing extended mapping of new vocabulary is supported by active-learning strategies. The development of vocabulary is an ongoing, daily responsibility in every classroom. Vocabulary activities are a vital part of every part of the school day, reading, science, social studies, recess, and even lunch.

Fluency, both spoken and reading fluency, is highly related to vocabulary knowledge and comprehension. Teaching students to reread when necessary and to read with expression and effective phrasing is closely related to the development of successful classroom participation. Teachers must build a rich repertoire of strategies to engage students in word study throughout the day. That is the main purpose of this section.

MODELED TALK: Showing While You Talk

27

This strategy addresses the following TESOL Standards:

Goal 2: To use English to achieve academically in all content areas

Standard 1: Students will use English to interact in the classroom.

Standard 2: Students will use English to obtain, process, construct, and provide subject matter information in spoken and written form.

Standard 3: Students will use appropriate learning strategies to construct and apply academic knowledge.

Modeled talk (Herrell, 1999), the concurrent verbal explanation and physical demonstration of directions or concepts, is one of the simplest and most powerful strategies for use with English language learners. It takes some planning and practice but can soon become a habit for effective teachers. Modeled talk is the use of gestures, visuals, and demonstrations as explanations are made. Gestures and modeling provide examples for learners to follow and lower their anxiety since they know exactly what to do because they have seen the directions or content modeled.

STEP BY STEP

The steps in implementing modeled talk are:

- *Identifying the lesson and gathering materials*—Identify the lesson to be taught and the materials to be used. Think about what you plan to say to explain the lesson and the directions to the students. Prepare the materials the students will use so that you have an example to show and, if necessary, examples in various stages of completion. Design gestures that will help the students understand exactly what will be expected of them without having to rely on English vocabulary for understanding.

- *Practicing your modeled talk*—Practice your talk in front of a mirror to determine if your instructions, modeling, and gestures convey the message you want the students to understand.

- *Designing a visual of directions*—Design a standard visual that will be used regularly if the lesson or directions require that the students follow a sequence of instructions. This will help

151

Props	Visuals
Any textbooks to be used Scissors, tape, rulers, pencils, notebooks that will be needed Realia whenever vocabulary will be new Word cards for any new vocabulary to be written Maps, globes, manipulatives, examples of products to be made	Numbered charts showing sequence to be followed Diagrams showing a recap of directions given Standard illustrations for scissors (for directions to cut), crayon (for directions to color), pencil (for directions to write), computer (when it is to be used), ruler (for directions to measure), paintbrush (for directions to paint)

Figure 27.1 Props and Visuals to Support Modeled Talk

the students become accustomed to looking for this visual for support in remembering the sequence. Simple numbered drawings work well for this. A set of standard drawings, laminated and placed in sequence on the chalkboard, can be used again and again for different activities. A picture of a pair of scissors, for example, always reminds the students that the next step is to cut, while a picture of a crayon reminds them to color.

• ***Reviewing the steps to be taken***—Review the steps the students are to take after you have delivered your modeled talk. Use the visuals you have created to reinforce the students' reference to them for support in remembering what to do. When the students are performing the activities you have explained, refer to the visuals whenever there is a question about what to do next so that the students practice the use of them. See Figure 27.1 for suggestions of props and visuals that support modeled talks.

APPLICATIONS AND EXAMPLES

Ms. Milsovic is using modeled talk to explain the day's learning centers to her kindergarten class of English language learners. She begins by sitting in a small chair with the students sitting on the floor in front of her.

"When I play the music," Ms. Milsovic says as she points to herself and then touches the play button on the tape player so the children hear a short section of the music they use as a signal to change activities, "you (indicates the children) will go to centers (she motions toward the centers)."

"First (she holds up one finger), you will go to the planning board." As she says this she signals for them to follow her to the planning board. The planning board is made of a large automotive drip pan. It has photographs of each of the centers attached by magnetic tape across the top of it and room for children's names on magnets under each of the center pictures.

"You will look for your name," Ms. Milsovic continues as she shows the children the name cards, which are not yet attached to the board. She reads a few of the names so the children understand what is written on the name cards.

"If Cher's name is under this center," she points to the picture of the art center, "she will go to the art center first." She motions for the children to follow Cher to the art center.

At the art center Ms. Milsovic shows the children exactly what they will do there. She demonstrates each step as she talks about it. On this particular day the children are studying frogs and toads and they are using green paper plates to make frogs with long curled tongues. Ms. Milsovic shows them how to make the frog and posts a visual with drawings that demonstrate what to do first, second, and third. After she demonstrates, she refers to the visual and asks one of the children to tell her what to do at each step. See Figure 27.2 for an example of the visual Ms. Milsovic used.

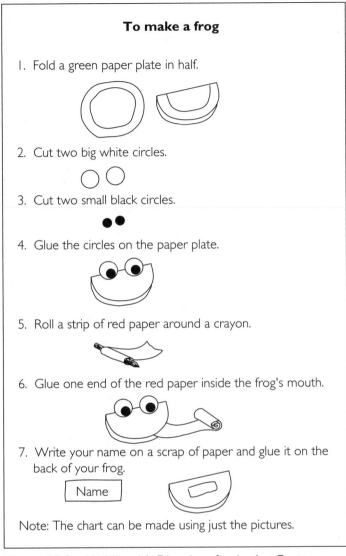

To make a frog

1. Fold a green paper plate in half.

2. Cut two big white circles.

3. Cut two small black circles.

4. Glue the circles on the paper plate.

5. Roll a strip of red paper around a crayon.

6. Glue one end of the red paper inside the frog's mouth.

7. Write your name on a scrap of paper and glue it on the back of your frog.

Name

Note: The chart can be made using just the pictures.

Figure 27.2   Ms. Milsovic's Directions for the Art Center

Each center is carefully modeled and key English vocabulary is taught and practiced. When all the centers have been explained, the children and Ms. Milsovic return to the planning board and the names of the children are placed on the board so they know where to go first. Once this is done, Ms. Milsovic plays the music on the tape recorder, signaling that it's time to move to centers. Since the children know what to do at each center and there are visuals available at each center to remind them in case they forget, Ms. Milsovic is able to work with small groups of students at the writing center using interactive writing to teach them how to write words describing frogs. The children are secure in their understanding of what is expected of them.

Ms. Delgado is demonstrating how to make four-corner books for her fifth graders, who are always looking for new ways to celebrate the books they have read. Since the students will be making their books while Ms. Delgado is holding literature discussions, she wants to make sure that they know exactly what to do. She displays a poster that shows each of the steps in their assignment and then she gives a modeled talk demonstrating the steps in the process. Figure 27.3 shows the poster Ms. Delgado displays.

As Ms. Delgado demonstrates the making of a four-corner book, she refers to the steps listed on the poster. "First," she says as she points to the number "1" on the poster, "you fold a piece of paper

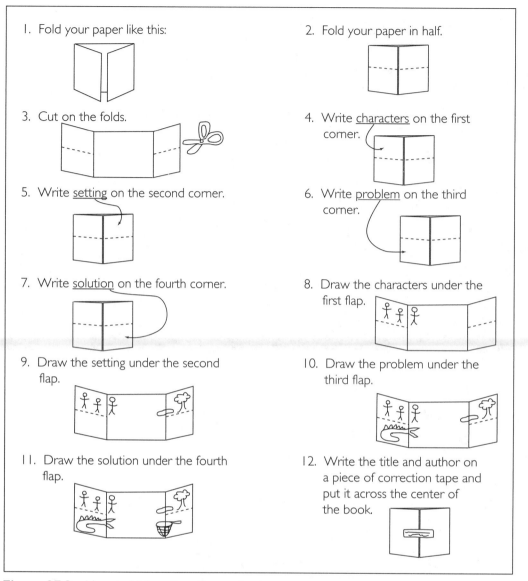

1. Fold your paper like this:

2. Fold your paper in half.

3. Cut on the folds.

4. Write <u>characters</u> on the first corner.

5. Write <u>setting</u> on the second corner.

6. Write <u>problem</u> on the third corner.

7. Write <u>solution</u> on the fourth corner.

8. Draw the characters under the first flap.

9. Draw the setting under the second flap.

10. Draw the problem under the third flap.

11. Draw the solution under the fourth flap.

12. Write the title and author on a piece of correction tape and put it across the center of the book.

Figure 27.3   How to Make a Four-Corner Book

like this." She demonstrates and then points to the drawing on the poster. Ms. Delgado writes "1" on the chalkboard and puts the sample she has started under the number.

"Second," she continues, as she points to the number "2" on the poster, "you fold the paper in half, this way." She takes a premade sample that was completed in step 1, demonstrates step 2, points to the drawing on the poster, writes the numeral "2" on the chalkboard, and puts the second sample under it.

"Third," she says as she points to the number "3" on the poster, "you cut on the folds you just made." She demonstrates the cutting on an additional sample, makes a "3" on the chalkboard and puts the third sample under it. At this point she has a sample at each stage of the preparation sitting along the chalk tray for the students to examine if the need arises.

Next she takes a premade sample of the four-corner book she has just shown how to make and writes CHARACTERS on one corner. "You write the word *characters* on the first corner," she says as she demonstrates.

Ms. Delgado models each step, adding the word *setting* on the second corner, the word *problem* on the third corner, and the word *solution* on the fourth corner. She then lifts the flap on which the word *characters* is written and demonstrates the drawing of the main characters of her book. She repeats the process with the rest of the four corners.

Last of all, Ms. Delgado takes a piece of wide correction tape and puts it across the middle of her four-corner book and writes the title and author of the book on it. As she does each of these steps she refers the students to the poster and leaves a sample on the chalkboard for them to examine as they are making their own books. Once she has completed the modeled talk, she puts the supplies on a table for the students to use and calls a literature discussion group together. The rest of the class is busily engaged in making four-corner books and her group is not disturbed. They know how to make their books and know they will have an opportunity to share the books after Ms. Delgado finishes working with her groups. This was explained to them as a part of the modeled talk—and it's on the poster.

CONCLUSION

Modeled talk is helpful in lowering students' anxiety because they know what is expected of them. It serves another important function when the teacher uses it consistently. English-speaking students often learn how to model talk and use it when explaining procedures and concepts to English language learners in the classroom. Students' use of modeled talk to other students increases the opportunities for English language learners to interact successfully with their peers and it builds feelings of community within the classroom.

EXAMPLES OF APPROXIMATION BEHAVIORS RELATED TO THE TESOL STANDARDS:

Pre-K–3 students will:

- follow instructions from verbal and nonverbal cues.
- gather and organize materials needed to complete a task.

4–8 students will:

- follow a sequence of instructions based on verbal directions and physical actions.
- generate and ask questions to clarify expectations.

9–12 students will:

- compare and classify information based on verbal instructions and physical modeling.
- construct a chart or visual representation of information gained through oral directions and physical modeling.

Reference

Herrell, A. (1999). Modeling talk to support comprehension in young children. *Kindergarten Education: Research, Theory, and Practice, 3,* 29–42.

REPORTING BACK:
Verbal Practice in Curricular Connections

28

Reporting back is a strategy used to support students in bridging the gap between spoken and written language (Gibbons, 1993). This strategy can be used as a follow up after any active learning experience. The students describe their experience, using vocabulary that is connected with the experience so that the rest of the class has a clear understanding of the materials and sequence of actions that were used. The students then write their reporting-back summary to be included in the class daily news, or their daily learning log. See Figure 28.1 for suggested activities appropriate for reporting back.

STEP BY STEP

The steps in using the reporting-back strategy are:

• *Preparing the students for action*—Prepare the students for an active-learning experience by giving directions for the activity and modeling what is expected. Follow up your demonstration by saying, "After you finish your activity, you will report back to the class describing what happened. For example, if you were reporting back to the class on the experience just demonstrated, you would say, 'I opened the jar of red paint and I opened the jar of blue paint. I took an eyedropper and used it to draw up some of the red paint and dropped two drops of red paint into the plastic cup. Next, I used the eyedropper to draw up some blue paint and put two drops of blue paint into the plastic cup. I took a toothpick and swirled the two colors together in the cup. When they mixed together they turned into purple paint. I learned that red and blue paint mix together to make purple paint.'

Curricular Area	Activity	Adaptation
Art	Create a summer art activity book for younger students by trying out art projects and then writing step-by-step instructions of how they were done.	Computer use; photos or drawings to accompany text
Dance	Create a dance to demonstrate the connections between movement and content area study, research dance in various cultures and historical periods, present an oral summary of the research along with the dance created.	Videotape the presentations; create a book describing the research done and the connections found
Theater	Research and write a play related to a period of history, such as the American Revolution, Civil War, World War II, "Roaring Twenties."	Publish the scripts along with the reports on the research done
Language arts	Research and write informational books. Require the students to report back on their research along with the steps they used in writing and illustrating the book.	Publish the books along with pages from their learning logs describing the process used to research; write and illustrate it, including any collaboration they did
Science	Use experiments as a topic for writing a children's science activity book for younger students to use as summer science activities.	Add diagrams, photos, and learning log examples to the book
Social studies	Teach the students to write anecdotal records as they observe interactions among people in public places such as the school cafeteria or the local mall. Focus on describing body language and facial expressions as well as clothing and physical attributes.	Add drawings of the situations

Figure 28.1   Suggested Activities for Reporting Back

After you finish your activity, you and your partner need to decide what to say when you report back to the class."

• *Listing and reviewing the steps*—After explaining the procedure to the students, list the steps on the chalkboard or on a chart. The steps might be:

1. Mix your two colors together in the cup.
2. Make a list of the steps you used.
3. Practice reporting back with your partner.
4. Ask for help if you need it.

• *Verbalizing the action*—During the activity, circulate throughout the classroom, reinforcing the vocabulary being used and scaffolding language by verbalizing what you see going on. For example, as one pair is dropping paint into the cup you might say, "You are dropping the paint into the cup. I see you dropping one, two, three drops of yellow into the cup."

• *Pairing for verbal practice*—After the activity, give the pairs time to practice their reporting-back dialogues. Then, ask each pair of students to report back to the group. This works best if each pair has a slightly different task. In the color-mixing activity each pair might have different colors or different numbers of drops to use so that the reporting back stays interesting and nonrepetitive.

• *Celebrating the achievements*—After each pair reports back, list important words that they used on the chalkboard and celebrate their use of interesting and important vocabulary. Emphasize the role the vocabulary plays in helping the audience to visualize exactly what the pair did.

• *Writing the reports*—After completing the reporting back, students write their verbal report and use it either as news items for the class daily news or as daily entries in their learning logs.

• *Assessing student progress and understanding*—While the students report back, take time to take brief notes to include in anecdotal records. Anecdotal records taken periodically over time serve as rich descriptions of students' verbal communication progress and are important additions to individual student portfolios.

APPLICATIONS AND EXAMPLES

Ms. Christensen's sixth-grade students are creating a class Rosetta stone and then using the alphabet they inscribe on the stone to write messages in hieroglyphics as a part of their study of ancient Egypt. The Rosetta stone is created as a class project, but the individual messages are transcribed by pairs of students writing in clay using sticks as styluses.

Ms. Christensen has modeled the use of the Rosetta stone to create her message and how the stone must also be used to decipher other messages. She has left the instructions for the activity on a chart in the room, but it is also written in hieroglyphics. She models her reporting back to the class with the directions, "Tell us what you did, step by step. Be sure to use words like *first, second,* and *next* so we can follow the sequence of what you did."

After the pairs complete their messages and report back orally, they write their messages in their social science learning logs, along with their translations and step-by-step descriptions of what they did.

Ms. Christensen has provided an activity that emphasizes the difference among casual spoken language between working partners, more formal spoken language used for class reports, and written language. As a closing activity she engages the students in a discussion in which they compare the types of things they said to each other while they were working on the messages, the kinds of sentences they used when they reported back orally, and the sentences they wrote in their learning logs. They also discuss the vocabulary they used in the more formal reporting back and writing. The students decide that the language used in the formal oral presentations was more like the language used in the writing in the learning logs than the language they used while talking to their partners.

One student says, "When I was working with Jonathan, I used a lot of words like *this* and *that* because we were pointing to objects and talking about them. When I talked about the objects in the reporting back, I had to use the names for them and say what I was doing instead of just doing it."

Ms. Carlson is an art teacher at Johnson Junior High. Johnson has an extremely diverse population of students and the school has established a schoolwide goal of developing students' oral and written language. Ms. Carlson has decided to use reporting back as a strategy after each project, requiring the students to write descriptions of their projects and how they were made. This month, the classes are using clay to create three-dimensional figures showing their favorite recreational activities.

Ms. Carlson demonstrates the use of clay to make a tennis player in position to serve the ball. She then reports back to the students, modeling the use of sequence words to describe her step-by-step procedures. She uses the reporting-back sequence to model the problem solving she had to engage in to create a sculpture that showed the arm and racket extended into the air. Using the overhead projector, Ms. Carlson then demonstrates how she will transcribe her oral reporting into her art learning log. She also includes a photo of her sculpture in her learning log.

The students spend about a week completing their sculpture. They work on their reporting-back assignments and practice in pairs while the slower sculptors are finishing their projects. Ms. Carlson invites Mr. Gobel, the principal, to come in to hear the reporting-back presentations and view the sculpture. Mr. Gobel is very impressed with the art, the descriptive ways the students found to describe the steps they used, and the problem solving they were required to do. He suggests they repeat the process for their parents the night of parent conferences.

CONCLUSION

Reporting back provides a step in the learning process that is frequently overlooked. It requires the students to use the lesson-related vocabulary to review the steps that were used in completing the assignment. It provides a direct connection between instruction and language.

English language learners are supported, when necessary, by being encouraged to use visuals that illustrate the steps and supply the vocabulary so that they have a scaffold when they report back to the teacher or the class.

EXAMPLES OF APPROXIMATION BEHAVIORS RELATED TO THE TESOL STANDARDS:

Pre-K–3 students will:

- verbally describe the steps taken to complete an assignment.
- listen and add to a peer's report of an activity.

4–8 students will:

- use academic language to describe content knowledge gained from a class assignment.
- verbally describe the actions and contributions of each member of a group following a group activity.

9–12 students will:

- write a written report describing steps taken to complete a long-range assignment.
- analyze and evaluate personal contributions to a group task.

Reference

Gibbons, P. (1993). Learning to learn in a second language. Portsmouth, NH: Heinemann.

Suggested Readings

Hernandez, H. (1997). *Teaching in multicultural classrooms*. Upper Saddle River, NJ: Merrill/Prentice Hall.

Peregon, S., & Boyle, O. (1993). *Reading, writing, and learning in ESL*. New York: Longman.

VOCABULARY ROLE PLAY: **29**
Building Vocabulary Through Dramatization

This strategy addresses the following TESOL Standards:

Goal 1: To use English to communicate in social settings

Standard 3: Students will use learning strategies to extend their communicative competence.

Goal 2: To use English to achieve academically in all content areas

Standard 1: Students will use English to interact in the classroom.
Standard 2: Students will use English to obtain, process, construct, and provide subject matter information in spoken and written form.
Standard 3: Students will use appropriate learning strategies to construct and apply academic knowledge.

Goal 3: To use English in socially and culturally appropriate ways

Standard 2: Students will use nonverbal communication appropriate to audience, purpose, and setting.

Vocabulary role play (Herrell, 1998) is a strategy used to encourage learners to make connections among their past experiences, the content currently being studied, and vocabulary that is new or being used in an unfamiliar way. Students are introduced to new vocabulary and given an opportunity to discuss and use the vocabulary in context through role playing. Often several groups of students are given the same vocabulary and asked to write and perform a skit in which the words are used and demonstrated. Since the groups are likely to write and perform skits in which the vocabulary words are used in different contexts, the skits serve to show multiple uses of the same words. In this way, English language learners are given an opportunity to see the vocabulary words used in context, as well as demonstrations of several contexts in which the words may be used appropriately.

STEP BY STEP

The steps in implementing vocabulary role play are:

- *Identifying key vocabulary*—Determine the vocabulary words that will be used in a lesson or reading. Make cards with the words written on them.

- *Teaching the lesson or reading the book*—As you teach the lesson or read the book—either reading aloud, or having the students read—stop as you encounter key vocabulary and discuss and act out the words. Pronounce the words carefully and have the students practice pronouncing them, especially if the words contain sounds difficult for them. Be sure to reread the page fluently after the vocabulary is explored. As each word is explored, place it in a pocket chart so students can see it clearly.

- *Connecting the vocabulary to past experiences*—After the lesson is complete or the story is read, show the cards to the class, one by one, and ask the students to talk about ways in which they have seen the words used. Use this opportunity to explore multiple meanings of words.

- *Sorting the words*—Further explore the words by engaging the students in word sorting. Ask them if any of the words have similar meanings, or if any of them are names for things—nouns. Identify the movement words—verbs—and place them together. Review the word meanings in several different ways to help the students remember them. See Figure 29.1 for a typical word sort.

- *Planning ways to use the words*—Leave the words on display in the pocket chart. Use the words in directions during the day. Encourage the students to use the new vocabulary in their writing and celebrate verbally when they do. Involve the students in creating scenes using the new vocabulary by dividing the class into small groups of three to five students and giving each group a set of four or five words. Make sure that each group has at least one member who is a strong reader. Instruct each group to create a scene in which all their words are used.

- *Giving the students time to practice*—Give the groups time to work on their scripts and practice performing their scenes. Encourage the groups to make and use simple props.

- *Performing the scenes*—Give each group a chance to perform the scenes that they have written. Discuss how the words were used after each scene is performed, celebrating innovative uses of the new vocabulary.

- *Focusing on multiple word meanings*—Compare and contrast the uses of the words by the groups, emphasizing the differing contexts used in the skits and the similarities and differences in the ways in which the words were used.

Movement Words	Names for Things	Descriptive Words
VERBS	NOUNS	ADJECTIVES/ADVERBS
paraded	ledge	scary
prowled	geranium	slowly
stroked	statue	quickly
winked	puddle	sparkling
stretched	park bench	leisurely

Figure 29.1   A Word Sort Using Words From a Vocabulary Role Play Lesson

Words taken from *The Third-Story Cat* (Baker, 1987).

APPLICATIONS AND EXAMPLES

Ms. Lee has brought her calico cat, Muffin, to school to visit the children in her first-grade class. Many of the children express fear at the possibility of handling Muffin, but Ms. Lee wants them to become more comfortable with her. She chooses a special book about a calico cat to share with her class. As she sits in the big rocking chair in the corner of the classroom with Muffin sleeping in her lap, Ms. Lee shows the cover of the book she holds, which has no picture on it.

"The title of this book is *The Third-Story Cat* (Baker, 1987)," Ms. Lee says. "There is no picture on the cover to help us guess what it is about. What do you think it might be? What is a third-story cat?"

"Maybe there were two other stories about the cat," Jacob suggests.

"That's an idea," Ms. Lee agrees.

"Have you ever heard the expression *third-story* before?" she asks.

"I think my uncle lives on the third-story," Tony answers tentatively. "You have to go up a lot of stairs to his apartment."

"That's right, Tony. Third-story means the same thing as third floor." Ms. Lee opens the book to the title page where the students can see a lovely watercolor painting of an apartment building with three floors. In the apartment on the third floor you can see a calico cat sleeping on the window sill.

"Look up here in the window," Ms. Lee says. "Do you see a cat that looks just like Muffin?"

"O-o-o-h," the students sigh. "It does look like Muffin."

Ms. Lee then uses the illustration of the apartment building to show the meaning of the word *third-story*. She sweeps her hand across the first floor of the apartment building in the picture and says, "The people who live on this floor can walk out their doors and be on the sidewalk. This is the first floor or first story." She points to the doors that open onto the sidewalk and to the sidewalk itself as she says the words.

"The people who live on the second floor, or second story, have to go up some stairs to their apartments." Ms. Lee points to the doorway and moves her hand up to the second floor as she explains.

"The people who live on the third story have to go up even more stairs," Ms. Lee explains as she points to the third floor.

"There are a lot of big words in this story," Ms. Lee says. "The author of this book, Leslie Baker, uses a lot of wonderful words to tell us about all the exciting things this cat does one day. Let's read the story and find out what adventures the cat has."

Ms. Lee reads the story aloud to the students, using the beautiful illustrations to help them understand the new vocabulary that is introduced in the story. She stops to demonstrate the meaning of the word *startled* as the cat is surprised by a butterfly flying up out of the geranium box. She has one of the children demonstrate the word *crept* as the cat is balancing along the ledge on the three-story building. As the story is read the children are exposed to a number of new words describing the ways in which cats move: *paraded, prowled, twitched, leaped*. Some other words require some physical practice, like *winked* and *stroked*.

After the story is read, Ms. Lee goes through the new words again and has the children make a large circle. They walk around the room and act out the movements the cats made in the story. They wink, and creep, and twitch, and parade until they are all very silly. They show the difference between being startled and being frightened, between winking and blinking, between parading and prowling, and between patting and stroking. When they sit back down in the circle, Ms. Lee shows them cards with the new words printed on them and as she holds each card up a child volunteers to act it out.

Ms. Lee leaves the new vocabulary word cards in a part of the room near the pocket chart and shows the children how they can use the cards to fill in the blanks in the pocket chart story.

They are invited to make new sentences with the cards during center time and they even have a new pointer with a calico cat on the end of it to use as they read the sentences they are making. Ms. Lee smiles as she watches the children busily building sentences with the new vocabulary words. One of the children is carrying Muffin around the room with her as she acts out the new words she has learned from *The Third-Story Cat.*

Mr. Valdez's fourth graders are studying Florida history. They are reading about the barefoot mail carriers who brought the mail down the beaches to the first settlements and the ways in which the various people came to Florida to establish permanent residences. Some of the vocabulary is unfamiliar to the students and Mr. Valdez wants to make sure that the words are understood by all his students. Going through the Florida history book, Mr. Valdez selects the words *barefoot, cypress, brackish, humid, Everglades,* and *tidepools,* and writes the words on sentence strips.

After he reads the section from the Florida history book aloud to his class, Mr. Valdez asks the students to talk about the ways in which they have heard the words used before.

Jonah starts the discussion by saying, "I like to go barefoot in the summertime. My mother is always telling me to put my shoes on."

"I know what is means to go barefoot," Katie adds. "I just don't understand why the mail carriers were barefoot."

Mr. Valdez takes the time to explain that since there were very few roads in the early days, the easiest route down the state was walking along the beach and so the mail carriers often got their feet wet. To protect their shoes, they walked barefoot until they came to places where they needed to wear shoes. Then they would stop and put their shoes back on.

Carla talked about brackish water and how her dad is often worried about the salt water at their beach house invading the drinking water. "That's what he calls brackish water," she explains. "It's when the salt water invades the fresh water."

"Yes," Mr. Valdez agrees. "But in some places in the state it's a natural thing for water to be brackish. Some of the rivers empty into the ocean and there is an area in which the salt water and fresh water mix. That's also brackish water."

The discussion continues until each of the words has been discussed. Mr. Valdez then divides the students into groups of three and asks them to write a short skit in which they use as many of the new vocabulary words as they can. One member of the group is assigned as the note-taker and the skits are written. The students are given 15 to 20 minutes to make simple props and each group is given a chance to act out its skit. Some of the groups have one of the members read the script while the other two do the acting. One group chooses to do a charade and asks the class to guess which word they are portraying. Another group has a complete dialogue with each of the speakers emphasizing a few of the new vocabulary words. One of the groups even performs a rap routine using the new words. By the time all six groups perform, all the new words have been demonstrated multiple times in many different contexts. Mr. Valdez is confident that the new vocabulary is thoroughly understood by everyone.

CONCLUSION

Vocabulary role play provides the link between learning a new word and using the word in context, or multiple contexts. Role play enables the student to create experiences with which to link the new vocabulary. The study of words, their multiple meanings, and origins can also be effective with the use of vocabulary role play. Students can add brief videos to illustrate word meaning, create animated computer dictionaries, publish vocabulary books, and illustrate word posters—all of which increase their interactions with and understanding of English vocabulary and multiple meanings.

EXAMPLES OF APPROXIMATION BEHAVIORS RELATED TO THE TESOL STANDARDS:

Pre-K–3 students will:

- act out common verbs.
- recreate a scene from a storybook with dialogue and action.

4–8 students will:

- create a scene demonstrating multiple meanings of common words.
- communicate the meanings of words through verbalization and action.

9–12 students will:

- interact with a group to write a script demonstrating word meanings.
- use appropriate language structures to depict a variety of social contexts in dramatic action scenes.

References

Baker, L. (1987). *The third-story cat*. Boston: Little, Brown.

Herrell, A. (1998). *Exemplary practices in teaching English language learners*. Fresno: California State University.

Jordan, M., & Herrell, A. (2002). Building comprehension bridges: A multiple strategies approach. *California Reader, 35*(4) 14–19.

VOCABULARY PROCESSING: **30**
A Multistrategy Approach to Building and Using Vocabulary

This strategy addresses the following TESOL Standards:

Goal 1: To use English to communicate in social settings

Standard 1: Students will use English to participate in social interactions.
Standard 2: Students will interact in, through, and with spoken and written English for personal expression and enjoyment.
Standard 3: Students will use learning strategies to extend their communicative competence.

Goal 2: To use English to achieve academically in all content areas

Standard 3: Students will use appropriate learning strategies to construct and apply academic knowledge.

Vocabulary processing (Jordan & Herrell, 2002) is an approach to vocabulary building especially appropriate for English learners because the vocabulary is introduced in several contexts and the students are given multiple opportunities to use the words in their everyday interactions both in and out of school.

The vocabulary being studied can be drawn from a book that is read aloud to the class, reading assignments, or curricular-specific words such as science or social studies vocabulary. Word collections (Herrell & Jordan, 2002) are written on chart paper or overhead transparencies so that the students make connections between and among words with which they are familiar and the new vocabulary being introduced. Word collections are a special type of word wall where the words are all related in some way. For example, if the new vocabulary is *amble,* the word is written on a word collection for ways to walk. The students are involved in thinking of all the different ways they can think of to walk.

As each word is written on the chart, someone demonstrates it and then everyone practices saying the word, acting it out, or relating it to something with which they are familiar. After the word collections are made, students choose one to three words to practice in their everyday verbal interactions. The words chosen by each individual are written into a vocabulary journal and then each student documents the ways they found to use the words.

The teacher also has a responsibility to find ways of using the new words as a part of the word processing strategy. In addition to using the words in the classroom setting, students are encouraged to find ways to use them and document their use outside of class.

This multiple-strategy approach to vocabulary supports students' understanding of the nuances of words that have the same or similar meanings. Research clearly indicates that the development of extensive vocabulary and understanding of word meanings is essential to successful and fluid comprehension in reading and verbal interactions (Allen, 2000). By collecting and actively using words, students are constantly building a repertoire of words and word meanings that will increase their understanding of oral language as well as stories and improve and strengthen their spoken vocabulary and eventually their writing skills.

STEP BY STEP

The steps in implementing vocabulary processing are:

- *Choosing vocabulary to explore*—The teacher preselects some words to be used in read-aloud or other content-area lessons. As the lessons are taught, additional words can be added to the lesson whenever it appears that students are in need of additional support in understanding the words.

- *Charting and categorizing the words*—As the story is read, or the lesson taught, vocabulary is written on charts on sentence strips. Sentence strips work especially well because the words can be moved around in pocket charts to categorize them into collections of similar words.

- *Adding context to the words*—Whenever possible, the words are acted out, related to real objects or pictures, or related to experiences the students have had. The charting and physicalization of the words supports students' understanding of the meanings of the words as they are categorized, acted out, or connected to objects and context.

- *Finding ways to use the words*—The teacher keeps the word collections on display in the classroom for several purposes. The students are encouraged to use the words in both speech and writing and document the ways in which they use them. The teacher uses the words frequently during the day and the chart helps to remind her of the words to be used. The word charts provide a record of the words students acquire as they add to the collections as well as acting as a reference for themselves and other students.

- *Encouraging additions to the word collections*—As students read and write they often locate words that can be added to word collections, and the teacher encourages them to add words to the charts. If they add a word to the collection, they are responsible for helping other students understand the meanings and nuances of the new words. This may be accomplished through simple explanations, or may require more elaborate illustration such as drawing, miming, or acting out scenes to demonstrate the word meanings.

- *Building vocabulary journals*—While the words are being collected on charts within the classroom, the children are engaged in finding ways to process or use the new words. As they discover new words, the children are encouraged to find ways to use the words and report back to the teacher and other students the ways in which they were able to use them in speech or in writing. The teacher sets aside some time each day for word study and part of this time is spent discussing the ways in which the new words have been used by the children. In kindergarten and beginning first grade, this is done orally or by having the teacher take the children's dictation to document the word usage in a double-entry journal created by the class. As the children become able to write for themselves, they take over the writing of the journal. See Figure 30.1 for an example of a double-entry word journal.

- *Using cognates*—As a part of word study, the teacher should make students aware of words in their native language that have English cognates—words in the native language that are close in meaning and pronunciation to English words. Most romance languages have a number of cognates

Kindergarten version (teacher takes dictation)	
Word	The ways we used it
Tiptoe	Miss McCloskey said, "Please tiptoe to your seats."
Parade	"We look like a parade when we walk with our heads and knees held high," Miss Vang said.

Upper-grade version (students write their own entries)	
Word	How I used it
Intently	I asked my dad why he was looking at the paper so intently. (He was impressed.)
Flung	I told my mom I had flung my towel over the porch rail.

Figure 30.1   Double-Entry Vocabulary Journals

that can be used to build English vocabulary (Williams, 2001). Teachers of students who speak Spanish, Italian, or Portuguese as their first language need to keep a multilanguage dictionary in the classroom so they can identify cognates and add to the students' understanding of the connections in meaning and pronunciation between the languages. The teacher writes the Spanish and English words on the chalkboard and talks about the meanings and pronunciations. The words can then be added to a chart of cognates in the classroom so that students are reminded of these connections. See Figure 30.2 for a list of common Spanish cognates. When cognates are added to word walls in the classroom they should be marked in some way to support English learners in making connections to their native vocabularies.

- ***Assessing growth and understanding***—Student vocabulary journals provide good entries for their portfolios. Teachers can also keep checklists of vocabulary usage in student writing and verbal interactions. Observing and documenting the words students include in their vocabulary journals and the ways in which they use the words is easily done during the time when they share their vocabulary journals. Students will enjoy keeping a running count of the new words they use in their vocabulary journals, as well.

- ***Adding technology***—Both the word collections and vocabulary journals may be done with a word processor. Students can access the word collections when they are writing on the computer or print out hard copies of the word collections to include in their individual writing folders. Some teachers have been successful in having students find artwork online to use in illustrating their vocabulary journals as well.

 APPLICATIONS AND EXAMPLES

To introduce her kindergarten/first-grade class to word study, Miss McCloskey asks them to stand up and walk around the classroom in a circle. "Now I want you to tiptoe around the room," she says, and the children immediately get up on their tiptoes and continue around in the circle. Even her English language learners respond quickly because they see what the others are doing. To reinforce the connection of the new word to their actions, Miss McCloskey begins a quiet chant. "Tiptoe, tiptoe, tiptoe," she chants softly as the children join in while they continue around the circle.

Animals

English	Spanish
animal	animales
human	humano
kangaroo	canguro
elephant	elefante
dinosaur	dinosaurio
eagle	aguila

Math

English	Spanish
decimal	decimal
double	doble
fraction	fraccion
circle	circulo
equal	igual
triangle	triangulo
vertical	vertical

Science

English	Spanish
hypothesis	hipotesis
acid	acido
metal	metal
corrosion	corrosion
plastics	plastico

Social Studies

English	Spanish
civilization	civilizacion
history	historia
pioneer	pionero
colonial	colonial
diary	diario

Common Words

English	Spanish
actor	actor
hospital	hospital
alphabet	alfabeto
television	television
opportunity	oportunidad
popular	popular

Books

English	Spanish
appendix	apendice
atlas	atlas
volume	volumen
title	titulo
page	pagina
introduction	introduccion

Figure 30.2 Common English/Spanish Cognates (From NTC's Dictionary of Spanish Cognates)

"Now let's parade," Miss McCloskey says. "Lift your head and your knees up high as you pretend to be in a parade. Parade, parade, parade." The chant changes as the children get into the parade mode. Miss McCloskey changes the commands a few more times and then asks the children to sit down in the circle. She says, "We have been walking in many different ways today. Who can remember all the ways we walked?"

"I know," Moua says as she raises her hand. "We tiptoe."

"Yes we tiptoed," Miss McCloskey confirms as she writes the word on the big chart she has beside her seat. "Moua, can you show us how to tiptoe?"

Moua gets up quickly and tiptoes around the edge of the carpet. The children softly begin to chant, "Tiptoe, tiptoe, tiptoe."

Miss McCloskey continues to add words to the chart as the children remember all the ways they walked. She asks the children to demonstrate their words as they contribute them to the chart.

"Now, I want to tell you a secret," Miss McCloskey says quietly. "If you want these words to be your words you have to find ways to use them. All day today I want you to remember to use the words we have written on our word chart. Do you see what I wrote at the top? What does it say?"

"I know," says Marco, one of the first graders. "It says 'ways to walk'."

"That's exactly right," Miss McCloskey says with a smile. "We found five different ways to walk today. Let's read them together." As she points to each word, the children read, "Tiptoe, parade, prowl, march, stomp."

"Before we go home today, we will have time for you to tell me about the ways you find to use these five words today," Miss McCloskey reminds them.

All during the day, Miss McCloskey finds ways to use the words on the word collection chart. She asks the children to parade into line for recess. She has them prowl down the hall to lunch. They tiptoe to their literacy centers and march to the music during their P.E. activity time. At the end of the day she gathers the group together to start their word study journal. She shows the class a piece of chart paper divided into a "T" chart. She writes "Word" over the left side of the "T" and "Ways we used it" over the right side of the chart.

"This is our word journal," Miss McCloskey says. "We are going to celebrate all the ways we used our new words today. Who found a way to use one of the words?"

"I did!" Tonio says. "I told Miss Vang that I was going to prowl over and get a drink."

"Very good, Tonio," Miss McCloskey says. "You used the word *prowl* so I write it under the word *word* on our chart." She writes *prowl* on the left side of the "T" chart. "And you said, 'I am going to prowl over and get a drink.'" Miss McCloskey writes, "Tonio said, 'I am going to prowl over and get a drink.'" She says the words very slowly as she writes them so that all the children can see how to write the words. She continues to ask the children to talk about the ways they used the new words and she writes the words and the ways in which they were used on the "T" chart or double-entry word journal.

"Now," she says after many of the words have been written on the word journal chart, "When you go home today I want you to continue to practice using your new words. Remember how you use them so we can add your words to the chart tomorrow. Also, I want you to be thinking of other ways to walk so we can practice walking in even more different ways tomorrow and add some new words to the chart."

Miss McCloskey's class builds the word collections and word journal each day. Before long they have collections of words for *walk, talk, smells, sounds, tastes, toys, flowers, clothes, food,* and *drinks.* Before long the children are keeping their own word journals with the first graders and kindergartners working together to make the entries. Of course, Miss McCloskey and her aide are very happy to take their dictation if they are needed.

Miss McCloskey is very pleased with the progress the children are making as they build their vocabularies through word collections and word processing. She is especially pleased with the progress of her English language learners who benefit enormously from this active approach to word study.

Mr. Cha's ninth graders are preparing for their district writing assessment. To help them write more interesting essays, Mr. Cha begins a word study unit so that his students will use a wider variety of descriptive words in their writing. Each day he gives the class a basic paragraph and they must find ways to create visual images as they add description and feeling to the paragraph. The first day of the study, Mr. Cha presents this paragraph to the class:

> A boy was walking through the field. He came to a tree and stopped to rest. All of a sudden, he heard a sound. He was scared. He stopped and listened. It was just a small animal climbing the tree.

"Can you see the boy in your mind?" Mr. Cha asks the class.

"No," Jesse answers.

"How can we add to the first sentence to help you see the boy?" Mr. Cha asks.

"We can describe him," Ana replies.

"Exactly, Ana. How do you think he looks?" Mr. Cha asks.

"We can say, 'A small boy with bright red hair and freckles was walking slowly through the field.'" Ana says.

"OK, that helps," Mr. Cha replies. "But let's do some brainstorming. What other words can we use instead of *small?*"

As the students call out words such as *little, tiny, miniature, petite,* and *elfin,* Mr. Cha smiles. "Now you've got the idea," he says as he writes the words on a chart. He labels the list "Other words for small."

"These are the kinds of words you can use to make your essays more interesting. When you use the same words over and over, your writing is not too interesting to read."

The class goes through the basic paragraph together making lists of other words for *walking, field, came, tree, stopped, rest, heard, sound, scared, stopped, listened, animal* and *climbing.* See Figure 30.3 for the lists they made.

walking	_field_	_came_	_tree_
stomping	meadow	encountered	pine
lumbering	pasture	returned	oak
ambling	grassland	approached	willow
stopped	_rest_	_heard_	_sound_
halted	relax	deciphered	noise
hesitated	take a breath	heeded	stirring
waited	pause	took in	shuffling
scared	_listened_	_small animal_	_climbing_
frightened	tuned in	rodent	scampering
startled	focused	squirrel	ascending
terrified	heard	mouse	clammering

Figure 30.3 Sample Word Collections

"Now I want each of you to rewrite the basic paragraph using some of the words from our word collections," says Mr. Cha. "You may use other words you think of, also. If you think of another word to use, be sure to come up and add it to our collection."

After the class completes the writing practice using words from the charts, Mr. Cha hands out college blue books. "These blue books are used in college for writing exams, but we're going to use them to create vocabulary journals. I want each of you to choose three words that we put in our word collections today. Choose three that you don't normally use. You will practice using them in your conversation and in your writing and then make notes in your vocabulary journals to tell how you used the words. Let me show you what I mean." Mr. Cha demonstrates making a "T" chart on the first page of his vocabulary journal and writes the word _elfin_ on the left side of the page. On the right side next to the word he writes, "I said to Jesse, 'I saw a girl today so small that I would call her elfin; she was small like an elf.'"

"Each day we will be sharing the ways that we have found to use our new words. You will get to choose new words to practice each day. Practice them here at school but also practice them at home. Your practicing new words will help your younger brothers and sisters to build their vocabularies too."

CONCLUSION

Miss McCloskey and Mr. Cha have found that building vocabulary involves many exposures to new words. They keep their word collections on display in their classrooms because they see the students using the words in spoken and written assignments. The charts in the room help the teachers remember to use the words in directions and explanations as well. They know that these strategies are effective because they hear the students using the words in verbal interactions in class and on the playground. They also see students finding new words for the word collections and adding the words to the charts.

EXAMPLES OF APPROXIMATION BEHAVIORS RELATED TO THE TESOL STANDARDS:

Pre-K–3 students will:

- explain ways to use new words.
- add words to category lists.

4–8 students will:

- document use of new vocabulary in a vocabulary journal.
- use words from word walls and charts to enhance writing.

9–12 students will:

- explore precise meanings of words and document their proper use in a personal vocabulary journal.
- revise written work to use a variety of descriptive and active words.

References

Allen, R. (2000). *Report of the national reading panel.* Alexandria, VA: ASCD.

Herrell, A., & Jordan, M. (2002). *Fifty active learning strategies for improving reading comprehension.* Upper Saddle River, NJ: Merrill/Prentice Hall.

Jordan, M., & Herrell, A. (Fall/Winter 2000). Collecting and processing words: Strategies for building vocabulary in young children. *Kindergarten Education: Theory, Research and Practice,* 145–151.

Jordan, M., & Herrell, A. (2002). Building comprehension bridges: A multiple strategies approach. *The California Reader, 35,* 14–19.

Williams, J. (2001). Classroom conversations: Opportunities to learn for ESL students in mainstream classrooms. *The Reading Teacher, 54*(8), 750–757.

WORD WALLS: Displaying and Organizing Words for Easy Access

31

This strategy addresses the following TESOL Standards:

Goal 1: To use English to communicate in social settings

Standard 3: Students will use learning strategies to extend their communicative competence.

Goal 2: To use English to achieve academically in all content areas

Standard 1: Students will use English to interact in the classroom.
Standard 2: Students will use English to obtain, process, construct, and provide subject matter information in spoken and written form.
Standard 3: Students will use appropriate learning strategies to construct and apply academic knowledge.

Goal 3: To use English in socially and culturally appropriate ways

Standard 3: Students will use appropriate learning strategies to extend their sociolinguistic and cultural competence.

Word walls (Tompkins, 1997) are alphabetical lists of words created in the classroom for the purpose of word study and vocabulary development. They can be as simple as a list of words written on a large sheet of butcher paper. In classrooms where students are learning English as a second language it is helpful to create bilingual (or multilingual) word walls with the words written in several languages and illustrated. These word walls then serve as a reference for students as they write or interact verbally. Some teachers prefer to create a number of different word walls in the classroom, one containing high-frequency words, which the students use for reference in writing, and others related to words being studied in connection to a literature or science focus unit. When the class moves on to another literature focus the words collected for the previous study can be placed on a word ring and kept for the students' reference. Placing a picture of the cover of the book to which the words are related helps the students to locate words by simply recalling the context in which the words were studied. See Figure 31.1 for suggestions on types of word walls and ways to display them.

High-frequency words	Alphabetical lists on large sheets of butcher paper.
	Laminated sheets of construction paper onto which individual word cards are attached.
	Large bulletin boards onto which individual words are added in alphabetical order.
	Clotheslines strung across the room onto which large cards with a single alphabet letter are attached. Word cards are then stapled to the alphabet letter to form the word list for each letter.
Literature word walls	Interesting, difficult, and unusual words from the story being studied are placed in a pocket chart and arranged alphabetically.
	The words may be arranged on a sheet of butcher paper in the shape of something related to the story like a covered wagon or hot-air balloon.
	The words may be collected in a container that relates to the story such as a witch's cauldron or miniature windmill.
Content-area word walls	Interesting words are written on cards and displayed on a pocket chart.
	Words are collected by entering them in the computer and printing out a large poster that is updated periodically. If the computer has a display screen attached, the list can be projected on a blank wall or projection screen.

Figure 31.1   Types of Word Walls and Suggestions for Displaying Them

STEP BY STEP

The steps in implementing a word wall are:

• ***Beginning word study***—Decide on the format you wish to use (see Figure 31.1) and begin by brainstorming a list of words with the students. To arrange the words in alphabetical order for easy access, write the words on individual cards and tape them on a wall or place them in a pocket chart. For a multilingual classroom add translations and illustrations to support the students' use of the words in writing and speaking. Involve the students in selecting words to be added to the word wall. With young children, you might want to begin your word wall by placing the students' names on the wall alphabetically and then adding words they encounter in the books they are hearing read aloud.

• ***Using the word wall***—Refer to the word wall whenever a word is discussed. Help the students to see the possibilities for the use of the word wall. If a student asks for the spelling of a word that is posted, draw the students' attention to it. If it is a word that is not on the word wall, add it (along with translations and an illustration when appropriate).

• ***Keeping the word wall interactive***—Use the words for activities such as word sorts, definition games, practicing syllabication, and phoneme segmentation. As word studies in literature, science, and social studies are completed, the words should be transferred to word cards and placed on a metal ring by punching a hole in the corner of each card. The ring can be stored on a nail or hook in the classroom placed at a level the students can easily reach.

APPLICATIONS AND EXAMPLES

The lizards are crawling all over the terrarium in Ms. Romero's first-grade classroom. The students are watching intently as the lizards crawl on the rocks and hop from plant to plant. As they observe, the students are writing their observations on sheets of paper attached to clipboards and trying to spell words like *lizard* and *amphibian*. Ms. Romero has started a science word wall by placing key words in a pocket chart near the terrarium. Because a number of her students speak Spanish at home, she has the Spanish words alphabetized on the same chart. The English words are written in green, the Spanish words in blue. All the words are illustrated, some with small magazine pictures the students have found and cut out, others by drawings made by the students.

Every day Ms. Romero and the students reread the words from the wall and use them for some type of activity so that the students will gradually come to recognize them all.

Ms. Romero has another word wall in her classroom. This wall is arranged on the doors of the closets and organized by using 9-by-12 sheets of laminated construction paper in a checkerboard pattern of primary colors. The first words added to this word wall are the students' names, then during the first few months of school the color and number words are added. Gradually more and more high-frequency words are added. Because the high-frequency word wall is filling quickly, Ms. Romero decides to keep her science and literature word wall separate and build them on word cards in the pocket chart. She's glad she made that decision because she now has 20 different word rings holding the words the class has studied in various subjects. Her students seem to know just where to go to locate a word when they need it for something they are writing.

Jonathan comes up to Ms. Romero with his observation log in hand. "I have a new word for the science word wall, Ms. Romero," he says. "The green lizard just *torpedoed* off the top of the plant into the pond. How do you write *torpedoed*?"

"I think you can spell that one, Jonathan," Ms. Romero says. "It just sounds hard. Let's sound it out." Ms. Romero picks up a card and she and Jonathan sound out the word as she writes it.

"It wasn't hard at all," Jonathan says, grinning. "I spelled it!"

"Now the hard part," Ms. Romero says. "Where does it go in alphabetical order?"

"That's not hard, Ms. Romero. It goes right after *terrarium*," Jonathan says.

"I see I can't fool you," Ms. Romero replies. "Can you draw a picture for your new word? And don't forget to ask Alberto if he knows the Spanish word for *torpedoed*."

"If he doesn't know it, his father will," Jonathan says as he trots off to talk to Alberto.

Later that day, Ms. Romero uses the words on the science word wall for a word-sorting activity. The students choose a group of words from the wall and tell how the words are related. Jonathan chooses *jumped, hopped, climbed,* and *torpedoed* and explains that he has chosen these four words because they are all things he has seen the lizards do.

Alberto chooses the words *verde, amarillo, anaranjado,* and *pardo* because they are all words that tell about the colors of the lizards.

Teresa chooses *tiny, bumpy, spotted,* and *striped* because they all tell about the way the lizards look.

Once everyone has a chance to select words and tell how they go together, Ms. Romero and the students recite the alphabet and the words are replaced on the pocket chart in alphabetical order. See Figure 31.2 to see how Ms. Romero's word walls are displayed.

Valentina is standing in front of the word wall in her seventh-grade classroom with a puzzled look on her face.

"What is the problem?" Mr. Stalvo asks.

"I can't find exactly the word I need for the story I am writing. I thought maybe I could locate one on the word wall," Valentina says.

"That's a good strategy, Valentina," Mr. Stalvo says with a smile. "What other possibilities do you have?"

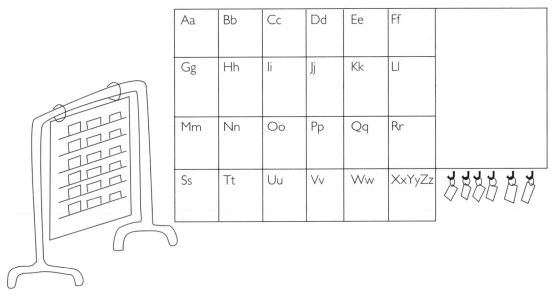

Aa	Bb	Cc	Dd	Ee	Ff	
Gg	Hh	Ii	Jj	Kk	Ll	
Mm	Nn	Oo	Pp	Qq	Rr	
Ss	Tt	Uu	Vv	Ww	XxYyZz	

Figure 31.2 Ms. Romero's Word Walls

"I could use the thesaurus," Valentina says, grinning, "but I can usually find a word on the word wall."

"You're right, Valentina. Our new literature focus book has a lot of interesting words in it."

Mr. Stalvo's seventh graders are reading . . . *and now Miguel* by Joseph Krumgold (1953). They are combining the literature study with a study of geography and finding a number of fascinating words. The word wall in front of which Valentina is standing is almost full. Soon they will have to take it down. See Figure 31.3 for the list of words on the word wall.

Since Valentina seemed reluctant to consult the class thesaurus, Mr. Stalvo decides to use the word wall to help the students create their own personal thesaurus. Later that day he gives directions for the students to bring a new three-ring folder to class the next day. "You don't need a huge one," he says. "A half-inch notebook and 50 pages of notebook paper will be enough."

The next day Mr. Stalvo and the students begin their classroom thesaurus project by labeling their notebooks and brainstorming all the ways they can say *walk* when they are writing. The students come up with *saunter, creep, tiptoe, parade, shuffle, prowl,* and *stomp.* After they brainstorm the list they go back and write a short descriptive phrase explaining the words. When they are finished they have a list that looks like this:

saunter—to walk at a slow, casual pace

creep—to walk at a snail's pace

tiptoe—to walk on the tips of your toes

parade—to walk proudly with head held high as if marching in a parade

shuffle—to walk slowly dragging your feet

prowl—to walk slowly and carefully as if trying not to be heard

stomp—to walk as if angry, banging your feet on the ground and making a loud noise

Once the class completes this exercise, Mr. Stalvo gives them their next assignment. "Over the next few weeks we are going to write our own thesaurus, beginning with the words we have collected from our literature focus book. Once we get some basic words entered we will be updating our vocabulary books regularly all year. I can't wait to see how many new words you can learn this year. I expect you to be using these books for many years to come. They should be very helpful in making your writing more exciting, too."

The first things the class does is match up the words on their literature word wall, putting words together that mean the same, or approximately the same, thing. Mr. Stalvo arranges the class into

A	B	C	E	F	G
absolutely adobe alfalfa apron arrange arroyo	balance bare beneath bundle burlap borracho burro	cactus canvas canyon champion corral coyote crawl cyclone	elbow engineer ewe	fetch flock fractions	grain graze government
H heave huddled	**I** imagine	**L** lamb liniment lonesome	**M** mesa mesquite mistake mutton	**N** necessary	**O** orphans
P partidero particular pasture peeping perfect permission permit pickaxes promised pueblo	**R** reason remarkable remembered remind	**S** scratch shearers shepherd shivering shovels skidding sopapillas squeaks stamped stovewood straggling stretched	**T** traitor trout	**U** underneath	**V** vamanos veranda
W windshield whisper wrestling					

Figure 31.3 Wordwall for . . . and now Miguel

cooperative groups, making sure that each group has at least one fluent Spanish speaker in it. They then divide up the words from the word wall and begin to create their new vocabulary notebooks— or thesaurus. The Spanish speakers are assigned the task of explaining the nuances in meaning for the Spanish words and making sure that the translations for the English words are accurate.

"Mr. Stalvo, I'm sure glad my dad insisted we speak Spanish at home!" Tomas exclaims. "I couldn't do this assignment if I hadn't kept up in Spanish."

"Your father is a wise man," Mr. Stalvo says with a smile.

CONCLUSION

Word walls can be very supportive to students in their study of words and the expanding of their vocabularies. However, it is important that the students be made aware of the ways in which the word walls can be used. Students will use the word walls when the teacher models the ways in which they can be used as resources.

Teachers encourage the use of the word walls by referring to them frequently, calling attention to the words, playing guessing games by giving clues related to the words on the wall, adding new and interesting words regularly, and relating content-area words to special word walls reserved for this use. The students should play an active role in the building of the word walls, suggesting words to be added, writing words themselves, even creating their own "special word walls" with small cards taped to the sides of their desks.

EXAMPLES OF APPROXIMATION BEHAVIORS RELATED TO THE TESOL STANDARDS:

Pre-K–3 students will:

- use word walls to find words in specific categories.
- use word walls to obtain correct spellings for words they want to write.

4–8 students will:

- categorize words from a word wall by parts of speech.
- select synonyms from a word wall.

9–12 students will:

- add synonyms to a word wall.
- select words from a word wall to enhance written products.

References

Krumgold, J. (1953). . . . *and now Miguel.* New York: Harper Collins.

Tompkins, G. E. (1997). *Literacy for the 21st century: A balanced approach.* Upper Saddle River, NJ: Merrill/Prentice Hall.

STORY REENACTMENT:
Making Stories Come to Life!

32

This strategy addresses the following TESOL Standards:

Goal 1: To use English to communicate in social settings

Standard 1: Students will use English to participate in social interactions.

Standard 2: Students will interact in, through, and with spoken and written English for personal expression and enjoyment.

Standard 3: Students will use learning strategies to extend their communicative competence.

Goal 2: To use English to achieve academically in all content areas

Standard 1: Students will use English to interact in the classroom.

Standard 2: Students will use English to obtain, process, construct, and provide subject matter information in spoken and written form.

Standard 3: Students will use appropriate learning strategies to construct and apply academic knowledge.

Goal 3: To use English in socially and culturally appropriate ways

Standard 1: Students will use the appropriate language variety, register, and genre according to audience, purpose, and setting.

Standard 2: Students will use nonverbal communication appropriate to audience, purpose, and setting.

Story reenactment is a strategy that encourages students to act out stories after they have read them or have heard them read. This strategy involves creating props for the students to use in reenacting stories so that they can use the book language they have heard or read, and better comprehend the text by acting it out in sequence.

Props for story reenactment may consist of costumes for the students to wear or prop boxes containing props made of clay, flannel, or laminated photos. Part of the effectiveness of this strategy is the planning and active involvement of the students in discussing the stories and creating the needed props.

STEP BY STEP

The steps in story reenactment are:

- **Reading the story**—Read a story to the students or have them read the story independently.

- **Retelling the story**—Have the students retell the story in sequence and list the props they will need to accurately reenact the story.

- **Gathering or making the props**—Provide materials for the students to use in creating the props for the prop box. The materials might be clay, dough for baked dough-art, felt, or drawing materials. Encourage the students to sign up for the props they will make. See Figure 32.1 for instructions for making dough-art props.

- **Storing the props**—After the props are made, painted, and sealed, decorate a shoebox in which to store the props. The box can be labeled with a photograph of the cover of the book so the students can easily identify the story props.

- **Using the props for retelling**—Encourage the students to use the prop boxes to retell and reenact the stories, working in pairs or small groups.

- **Assessing the retellings**—Listen to the story retellings and encourage the students who are using the "book language" and vocabulary. This is a good opportunity to document language usage and take anecdotal records. Note the completeness of the students' retellings and their inclusion of main events, characters, and inference.

APPLICATIONS AND EXAMPLES

Ms. Brown's kindergarten students are making dough-art props for the Gingerbread Man story. They are rolling out the dough and using cookie cutters to make the props. After the props are baked and cooled, the students paint them using a mixture of tempera paint and white glue. Once the props are dry they enjoy retelling the story, loudly proclaiming, "Run and run as fast as you can. You can't catch me. I'm the Gingerbread Man!"

Once the props for the Gingerbread Man are made, the students ask Ms. Brown, "Can we make props for The Little Red Hen now?" Ms. Brown decides to have an ongoing center where the students can make story retelling props. They are enjoying the props and she sees a lot of language practice going on as they use the props to retell the stories they have read.

---

4 cups flour (NOT self-rising)   1 cup salt
1½ cups water
Mix ingredients together. Mixture will be stiff.
Knead for 10 minutes.

Make shapes desired, separate by thickness (poke holes in thick pieces).
Bake at 325–350 degrees (½ hour per ¼-inch thickness)
Cool.

Paint to resemble figures in the storybook.
Use acrylic paints or tempera mixed with Elmer's glue (half and half).

Other suggestions for prop boxes: Paper doll figures, flannel board figures, magnetic tape on the back of pictures, overhead transparency pictures, actual dress-up clothes, and larger props.

Figure 32.1 Baked Dough Recipe

Story reenactment is a strategy that seems to be made for English language learners. It provides a script for them to follow as they retell favorite storybooks. The props or costumes give them support in remembering the sequence of events. They gain confidence in their oral English abilities with each new retelling.

Mr. Zarras's sixth-grade English language learners are making props for the story *Where the Wild Things Are* (Sendak, 1963). The students read and reread the story many times so that they can tell it by heart. After the props are complete, the students will retell the story, with props, to their first-grade book buddies. The day finally comes when all the props are complete.

The sixth graders enter the first-grade classroom with broad smiles on their faces. The first graders sit enthralled as they listen to their sixth-grade friends reenact one of their favorite stories with the small clay props they have created. As soon as the sixth graders finish their production, Janey, one of the quietest of the first graders, shyly raises her hand. "Can I do it?" she asks. Soon all the first graders are clamoring for a turn to retell the story using the props. The lesson is a great success.

The first graders are in awe when the sixth graders announce that they will leave the prop box in the first-grade class for the first graders to use. The book and the prop box are presented solemnly to the first-grade class as a gift from their book buddies. The sixth graders are very proud of their ability to present the story so well and of their handmade gifts. Mr. Zarras is even prouder of his wonderful idea. It has boosted the self-confidence of his English language learners immensely.

CONCLUSION

Story reenactment can be used at any grade level. High school students enjoy the reenactment of literature they have read by using minimal costumes and props and by acting out the parts. Students can create overhead transparency props or computer graphics that they can use to reenact stories in the form of a slide show as an alternative to actual role playing.

Story reenactment provides a unique opportunity for the teacher to observe and evaluate the students' comprehension of the stories reenacted and the students' use of unique vocabulary and sentence structures. No matter which mode of prop is used in story reenactment, the students benefit by increased interaction with story plot, language, and structure.

EXAMPLES OF APPROXIMATION BEHAVIORS RELATED TO THE TESOL STANDARDS:

Pre-K–3 students will:

- use props and book language to retell a story.
- generate a list and make props to support story reenactment.

4–8 students will:

- write new versions of familiar stories.
- sequence and reenact complex story plots.

9–12 students will:

- create dramatic reenactments of historic scenes.
- create scenes demonstrating a variety of points of view centering on an issue.

Reference

Sendak, M. (1963). *Where the wild things are.* New York: Harper Collins Juvenile Books.

SCRIPTING:
Practicing Verbal Interactions

This strategy addresses the following TESOL Standards:

Goal 1: To use English to communicate in social settings

Standard 1: Students will use English to participate in social interactions.
Standard 2: Students will interact in, through, and with spoken and written English for personal expression and enjoyment.
Standard 3: Students will use learning strategies to extend their communicative competence.

Goal 2: To use English to achieve academically in all content areas

Standard 1: Students will use English to interact in the classroom.
Standard 2: Students will use English to obtain, process, construct, and provide subject matter information in spoken and written form.
Standard 3: Students will use appropriate learning strategies to construct and apply academic knowledge.

Goal 3: To use English in socially and culturally appropriate ways

Standard 1: Students will use the appropriate language variety, register, and genre according to audience, purpose, and setting.
Standard 2: Students will use nonverbal communication appropriate to audience, purpose, and setting.
Standard 3: Students will use appropriate learning strategies to extend their sociolinguistic and cultural competence.

Scripting (Lozanov, 1982) is a strategy that prepares English language learners with sample language interactions or situational dialogues appropriate for upcoming events. These sample language interactions, called *scripts,* are presented and practiced prior to the students encountering the situation when the scripts will be needed. Preparing and practicing scripts in advance of events is supportive of the learner because it lowers anxiety and builds confidence in the ability to communicate in English.

To use scripting, the teacher must be able to identify or create opportunities for verbal interaction and engage the students in verbal and role play so that the students understand the situation in which the script is appropriate and practice delivery of the basic script as well as several possible alternate responses to ensure communication. Preparing the students for alternate responses sometimes involves the preparation of a ready-made template, which students can use in their own particular situation. The students do this by filling in the slots in the template with specific information to communicate. Suggestions for possible scenarios for scripting experiences are shown in Figure 33.1.

STEP BY STEP

The steps in using scripting with students are:

- *Identifying an opportunity for verbal interaction*—Identify a situation where a script will be helpful to English language learners or other students. Carefully plan the normal verbal interactions that would occur in the situation and write the words in the form of a short dialogue. Duplicate the script for the students.

- *Explaining and modeling the script*—Explain the situation to the students and enlist one student to walk through the script with you. Read the script with the student, acting out the physical

Situation	Scripting Needs
Greeting classroom visitors	One person should be designated (students take turns); what to show, how to explain, how to introduce teacher, students, visitor; when to interrupt teacher, where to take the visitor at the end of the visit
Celebration visits to principal	What to say to the school secretary; how to introduce yourself and talk about why you're there
Field trips	What to expect, any special protocol, when talk is appropriate, when quiet is expected; special terminology needed
Parent nights at school	What is expected of each student; individual assignments as far as explaining the curriculum, classroom routines, providing commentary
Any situation where certain behavior or language is expected	The actions, language that is expected

Figure 33.1   Suggestions for Scripting Activities

A student prepared is a student empowered, relaxed, and ready to learn.

You ask, "How are you today?"

1. If the response is, "Fine, thank you."
   You say, "I'm happy to hear that."
2. If the response is, "Not too good."
   You say, "I'm sorry to hear that. Are you sick?"
3. If the response is, "OK."
   You say, "Oh, is something wrong?"
4. If the response is, "Wonderful, I'm having a great day!"
   You say, "That's great! What has happened to make it a wonderful day?"

Figure 33.2 A Dialogue with Alternate Responses

actions that will normally be a part of the situation such as opening the door, pulling out a chair, or motioning for the other person to walk ahead of you. Be sure to emphasize that people's responses may not be exactly the same as the words in the script and the importance of listening to their responses. Provide some practice in listening to people's responses and choosing alternative words as appropriate. This step involves the analysis of possible responses by the teacher and providing practice for the students in which the teacher emphasizes the importance of listening to the speakers' response and choosing among the possible dialogues according to the direction the interaction takes. See Figure 33.2 for an example of dialogue with alternate responses.

• *Practicing in pairs*—Pair the students and encourage them to practice the use of the scripts as they play the roles. Begin the practice with English language learners paired with more fluent speakers of English. The first few times English language learners encounter the situation and use the script they may be more comfortable with a more fluent English speaker's presence for support as long as the more fluent speakers understand their roles as backup supporters in case the script is forgotten or the communications don't follow the normal course of events.

• *Assessing student progress and understanding*—Watch and listen as students practice in pairs, noting each student's use of the script as well as their ability to adapt responses. Make a videotape of the paired practice and watch the video with the students involved, helping them to identify their strengths and ways they can improve. Place the videotape in individual students' portfolios along with your anecdotal analysis of their progress. Placing periodic samples on the videotape allows the students—and their parents—to see the progress being made in verbal interaction skills in English.

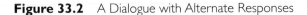

APPLICATIONS AND EXAMPLES

Ms. Casias' first graders are preparing for their Mother's Day tea. They have drawn portraits of their mothers and written short descriptions of them. Ms. Casias plans to have the students read their descriptions and then ask the mothers if they can find their portraits on the portrait wall.

The students have made cookies and tea, carefully measuring ingredients and following recipes. The day before the tea Ms. Casias gives the students a copy of a script they will use when a mother is escorted from the office into the classroom and another short script that gives the students practice in introducing their mothers at the tea. The first script says,

"Hello, my name is _____. I will take you to Ms. Casias' room. Please come with me." (Open the office door for the mother and motion for her to go first through the door.)

"I will show you the way to the room. We are very happy that you are here." (Walk to the classroom slowly so that the mother can walk with you.)

After the mothers arrive and everyone is served tea and cookies, the students will use the second script. (Student stands and motions to his/her mother as she is introduced)

"My name is _____ and this is my mother, _____. I would like to read something I have written about my mother." Students read the descriptions they have written about their mothers and then say to their mothers,

"Can you find your portrait on the wall?"

(The mothers identify their portraits and the descriptions are placed under the portraits after the mothers identify them.)

As the mothers leave be sure to say, "Thank you for coming to our tea."

Ms. Casias arranges a section of the room to look like the furniture arrangement in the office and the students practice the first script. The fluent English speakers play the parts of the mothers and the English language learners practice greeting a mother and bringing her to the classroom. Once the mothers have all arrived in the practice session the chairs are placed in the same way they will be arranged for the tea and the students practice introducing their mothers. Because some of the mothers do not speak English, some of the students practice introducing their mothers in English and their home language. Several of the students are able to read their descriptions in English and then translate them into the home language. For the students who need help with the translation, the school primary language tutors will be available to help at the tea.

The day of the tea, Ms. Casias takes time to practice the scripts before tea time and the students are all smiles as they serve as official greeters and later make introductions. The day after the tea the class talks about the tea and Ms. Casias decides that she will continue to ask students to go to the office to greet and escort visitors to the classroom. They seem to enjoy this experience.

Mr. LeBeau is taking his 10th-grade government class to the state capital on the train. After they arrive in the capital they will observe a legislative session and visit the local legislators in their offices. The students have prepared questions that they will ask the legislators during the scheduled interviews. Mr. LeBeau has prepared a script for the students so they will follow the proper protocol while entering the offices and participating in the interviews. Each group has a leader who will keep the group together and make sure that everyone has an opportunity to ask questions.

Mr. LeBeau stages a practice session the day before the trip so that everyone has a clear idea of the sequence of events. They walk through the procedures of boarding the train and learn who their group leaders are. Mr. LeBeau even practices the short walk from the train station to the capitol building, discusses expected behavior, and gives the students time schedules so they understand exactly what will be expected of them.

The students are given scripts illustrating the language that should be used when entering the offices of the legislators, and they are given instructions about their behavior in the offices and the government buildings. They practice entering the offices in small groups with a designated leader and a back-up leader in case one is needed. One of the students plays the part of the receptionist in the office and the groups practice the proper behavior and sequence of events that is likely to occur during the interviews. The students are given some possibilities of different scenarios just in case the script is not followed exactly. The groups all practice asking and answering questions.

The students seem confident that they are prepared for the field trip. They all arrive nicely dressed and carrying notebooks for their interviews. On the way home at the end of the day Mr. LeBeau asks them how things went.

"It was almost like you sent them the scripts, Mr. LeBeau," Marisea says. "I knew exactly what to expect."

"You forgot one thing, though," Helia adds. "I didn't know what to say when they asked us if we wanted coffee."

"Well, did you want coffee?" Mr. LeBeau asks, smiling.

"I said, 'No thank you,'" Helia answers. "I didn't know how I would hold it, drink it, and take notes."

"Well, 'No thank you' was the right thing to say then," Mr. LeBeau assures her. "Sometimes you have to go without a script. But you knew what to do."

CONCLUSION

Scripting provides English language learners with language they will need in a variety of situations. This strategy reduces anxiety when students are placed into unfamiliar situations or are asked to use new language structures. Once students are confident that they can fall back on the scripts, they will find that they are more relaxed and can begin to communicate more freely. The scripts remain in their memories as back-up words, just in case.

EXAMPLES OF APPROXIMATION BEHAVIORS RELATED TO THE TESOL STANDARDS:

Pre-K–3 students will:

- create a script for a common social interaction.
- use scripts to practice verbal interactions in a classroom activity.

4–8 students will:

- create and use scripts to interview experts in a specific academic discipline.
- create and use scripts to gain knowledge of family histories through interviews.

9–12 students will:

- create and compare scripts for formal and informal interactions in a variety of contexts.
- analyze scripts for their social and cultural appropriateness.

Reference

Lozanov, G. (1982). Suggestology and suggestopedia. In R. Blair (Ed.), *Innovative approaches to language teaching*. Rowley, MA: Newbury House.

TALK SHOW:
Practicing Verbal Communication to Build Confidence, Vocabulary, and Comprehension

34

This strategy addresses the following TESOL Standards:

Goal 1: To use English to communicate in social settings

Standard 1: Students will use English to participate in social interactions.
Standard 2: Students will interact in, through, and with spoken and written English for personal expression and enjoyment.
Standard 3: Students will use learning strategies to extend their communicative competence.

Goal 2: To use English to achieve academically in all content areas

Standard 1: Students will use English to interact in the classroom.
Standard 2: Students will use English to obtain, process, construct, and provide subject matter information in spoken and written form.
Standard 3: Students will use appropriate learning strategies to construct and apply academic knowledge.

Goal 3: To use English in socially and culturally appropriate ways

Standard 1: Students will use the appropriate language variety, register, and genre according to audience, purpose, and setting.
Standard 2: Students will use nonverbal communication appropriate to audience, purpose, and setting.
Standard 3: Students will use appropriate learning strategies to extend their sociolinguistic and cultural competence.

Talk show is a strategy that encourages the production of verbal English based on information and verbalizations studied ahead of time. The time to work in small groups and plan the presentation helps English language learners gain confidence and competence in the production of spoken English. This strategy involves three students working together to create an interview in which one plays the talk show host(ess), one plays the person to be interviewed, and the third provides a silent "acting out" or interpretation for the non-English speaker. The use of the third person in the group to provide nonverbal communication of the information being discussed often adds a very entertaining twist to the interview. The students begin to develop signals similar to those used in the party game charades.

Talk show can be used to give students motivation to research a group of explorers, literary characters, or even average people who have contributed something unique to society. It is an appropriate technique for reviewing characters at the conclusion of the reading of a piece of literature and is an interesting way to get students involved in research on the Internet. It is a versatile strategy that can be adapted for many purposes. Once the students have been involved they quickly learn to work together to create an interesting and informative interview situation.

STEP BY STEP

The steps in using talk show in the classroom are:

• **Choosing an appropriate topic**—The teacher identifies an appropriate topic for talk show implementation. The topic must be one where the students can gain information about the person to be interviewed from reading and/or researching. See Figure 34.1 for suggestions of appropriate topics for talk show.

• **Explaining and modeling the talk show strategy**—The teacher explains talk show by referring to a television talk show with which the students may be familiar, *Oprah,* for example. The teacher models the role of talk show host by having one student come up to be interviewed about a recent classroom event. Before interviewing the student, the teacher asks the rest of the class to brainstorm questions for the person to be interviewed. The teacher writes this brainstorming on a chart or chalkboard so all students can see ways to formulate questions for the interview. The teacher then models an interview with the student. After a model interview is given, the teacher calls another student up to be the "interpreter." The interpreter is given the job of acting out the questions and answers as they are given. The teacher models some signals for "question" and some other ways of interpreting visually. See Figure 34.2 for examples of visual interpretation signals.

• **Giving the groups guided practice**—The teacher divides the class into groups of three and gives them a topic to practice. Each group selects their interviewer, interviewee, and interpreter and brainstorms a list of questions. The interviewer must practice asking questions that cannot be answered with one word responses. See Figure 34.3 for examples of ways to rephrase questions for more complete responses. The teacher circulates around the room while the students practice their interviews, encouraging groups to think of interesting questions and responses.

Grade	Subject	Talk Show Use
K–12	Reading	Interview characters in books read
K–12	Social Studies	Interview historical characters
K–3	Social Studies	Interview community helpers
4–12	Current Events	Interview people in the news
9–12	Literature	Interview characters in plays read

Figure 34.1 Appropriate Topics for Use With the Talk Show Strategy

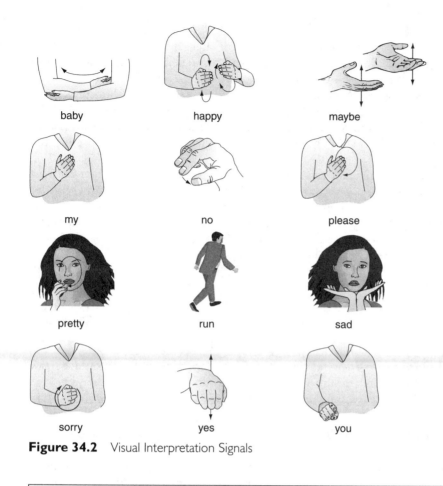

baby   happy   maybe

my   no   please

pretty   run   sad

sorry   yes   you

Figure 34.2 Visual Interpretation Signals

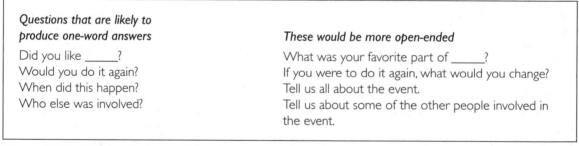

Questions that are likely to produce one-word answers	*These would be more open-ended*
Did you like _____?	What was your favorite part of _____?
Would you do it again?	If you were to do it again, what would you change?
When did this happen?	Tell us all about the event.
Who else was involved?	Tell us about some of the other people involved in the event.

Figure 34.3 Ways to Rephrase Questions

- ***Presenting to the class***—After the groups have had an opportunity to practice their interviews, they come up in front of the class and perform for the group. With groups with very limited English, this step may be skipped until the students have had more time and experience with English or may be limited to groups who volunteer. After each group performs, the teacher identifies especially good questions, responses, and interpreting signals.

- ***Adding technology***—Instead of having the interpreter use visual signals and signs, the group can find visuals on the Internet and use a program such as PowerPoint to create a series of visuals to support the class's understanding of the interview. If one of the students is adept at drawing, the group can use the overhead projector so the interpreter can illustrate the interview as it progresses. Digital or standard photographs might also be taken and printed out to add to the chart of visual interpretation signals (Figure 34.2). As new interpretations are discovered, they may be added to the chart. The groups might also videotape the interviews and show the tape instead of performing the interview live.

APPLICATIONS AND EXAMPLES

Mr. Workman's fifth graders have been studying a piece of literature titled *Holes* (Sachar, 1998). They have read and discussed the novel, comparing and contrasting the characters and their roles in the story. Mr. Workman introduces the talk show strategy by asking the students if they've ever watched a talk show on television. The students mention several talk shows they have watched but Mr. Workman focuses on Oprah and the way she interviews people who come on her show. He selects one character from *Holes,* X-Ray, as an example and says, "I know this character played a unique role in this story. What kind of questions would Oprah ask him?"

The students generate a list of questions such as, "Why couldn't you find anything in the holes?" and "Why did you think the third hole was the hardest to dig?"

After the students and Mr. Workman generate a number of questions, Mr. Workman brings one student up to play the part of X-Ray. Mr. Workman asks some of the questions generated by the students and then stops. "Jerry is doing a wonderful job of answering questions. This shows me that he really understands what happened in the story. Now I need to add one more person to this interview. I want someone to come up and stand behind us as we talk and use hand signals and gestures to "act out" what we are saying."

As Mr. Workman and Jerry continue the interview, exploring the events in *Holes,* Joanne acts out their interactions, often bringing the class to giggles. After they have finished the interview, Mr. Workman goes over some more visual signals and gestures that could be used by the interpreter and compliments Joanne on her innovative acting. He also talks about the ways in which Jerry answered the interview questions completely, showing how well he had read the materials that were assigned as well as using the Internet for additional details about the gold rush.

Mr. Workman then encourages students to choose another of the characters in the story for their interviews, places them into groups of three, and gives them time to practice their interviews.

"Remember, the class should learn more about the character you are interviewing as well as facts about the part of the world where the story takes place after they watch and listen to the interviews," Mr. Workman reminds the class. "We will all be taking notes during your presentations and keeping track of any new information you share. Be prepared to give us the sources for your information after the interviews are presented, as well."

Mr. Workman moves around the room as the students practice their interviews, listening and giving advice to each group of students. He is very pleased with the oral language practice and the support the students are giving one another in correcting English grammar and structure. He looks forward to their presentations to the class.

Mrs. Gutilla teaches American history in an inner-city high school where most of her students are English-language learners. In studying the Declaration of Independence and the U.S. Constitution, Mrs. Gutilla decides to use Jean Fritz' books *Will You Sign Here, John Hancock* (1976), and *Shh! We're Writing the Constitution* (1987), as well as some simple biographies of Thomas Jefferson, Benjamin Franklin, George Washington, Paul Revere, and Samuel Adams to help her students gain a better understanding of American history. She divides her students into small groups and has them read and discuss one of the assigned books taking notes of facts about the people involved in the writing of the Declaration of Independence and the Constitution.

After the groups have read and discussed their books, she has each group select one of the American heroes to research and helps them find Internet sources for more information about their selected hero. Mrs. Gutilla then gathers the class together to explain the talk show strategy that they will use to present their research to the class. She explains that each group of three people will present its hero in the form of an interview. One of the students will conduct the interview, one student will pretend to be the hero and the third will be the visual interpreter for the group.

Mrs. Gutilla helps the class to brainstorm a number of questions that they might ask the hero if they met him in person. She helps the group determine the type of information they would want to gather to better understand the hero's role in the process of writing the Declaration of Independence or the Constitution, or both documents. As these questions are formulated, Mrs. Gutilla writes them on a large chart which will remain on display during the guided practice time. She also reviews the role of the interpreter and some of the signals and gestures they can use to act out the interview. She displays an enlarged version of Figure 34.2 to help the interpreters remember some of the visual signals they can use.

Mrs. Gutilla gives the class time to practice their interview and enlarge their repertoire of questions to be asked. She moves around the class as the students are practicing to give them advice and support. She then meets with each group to help them create a visual to be used at the end of their presentation to share books and resources they used to gain their information. She schedules their presentations so that each group will know when they will perform and plans to videotape their presentations so they will have a chance to review their oral fluency and presentation skills and set goals for themselves in those areas.

CONCLUSION

Talk show is an interactive presentation strategy that provides focused practice in research and oral presentation skills. It provides a structure that allows participation at various levels. The interviewer must have a strong knowledge of how to ask oral questions to provide an opportunity for extended talk by the interviewee. The interviewee must know how to respond to specific questions. The interpreter must listen carefully and respond physically but need not have strong verbal skills. Because the implementation of this strategy depends heavily on teacher explanation and modeling and extended guided practice, English learners are supported in their participation and are more able to participate successfully. It is a strategy that is easily adapted to different curriculum areas and grade levels.

EXAMPLES OF APPROXIMATION BEHAVIORS RELATED TO THE TESOL STANDARDS:

Pre-K–3 students will:

- participate in an interview representing a viewpoint of a storybook character.
- use gestures and mime to represent a conversation between storybook characters.

4–8 students will:

- represent and maintain a point of view throughout an interview setting.
- engage in a conversation with a variety of historical figures, using a talk show format.

9–12 students will:

- formulate and ask questions to obtain information from a current political figure in a simulation activity.
- answer questions in a talk show simulation based on knowledge gained from reading and research.

References

Fritz, J. (1987). *Shh! We're writing the constitution*. New York: G. P. Putnam's Sons.
Fritz, J. (1979). *Will you sign here, John Hancock?*. New York: G. P. Putnam's Sons.
Sachar, L. (1998). *Holes*. New York: Farrar, Straus, and Giroux.

WRITING WORKSHOP: Supporting the Acquisition of English Writing Competence

35

This strategy addresses the following TESOL Standards:

Goal 1: To use English to communicate in social settings

Standard 2: Students will interact in, through, and with spoken and written English for personal expression and enjoyment.

Standard 3: Students will use learning strategies to extend their communicative competence.

Goal 2: To use English to achieve academically in all content areas

Standard 1: Students will use English to interact in the classroom.

Standard 2: Students will use English to obtain, process, construct, and provide subject matter information in spoken and written form.

Standard 3: Students will use appropriate learning strategies to construct and apply academic knowledge.

Goal 3: To use English in socially and culturally appropriate ways

Standard 1: Students will use the appropriate language variety, register, and genre according to audience, purpose, and setting.

Standard 2: Students will use nonverbal communication appropriate to audience, purpose, and setting.

Writing workshop (Graves, 1983) is an approach to teaching writing in which the students choose their own writing topics and move through prewriting, drafting, revising, editing, and publishing their work as though they were professional authors (Tompkins, 1994). Writing workshop is especially supportive to English language learners because students are encouraged to discuss their ideas, work with a partner or group in revising and editing, and interact verbally with others (Diaz-Rico & Weed, 2002). The classroom environment in which students work together to support each other as they work through the stages in the writing process provides the support necessary to lower anxiety and motivate students to write. The opportunity to write on self-chosen topics validates each student's experiences. The stages in process writing are shown in Figure 35.1 with suggestions for supporting English language learners.

STEP BY STEP

The steps in implementing writing workshop are:

- ***Introducing the writing process***—Introduce the writing process stage by stage, modeling each stage with your own writing. Talk about the need for prewriting to get ideas flowing and model a prewriting strategy such as webbing, listing, drawing, or brainstorming. Do your own prewriting using an overhead projector or chart so that the students can see the process and then give them an opportunity to prewrite. Follow this same pattern through each of the subsequent stages in writing, using your own developing piece as an example.

- ***Providing daily writing time***—Provide writing materials and time to write each day. As students complete first drafts, schedule writing groups to give them feedback and suggestions. Set the classroom up to encourage interaction among the students as they write, revise, edit, and publish. Provide resources such as dictionaries, thesaurus, and content-area reading for reports.

- ***Teaching minilessons***—As you see the need, teach minilessons on skills and additional strategies for each of the stages. These lessons can be whole-group, small-group, or individual. Encourage the students to work at their own pace, writing and publishing on topics that relate to other curricular areas or to their own experiences.

- ***Celebrating accomplishments***—As students complete the writing, find ways to celebrate their accomplishments and include their published works in the class library. Always give students an opportunity to share their published works and include their photos and an "About the Author" page in the published books.

- ***Adding technology***—The word processor is a natural addition to the writing workshop. Students can write their drafts by hand if only one computer is available and when they are ready to produce the final draft, they can type it on the word processor and print the final copy out—looking very professional. If more than one computer is available students can write their drafts on the word processor. Using the computer for writing workshop is motivational for a number of students and actually encourages students to write more. Making revisions is easier as well since the whole document does not need to be rewritten.

APPLICATIONS AND EXAMPLES

The fourth graders in Mr. Heil's classroom are using their writing workshop time to write plays for the dragon puppets they have created in art. Since the students are reading fantasy books in reading class, they have decided to write plays about dragons and damsels in distress. To prepare the students to write plays, Mr. Heil has brought in several scripts so the students can see the format they will use. The class brainstorms the elements of fantasy they remember from the stories they are reading and list several possibilities for plays. Mr. Heil organizes the students into groups so that each group has at least one strong writer and the English language learners have a language buddy who can translate for them if needed.

The groups start to work by looking at the puppets they have made and brainstorming a list of characters in their play. Each of the students is assigned an additional puppet to make and the script writing begins.

The students work in groups for several days, producing a rough draft, revising, and editing. Once their script is complete, they bring in the puppets they have made at home and begin to practice their puppet plays. Mr. Heil provides a puppet stage and the groups decide they must have backdrops to make the productions more realistic. At the end of the week, almost all of the groups are ready to perform.

Mr. Heil's class is using writing workshop to create a collaborative project. They are providing support for the English language learners by working as a group to support the creation of a play. Once

Writing Process Stage and Definition	Adaptations for English Language Learners
Prewriting. Strategies for getting and organizing ideas	Allow first language usage if needed. Model more than one strategy using visuals and actual writing ideas being developed. Include realia. Encourage first language partner or small-group work.
Drafting. Getting some ideas down on paper.	Model putting a draft down on paper using an overhead or chart. Think aloud as you write. Write on every other line to allow for revisions. Model crossing out ideas, writing between lines, making changes as ideas begin to flow. Encourage collaboration and discussion of ideas among students. Allow writing in first language.
Revising. Focusing on the content of the piece, asking questions if parts are not clear, giving suggestions to the writer. This stage can be repeated as needed.	Model a writing group using your writing. Encourage the students to give you feedback and ask questions about the piece of writing you are doing. Work with a small group. Encourage translation to English if the piece is written in another language. Authors can use student translators for both the reading of the piece and feedback and suggestions given. Authors decide which revisions to make based upon the group suggestions.
Editing. Correcting mechanics.	Model the editing process using your own writing. Teach proofreading symbols so that students can work together to correct all spelling, punctuation, capitalization, and other mechanical errors. Encourage partner work. Provide resources such as dictionaries, thesaurus, and English grammar textbooks. After student editing, teacher can serve as final editor.
Publishing. Putting the writing into a final form such as mounting for the bulletin board, binding into a book, creating a shape book, pop-up book, or other novelty form.	Model the publishing of your writing. Introduce the publishing possibilities by modeling each of them. Encourage the students to choose their publishing mode and work with a partner. Take photos of the authors for an "About the Author" page in the book.
Celebration. Sharing the finished work with classmates or others.	Student whose book is published sits in the Author's Chair and reads the newly published book or writing aloud. Principals, other teachers, and parents can be invited.

Figure 35.1   Writing Process Stages Adapted for English Learners

the script is complete all of the group members participate in the performance. Because the script provides a strong scaffold for the oral presentation, all the students are confident reading their parts.

Ms. Martin teaches a senior humanities class in a large high school. She finds the final grading period in the senior year to be difficult since the students are eager to graduate and move on. Ms. Martin decides to try a new project for her senior group. Using a writing workshop format, she suggests that the students look back at the past four years and create a scenario based upon a current event, stage play, or film that will encourage the other seniors to recall something memorable about their high school experience. They begin by brainstorming a list of possibilities and then a list of characters who might be included in the scenarios.

The final lists provide some hilarious suggestions and the students choose topics on which to write. Some of the students choose to write alone, others in pairs and small groups. Since the high school is named Hoover High, the students decide to produce a publication titled, "Hoover History Hash." Their stories change the history of the last four years in slightly wacky ways. One story has the principal as the hero of a local happening in which one of the students drove his car into the river. Mr. Posten, the principal, is hailed as the hero of the story and the events are changed just enough to make the story laughable.

Once the stories are written, Mr. Posten is so impressed with their originality that he chooses five to read over the intercom during the last week of school. The stories are so popular that the student publication is sold out.

CONCLUSION

Writing workshop is a strategy that has many possibilities. Because writing workshop is intended to simulate the procedures that real authors follow as they prewrite, write, revise, edit, and publish, students have multiple opportunities for context-based verbal interactions as they research, confer, and give and receive feedback on their own and their colleagues' writing. Because the students choose their own topics for writing, students' ideas and experiences are validated. Writing in students' home languages is valued and collaboration to create bilingual (or multilingual) books can contribute to the growing library of such books in the classroom. See Chapter 17, Bilingual Books and Labels, for more information on this topic.

For writing workshop to be effective, students must be given writing time daily. A structure must be set up in the classroom to support all the stages in the writing process and the students must be given instruction in ways to support one another in reading drafts, giving feedback, and editing collaboratively. When the workshop is encouraged and student interaction supported, nothing provides a more collaborative classroom environment than writing workshop.

EXAMPLES OF APPROXIMATION BEHAVIORS RELATED TO THE TESOL STANDARDS:

Pre-K–3 students will:

- use drawings to plan for writing activities.
- use resources in the classroom to support writing.

4–8 students will:

- discuss writing with peers and revise based on the discussion.
- edit writing for correct use of spelling and grammar.

9–12 students will:

- revise writing to enhance and clarify style and fluency.
- create written products based on research.

References

Diaz-Rico, L., & Weed, K. (2002). *The crosscultural, language, and academic handbook.* Boston: Allyn & Bacon.

Graves, D. (1983). *Writing: Teachers and children at work.* Portsmouth, NH: Heinemann.

Tompkins, G. E. (1994). *Teaching writing: Balancing process and product* (2nd ed.). Upper Saddle River, NJ: Merrill/Prentice Hall.

V

STRATEGIES FOR BUILDING COMPREHENSION

The 15 strategies contained in this section provide teachers with support in actively involving students in making sense of text. Making meaning from text is a complex act that requires a number of elements including vocabulary knowledge, automaticity—the automatic recognition of printed words—background knowledge, and the use of a combination of cueing systems. Judith Irwin's research (1991) has helped us understand the processes that good readers use to make sense of the printed word. The strategies in this section combine the knowledge we have gained about language acquisition with the theory and research about reading comprehension to provide structures that support the English learner in comprehending English text.

Beginning with simple lessons such as language experience, where students see their experiences and words used to create a written text, this series of comprehension strategies helps English learners understand that creating meaning requires active engagement. As English learners build knowledge and vocabulary in English, learning strategies to solve problems and relate reading text to past experiences helps create a repertoire of approaches that readers can use when they encounter unfamiliar words and concepts.

English learners have a great need to understand the English writing system and the ways in which ideas are expressed in English. It is important that they be familiar with problem-solving approaches, build confidence in their abilities to make sense of written text, and pronounce and read orally in the classroom without embarrassment.

Our ultimate goal in supporting English learners is that they become fluent in English reading and writing so that they have access to all the doors that open to truly well-educated people in an English-speaking nation. To accomplish this goal, teachers must provide daily, highly engaging instruction that builds these skills in an ever-increasing variety of texts and genres.

READ-ALOUD PLUS:
Using This to Support Understanding While Teaching Comprehension Strategies

This strategy addresses the following TESOL Standards:

Goal 2: To use English to achieve academically in all content areas

Standard 1: Students will use English to interact in the classroom.

Standard 2: Students will use English to obtain, process, construct, and provide subject matter information in spoken and written form.

Standard 3: Students will use appropriate learning strategies to construct and apply academic knowledge.

Read-aloud plus (Jordan & Herrell, 2001) is a strategy that can be used whenever the students must read "tough text." It is especially valuable for use with English language learners because it incorporates the modeling of fluent, expressive reading of English text with techniques for clarifying vocabulary, periodic checking for understanding, and the providing and activating of knowledge that helps students make connections between text and personal experience.

Read-aloud plus involves the teacher reading text aloud to students while adding visual support, periodic paraphrasing, and/or rewriting as the "plus" or extension to the read-aloud. The students are actively involved in the "plus" part of the lesson and so are more motivated to listen carefully as the teacher reads aloud. The read-aloud and extension activities allow the students to become familiar with strategies they can use independently whenever they must read difficult text, thereby providing them with reading comprehension instruction and practice in the process of interacting with required content-area or literature text. See Figure 36.1 for a variety of read-aloud plus extension activities.

STEP BY STEP

The steps in implementing the read-aloud plus strategy are:

• **Prereading and choosing support materials**—The teacher prereads the text to be explored and chooses appropriate support materials and extension activities. In preparing for the lesson, the teacher selects vocabulary and/or concepts that may be unfamiliar to the students. She identifies appropriate extensions such as visuals or rewriting activities that will be used and designs an approach

- Visuals—transparencies, photos, graphs, charts
- Realia—real objects related to the material being studied
- Paraphrasing—restating the material in simple language
- Rewriting—rewriting the material in simple language
- Rewriting and illustrating—adding illustrations to the rewritten material
- Comparing and contrasting—using graphics such as webs or Venn diagrams to compare and contrast material with previously read material
- Physicalization—acting out the material, sometimes adding simple props

Figure 36.1   Read-Aloud Plus Extension Activities

for presenting the materials to the students. Some of the support materials will be most effectively presented prior to the reading aloud of the text, others may need to be presented as the text is read, while still others will best be used after the reading. If visuals are needed, the teacher locates them and prepares them in the form of transparencies, charts, or posters. See Chapter 2 for visual resources. It is important that the teacher mark the text to be read so that she has a plan as to when she will stop reading and which visuals or other support will be presented at each stopping point.

   • *Explaining the process to the students*—The teacher explains the process to the students, telling them that she will be reading the text to them and that they will be expected to listen carefully so that they can participate fully in the extension activities. She gives an example or two of how they will participate.

   • *Reading and clarifying*—The teacher reads aloud, stopping at appropriate places for clarification or display of visuals that help to relate vocabulary and concepts to the students' background knowledge.

   • *Engaging the students actively*—The teacher engages students in active-learning extension activities periodically during the reading or immediately after the reading so that the students make connections between the new vocabulary and concepts presented.

   • *Reviewing key concepts*—The teacher reviews key concepts and vocabulary and leaves the visuals displayed in the classroom so students can refer back to them during any follow-up assignments. She may return to the visuals at a later time to further engage the students with the vocabulary or concepts as an additional review. See the chapter in this text on sorting activities for ideas for delayed review techniques.

   • *Assessing and monitoring growth*—Depending on the extension activities chosen for the lesson, students may create a paraphrased version of the reading materials, illustrations that demonstrate their understanding or other graphics or visuals. These products can be included in the student portfolios. The teacher can observe during the interactions and make anecdotal notes that demonstrate the students' understanding or need for additional instruction. After read-aloud plus has been taught and used a number of times, students can be asked to paraphrase a piece of text as a performance sample and the record of that sample can be included in the portfolio.

   • *Adding technology*—Students can use the Internet to search for illustrations to add context to the read-aloud materials. They can use the word processor for writing paraphrased versions of the text read-aloud. They can create PowerPoint presentations demonstrating their understanding of the text. All of these products can be included in the students' portfolios.

APPLICATIONS AND EXAMPLES

Mrs. Behrend's fifth graders have begun a unit on geometry. Mrs. Behrend has introduced the geometric concepts of circle, diameter, radius, square, and rectangle, but a number of her students are English learners and she wants to extend their understanding of the terms and build their math vocabularies. She finds a series of books that infuse math concepts into the story lines and decides to try a read-aloud plus activity during their read-aloud time. Mrs. Behrend prepares a 3-by-12-inch rectangle for each of her students and distributes the rectangles, scissors and tape to each student.

"We're going to listen to a story today," Mrs. Behrend says to the class. The title of the story is *Sir Cumference and the First Round Table: A Math Adventure* (Neuschwander & Geehan, 1997). As we read this story we will use our knowledge of geometry and follow the directions to build the tables along with the Sir Cumference's carpenter.

As Mrs. Behrend reads the story aloud, the students are directed to try to solve the problems Sir Cumference is having with his table. They use their rectangles to represent the original table used by Sir Cumference and his knights and they follow the directions given to the carpenter as they create a square, a parallelogram, an octagon, and eventually an oval to represent the table shapes being tried in the story.

When finally Sir Cumference finds a tree in the forest that has blown over and Lady Di (of Ameter) measures the felled tree by standing tall and reaching up to touch the very top of the circle, the students begin to giggle.

"I get it, Mrs. Behrend," Tua says, laughing. "Lady Di is measuring the diameter of the circle."

"You are so smart," Mrs. Behrend answers with a smile. "And do you know something else? Her son's name is Radius, and he's exactly as tall as half the diameter of the tree."

The students in Mrs. Behrend's class are excited about understanding the story of Sir Cumference because they know the math vocabulary. They are very excited that Mrs. Behrend has found some other math stories about Sir Cumference. Over the next few days Mrs. Behrend reads more math stories, always supporting the students' understanding of the vocabulary and concepts with read-aloud plus extensions such as realia, visuals, and active involvement materials.

Mr. Threlkeld's tenth graders are participating in a schoolwide exploration titled "Unlikely Heroes." The entire school is searching the library, newspapers, and the Internet for examples of teenagers who have made a difference. Roberto, one of Mr. Threlkeld's English learners, is having difficulty understanding the concept of an "unlikely hero."

"I know what a hero is," Roberto says. "I just don't know what an unlikely hero is."

"I am going to read a book to the class today, Roberto," Mr. Threlkeld replies. "I think this book will help you understand. We need to think about the word *unlikely* though. I could say that it is unlikely that you will grow up to be an opera singer. That means that you may become a baseball player. You're good at baseball. I just don't think you'll be a professional singer."

"Not an opera singer!" Roberto exclaims. "Maybe a rock star, though."

"Exactly," Mr. Threlkeld says with a grin. "It's likely that you'll be an athlete. It's not likely that you'll be an opera singer. *Unlikely* means it's probably not going to happen."

"OK, I get that. But what's an unlikely hero?"

"That simply means that people can be heroes when you wouldn't expect them to be. In the story I am going to read to the class, nine teenagers are heroes. They are just ordinary teenagers, but they do something very brave. They make it possible for other teenagers to do something after they do it for the first time. The book is called *Warriors Don't Cry* (Beals, 1995) and it's about the first black students to go to an all white high school in Little Rock Arkansas."

Mr. Threlkeld has prepared to read this story by finding newspaper photos on the Internet and downloading them onto transparencies. He shows his students the newspaper articles about the Little Rock Nine and the class discusses the political situation of 1957 and the courage it took for teenagers to break the racial barriers in Arkansas.

Mr. Threlkeld reads one chapter of the book aloud. When he has finished the first chapter he and the students talk about it. He asks one student to retell the events of the first chapter in his own words as he takes notes on the overhead. Marco says, "Melba tells about how she was born and how black people didn't get treated fairly in those days. She tells about having to pay high prices for day-old bread. She tells about her grandmother saying that she was born to do something great." When Marco stops, Mr. Threlkeld asks, "Does anyone have anything to add to Marco's retelling?"

Roberto says, "Melba didn't think she was doing anything special going to a white high school. She thought the soldiers would protect her. She didn't know she was going to have to be very brave."

"Very nice," Mr. Threlkeld says. He shows the pictures of the guardsmen barring the door to Central High as the black students approach. "Does this look as if the soldiers are protecting the black students?"

The students talk about why the guardsmen blocked the door. They look at the faces of the people in the angry mob and then Mr. Threlkeld has them act out the scene.

When they are finished with their reenactment, Mr. Threlkeld asks the students playing the Little Rock Nine how they felt.

"It's strange," Tisha says. "These are my friends and yet when they were yelling at me and pushing me, I was scared. It felt real. Those nine students were heroes."

Mr. Threlkeld keeps reading the book, chapter by chapter during the next week. His students listen intently; they act out some of the more compelling scenes; and they look up articles and photos in books and on the Internet. At the end of the book some of the students write their reactions in their reading journals. Roberto writes:

> I never think a teenager can be a hero unless they save someone's life. The black teenagers who went to white high school were heros. They were brave. They didn't have friends. It's hard to go to school and have everybody hate you.

Mr. Threlkeld is very pleased with the way his students have understood Melba's story. He notices his Mexican students talking to his Asian and black students more. He is hoping for more unlikely heroes.

CONCLUSION

Mrs. Behrend and Mr. Threlkeld have found ways to use read-aloud plus strategies to enhance their students' understanding of text. They have made their reading more comprehensible to their students, but more than that, they have taught their students some comprehension strategies in the process. Their students are using several of the comprehension strategies researched by Judith Irwin (1991) by relating their own experiences to the texts they are reading, paraphrasing text to make it more understandable, and by adding visuals and reenactment to make the text come alive. As the teacher models and explains these strategies, students have more learning strategies to employ whenever they come to text that is tough to understand.

EXAMPLES OF APPROXIMATION BEHAVIORS RELATED TO THE TESOL STANDARDS:

Pre-K–3 students will:

- use realia to support story understanding.
- discuss stories and relate them to personal experiences.

4–8 students will:

- compare story plots to personal experiences in double-entry journals.
- compare versions of stories using graphic organizers.

9–12 students will:

- compare fictional and factual versions of the same historical events.
- write a fictional version of an historical event.

References

Beal S. M. (1995). *Warriors don't cry*. New York: Simon & Schuster.

Irwin, J. (1991). *Teaching the comprehension processes* (2nd ed.). Needham Heights, MD: Allyn & Bacon.

Jordan, M., & Herrell, A. (2001). *Read aloud plus: adding understanding to tough text*. Presentation at the California Reading Association State Conference. San Jose, CA: November 2001.

Neuschwander, C., & Geehan, W. (1997). *Sir Cumference and the first round table: A math adventure*. Watertown, MA: Charlesbridge.

LANGUAGE EXPERIENCE APPROACH:

Building on an Experience to Create a Written Account

37

The **language experience approach** (Lee & Allen, 1963) is an activity-based writing lesson that helps students to see the connections between experiences, what is spoken, and the written language. The students participate in an experience such as a field trip, science, or art lesson. The teacher engages the students in a discussion of their experience and as they talk about what they did, the teacher models writing their words on large chart paper. The teacher demonstrates the connection between sounds and written letters by sounding the words out as she takes the students' dictation. The students are able to read the text because they participated in the activity and the written words tell what they said about their experience. For these reasons, language experience lessons are very appropriate for English language learners (Hernandez, 1997).

The texts that are created from language experience lessons are frequently used for rereading or creating books for the students to illustrate or use in reader's theater. Big books made by the students from a language experience text provide an opportunity for the students to work collaboratively as illustrators and make a contribution to the class library.

STEP BY STEP

The steps in implementing the language experience approach are:

• ***Providing an active experience***—Provide an active learning experience such as a field trip, science experiment, art lesson, or physical movement lesson. For individual students, language experience lessons are based on any experience the student wishes to share.

• ***Talking about the experience***—Seat the students so they can see the chart or chalkboard where you are writing. Engage them in conversation about the activity they have just experienced. Encourage them to use complete sentences as they describe the activity.

• ***Taking dictation***—Record the students' descriptions of their experience. The recording reinforces their understanding of the oral to written language connection best if you follow this sequence:

  • Repeat the sentence to be written and then say it again one word at a time as you write it.

  • Have the students read the sentence along with you, pointing to each word as it's read.

  • If sequence is important to the text, ask leading questions such as, "And then what did we do?"

  • If the students are not dictating the sentences in proper sequence, you may want to record their sentences on sentence strips so that they can be rearranged in sequence after all the sentences are written.

• ***Rereading and exploring vocabulary***—When the entire text has been dictated, reread it aloud with the students reading along. Celebrate the vocabulary contributed by the students and give the students who dictated sentences a special pat on the back. Involve the students in deciding how they want to publish their text.

• ***Providing time for expansion projects***—Provide time and materials for the students to use in creating a product from their dictation. Figure 37.1 shows ways that language experience texts can be published.

APPLICATIONS AND EXAMPLES

Ms. Chan's first graders are planting the bean seeds they brought back from their trip to the farm. Ms. Chan asks the students to tell her how they planted their seeds.

"We got some dirt," Lee says.

Ms. Chan picks up her marker and says, "Let's write this down so we can put it in our newsletter this week. We (she sounds the letters as she writes them) got—some—dirt."

The students dictate sentences about their experience as Ms. Chan writes the words, sounding them out as they are written. When they are finished, Ms. Chan and the students read the sentences together.

"You did a nice job. We will put this story in the newsletter this week. Your parents will like to read about what you did. Do you want to do anything else with this story?"

"Can we make a book and draw pictures?" Tia asks.

"Do you want to make a big book or little ones?" Ms. Chan asks.

"Big one!" the students reply.

Ms. Chan gets large pieces of construction paper, cuts the chart story apart and gives each student a sentence to illustrate. She helps them to glue the sentences to the bottoms of their papers, under their illustrations. They put the book together with large metal rings and place it in the reading center. The students all enjoy stretching out on the floor to reread their book.

Mr. Mejas and his seventh graders are reading *The Giver* (Lowry, 1993). The students are reading a few chapters and then meeting with Mr. Mejas to discuss the book. As a part of the literature circles that meet once a week to discuss the chapters that have been read, each student dictates a favorite phrase or sentence selected from the text. The sentences are displayed on the bulletin board in categories

Publishing Format	Instructions
Parent newsletter	Language experience lesson is taught and text is used to share class activities with parents. One of the students illustrates the text. Note that it is a collaboratively written text and list the students who contributed.
Wall story	After the text is written, copy it one sentence at a time onto large construction paper. Ask a different student to illustrate each page. Display the pages, in proper sequence, along a wall or hang from a display line in the room. After awhile the pages can be taken down and made into a big book.
Individual books	After the text is written, copy it, one sentence per page, onto a master that can be folded into a book. Make photocopies of the pages. Help the students fold them to make a small book, staple it together, and have the students illustrate it.
Pocket chart game	As the text is dictated, write the sentences on sentence strip paper, one sentence per strip. Mix the sentences up and have the students rearrange them in order. After awhile, cut the words apart and encourage the students to rebuild the original text or create a new one using the same words.
Walk on story	After the text is written, copy the sentences, one sentence per page of construction paper. Have the students illustrate the sentences and then laminate the individual pages. The students read the text by spreading the pages out on the floor and stepping from page to page, reading as they walk.

Figure 37.1   Ways to Publish Language Experience Texts

marked, *Beautiful Language, Powerful Language, Suspenseful Language,* and *Descriptive Language.* Often Mr. Mejas has the students close their eyes to listen to the sentences the other students are sharing. Listening with their eyes closed helps them to decide where the phrase or sentence should be placed on the bulletin board. As Mr. Mejas writes the words on the sentence strips, the students help him spell the words by sounding them out as he writes them. After the phrase or sentence is written they discuss other words that may be related to the words written such as *transport, transportation, transporter, transition,* and *porter.* Mr. Mejas thinks that by relieving the students of the writing in this approach, they are able to focus more on the meanings of the words and the cohesion of the text.

CONCLUSION

Language experience lessons support the development of English vocabulary, including the active participation and verbal interaction of students through the use of their personal experiences in the creation of a written text. Follow-up activities such as the publishing of the text for use in reading practice serves to provide low-stress reading support for students learning a new language. Seeing their own stories published and illustrated also provides motivation and validation for students. Language experience texts can be used in multiple areas of the curriculum and serve to strengthen the concept-language connections of all students.

EXAMPLES OF APPROXIMATION BEHAVIORS RELATED TO THE TESOL STANDARDS:

Pre-K–3 students will:

- verbalize an account of an experience.
- orally reread a written account of a collaboratively created experience story.

4–8 students will:

- participate in a collaborative revision of an experience story.
- create illustrations based on the reading of an experience story.

9–12 students will:

- add personal details to a collaboratively written experience story.
- write a personal view of a shared experience.

References

Lee, D. M., & Allen, R. V. (1963). *Learning to read through experience* (2nd ed.). New York: Meredith.

Lowry, L. (1993). *The giver.* Boston: Houghton Mifflin.

Hernandez, H. (1997). *Teaching in multicultural classrooms.* Upper Saddle River, NJ: Merrill/Prentice Hall.

INTERACTIVE WRITING:
Developing Writing Skills Through Active Scaffolding

38

This strategy addresses the following TESOL Standards:

Goal 2: To use English to achieve academically in all content areas

Standard 1: Students will use English to interact in the classroom.
Standard 2: Students will use English to obtain, process, construct, and provide subject matter information in spoken and written form.
Standard 3: Students will use appropriate learning strategies to construct and apply academic knowledge.

Interactive writing (Pinnell & McCarrier, 1994) is a form of shared writing or language experience lesson in which the teacher and students compose a story or text and share the pen in writing the words down on a chart or writing paper. The students are supported in using conventional spelling, capitalization, and punctuation. They are encouraged to write the parts of the text they are able to write. The teacher supplies the nonphonetic parts of words as she supports the students' decision making as they practice writing with conventional spelling and mechanics.

Interactive writing provides scaffolding for young children moving from invented spelling into conventional spelling or to older students who are in need of skill- and confidence-building. It is especially appropriate for English language learners because providing an experience about which to write is the first step in interactive writing. While discussing the experience, the students provide the language to be written. The teacher helps them in creating complete English sentences, sounding out the words to be written, and teaching the use of capitalization and punctuation. See Figure 38.1 for texts and skills that can be taught through interactive writing.

STEP BY STEP

The steps in conducting an interactive writing lesson are:

* ***Providing an experience on which to focus writing***—Provide an experience to write about. Interactive writing can be done after a field trip, to share daily news, or after reading a book.

Texts	Skills
Labels	Letter formation
Lists	Initial consonants
Daily news	Final consonants
Parent newsletters	Short vowels
Formula poems	Capital letters
Friendly letters	Punctuation
Business letters	Drafting
Reports	Revising
Book reports	Editing
Big books	Alliteration
Alphabet books	Varying word choice
Fact books	Writing dialogue
Autobiographies	Citing sources
New versions of old books	Conventional spelling

Figure 38.1   Texts and Skills Appropriate for Interactive Writing Lessons

The shared experience gives the group something to write about. If the interactive writing is done with an individual it still works best to have a recent experience to write about.

• *Gathering materials*—Display a piece of chart paper on which the text will be written, or a piece of writing paper if the text is to be written with an individual student. Gather markers and correction tape. Inch-wide correction tape is best when the story is written on chart paper.

• *Starting the process*—Negotiate a sentence to be written. In the beginning it is best to start with a fairly simple sentence. Have the students help you count the words in the sentence. This helps you remember it and helps the students to see the individual words as they are written.

• *Scaffolding the writing*—Say the first word in the sentence slowly, drawing out the sounds. Ask the students what letter they hear at the beginning of the word. Invite one student to come and write the beginning letter, but before it is written ask, "Will you write a lower-case letter or a capital letter?" If the student answers, "Capital," ask, "Why?" The idea is to provide all possible support for success as well as to verbalize the decisions to be made so that all students understand. Then, allow the student to write the letter. Note that with older—or more skilled—students you adjust this step, encouraging them to write whole words, or even phrases, and providing only the support necessary for the students to participate successfully.

• *Rereading after each word is added*—After each word is written, go back and reread the sentence so far, pointing to each word as it is read. Continue to compose and support the children in writing the story following the same procedures. Focus on decisions that must be made as the writing is done, such as when to leave spaces, when to use capital letters, commas, periods, and so on. Use the correction tape whenever necessary, but always offer support to the student who made the error and encouragement when the error is corrected.

• *Reading the story aloud*—After the text is written, celebrate with the students by having the group read it aloud. Choose a student or two to illustrate it and then display it proudly in the classroom. When completed, an interactive writing lesson should produce a story that is correctly spelled, spaced, punctuated, and capitalized. Every student in the group should be able to read it, pointing to each word as it is read.

APPLICATIONS AND EXAMPLES

Mr. Benning gathers his first-grade students on the carpet at the end of each day. He asks them to tell him about the activities they have enjoyed in school that day. As they talk about their experiences, Mr. Benning conducts an interactive writing lesson. Each student is encouraged to participate as they are able. Some students can supply beginning letters in words, others can write whole words and even some phrases. Mr. Benning supports the students in sounding out words, leaving spaces, and placing punctuation marks and capital letters. After the text is complete, the students reread it together and talk about information they want to share with their parents. This daily ritual brings closure to their school day and reminds them of stories they want to share with their parents. It also provides a daily model for the uses of writing, conventional spelling, and mechanics. Figure 38.2 shows an example of Mr. Benning's first-grade daily news texts written by students from nine different language backgrounds.

Ms. Jacobs teaches eighth-grade English. Her students are reading literature related to the Underground Railroad and she decides that an interactive writing lesson would help the students to summarize their knowledge of the railroad while simultaneously providing an opportunity for her to teach writing mechanics in an authentic way.

Ms. Jacobs provides each student with an individual white board and dry-erase marker. She begins the interactive writing lesson with a question about the book *The Story of Harriet Tubman, Conductor of the Underground Railroad* (McMullan, 1991), which she has been reading aloud to the class. The students help compose a narrative about the book and Tubman's participation in the Underground Railroad. One student is chosen to write on the chart paper provided, but all students are writing the text on their white boards. Ms. Jacobs is monitoring the white boards and noting the abilities of the individual students as they write. She also supports the students' composing skills by making observations such as, "We've already started two sentences with 'She.' Maybe we can think of another way to begin this sentence."

Ms. Jacobs' students can write entire sentences as they contribute to the interactive narrative, but she is helping them choose interesting words, complex sentences, and literary forms in their writing.

A fascinating fact comes to light as the students are composing the story and discussing the book. When Ms. Jacobs asks the question, "Where does the Underground Railroad run?" a number of the students answer, "From Mexico to California." This revelation provides an opportunity for Ms. Jacobs to use a United States map to correct a misconception among the students about historical information

Today we went to the zoo.
We saw lots of animals.
Jose liked the monkeys the best.
Paulie liked the elephant.
We sang songs and ate lunch at the zoo.
It was fun.

Figure 38.2 Mr. Benning's Daily News (Written Interactively)

that she may not have known about if it had not been for the discussion generated by the interactive writing discussion.

The English language learners in the group are participating actively and having great success in composing the story. Because a group is composing the story, the anxiety level is lowered considerably and the peer interactions make writing more enjoyable. The students learn that some of their peers are very good at finding interesting words to use, while others are more adept at deciding on good titles. They are learning to appreciate each other's unique contributions.

CONCLUSION

Interactive writing involves the students in a thought process that is converted to writing. By discussing what they will write, and when and why conventions of writing are used, students are consistently reminded of the rules of writing and spelling in English. Students soon become more confident in their ability to transcribe their thoughts into readable English text because the teacher provides support by asking questions and reminding the students to think about the rules. The conventions and thoughts they practice writing as a group are then transferred to their independent writing.

EXAMPLES OF APPROXIMATION BEHAVIORS RELATED TO THE TESOL STANDARDS:

Pre-K–3 students will:

- contribute a letter or word to an interactive writing activity.
- correct writing errors with the teacher's support.

4–8 students will:

- contribute a phrase or a sentence to an interactive writing activity.
- suggest changes in sequence or form to enhance interactive writing products.

9–12 students will:

- contribute ideas and format for interactive writing projects.
- collaboratively revise and restructure an interactive writing project.

References

McMullan, K. (1991). *The story of Harriet Tubman, conductor of the underground railroad*. New York: Bantam Books.

Pinnell, G., & McCarrier, A. (1994). Interactive writing: A transition tool for assisting children in learning to read and write. In E. Hiebert & B. Taylor (Eds.), *Getting reading right from the start: Effective early literacy interventions* (pp. 149–170). Needham Heights, MA: Allyn & Bacon.

Suggested Readings

Button, K., Johnson, M., & Furgerson, P. (1996). Interactive writing in a primary classroom. *The Reading Teacher, 49,* 446–454.

Collom, S. (Ed.). (2000). *Sharing the pen: Using interactive writing in primary classrooms*. Fresno, CA: San Joaquin Valley Writing Project.

Fountas, I., & Pinnell, G. (1993). *Guided Reading: Good first teaching for all children*. Portsmouth, NH: Heinemann.

GUIDED READING:
Providing Individual Support Within a Group Setting

This strategy addresses the following TESOL Standards:

Goal 2: To use English to achieve academically in all content areas

Standard 1: Students will use English to interact in the classroom.
Standard 2: Students will use English to obtain, process, construct, and provide subject matter information in spoken and written form.
Standard 3: Students will use appropriate learning strategies to construct and apply academic knowledge.

Guided reading (Fountas & Pinnell, 1996) is an approach to teaching reading in a small group setting, while providing individual coaching. The students are taught in groups of four to six, all reading at approximately the same level. Teachers use running records to determine the students' reading levels, their use of cueing systems (attention to phonics, meaning, word order, sentence structure, and the relation of the text to the students' prior experiences). Running records also determine the students' use of self-correction and their attention to self-monitoring of whether their reading is making sense.

A guided reading lesson begins with a book walk, in which the students and teacher look through the book and predict what will happen. It then progresses through multiple readings of the book with students reading to themselves at their own pace. During this time, the teacher moves from child to child in the group, listening to them read and coaching them on decoding, self-monitoring, and comprehension strategies. This coaching is done by asking the student questions like, "Does that word start with a 'd'?" or "Does that make sense?" The students continue to read until each child has been coached.

Teachers then conduct minilessons based on the needs of the students identified during the coaching sessions. A teacher uses this opportunity to discuss the story and determine whether the students need support in understanding what they have read. Vocabulary is discussed, clarifying and relating it to the story, the illustrations, and the students' background experiences. The group may then engage in writing, phonics, or other skills activities.

The guided reading approach is appropriate for English language learners because of the focus on vocabulary development, individual instruction, and opportunities for verbal interactions. Because the English language learners participate in a group discussion of the story and the vocabulary encountered, they benefit from the language interactions of the small group setting. Because their needs may be different from the native English speakers, the individual coaching provides the teacher with an opportunity to support their understanding, correct pronunciation, and clarify word meaning and misconceptions caused by reading in their second language.

STEP BY STEP

The steps in teaching a guided reading lesson are:

• *Grouping the students for instruction*—Place students in groups of four to six, based on information from running records. Choose a book at the appropriate reading level for the students in the group and based on their interests whenever possible. Although guided reading can be used with any text, it is most effective when used with authentic texts that are of interest to the students.

• *Beginning the process*—Gather the group at a table and take a book walk through the book to be read. A book walk involves looking at the illustrations on each page, predicting what will happen on that page, discussing and modeling the meaning of vocabulary that will be needed to read the page, and building background knowledge. Sometimes it will be necessary to use visuals, gestures, or realia—real objects—to support the students' understanding of the vocabulary. It is also very helpful to relate vocabulary words to words in the child's home language whenever possible.

• *Reading aloud but not in unison*—Give the students copies of the book and encourage them to read aloud at their own pace. Move from student to student, listening to their oral reading and giving them instruction as needed in decoding, reading fluently, or self-monitoring. Ask questions to help them learn to self-monitor. Encourage the students to reread the story if they finish before you have listened to and coached each child. See Figure 39.1 for suggested questions and prompts to use.

• *Pairing students for additional practice*—Pair the students up to read to each other and listen to their oral reading one more time, coaching and celebrating their successes.

• *Teaching minilessons based on student needs*—Introduce a minilesson based on the needs you see as you coach individuals. Focus on self-monitoring and problem-solving strategies. Conclude the lesson with a discussion of the story, writing the students' words down in the form of a dictated story or interactive writing lesson. Encourage all the students to participate in an oral rereading of the story written.

APPLICATIONS AND EXAMPLES

Although guided reading as described in this chapter is usually done in primary grade classrooms, it is appropriate for English language learners of all ages because of the comprehension instruction and language development it supports. In first and second grade, teachers are using this approach with all students. It is particularly valuable for English language learners because of the repeated reading it encourages and the vocabulary that is introduced, modeled, and connected to illustrations.

Student's Behavior	Sample Questions or Prompts to Use
Guessing words	Does that make sense?
Skipping words	Point to each word as you read it. Did it match?
Inserting extra words	Point to each word as you say it. Were there enough words?
Substituting words that start with the same letter	Does that make sense? Look at the whole word.
Appealing for help from the teacher	Give it a try. How does it begin?
Incorrect reading of a word	Try that again. You made a mistake. Can you find it?

Figure 39.1 Questions and Prompts to Promote Self-Monitoring and Comprehension in Guided Reading

For example, Ms. Garcia is using the little soft-back book *Where's Tim?* (Cowley, 1996) with a group of Southeast Asian students. The book tells of a child looking for his pet cat. He looks in many places, including the kitchen cupboard, and finally finds the cat under the bedspread.

Ms. Garcia does a book walk, showing the pictures and having the students predict where the boy might look next. When Ms. Garcia reaches the page where the boy is looking in the kitchen cupboard, she shows them the cupboard behind her, under the classroom sink.

She says, "This is a cupboard. It's like a closet, but it's usually found in a kitchen or bathroom. It's not as tall as a closet." She gestures toward the coat closet as she says the word *closet*. She repeats *cupboard,* pointing to the cupboard. She repeats *closet,* pointing to the coat closet.

When the boy discovers the lump under the bedspread, Ms. Garcia demonstrates a lump by covering a stuffed cat with a towel. She says, "The boy saw a lump. The cat made a lump under the bedspread." She has the students pull their hands up under their sleeves to show her how their hands make lumps under their sleeves. They then read the story. See Figure 39.2 for additional strategies for guided reading.

CONCLUSION

In upper grades, guided reading can often help students to understand content reading such as science and social studies where the vocabulary is often unfamiliar to the students. Using this approach, walking through the reading material, examining illustrations, charting and graphing, and discussing them is often very helpful in building comprehension. Reading in pairs and encouraging summary and discussion is also appropriate with older students.

Problem	Suggested Strategies
Insufficient background	Use realia, visuals, or videos to build background. Read-aloud picture books that relate to the same topic.
Unfamiliar vocabulary	Use realia, illustrations, or skits to act out meanings. Provide translation to home language for unknown words.
Word-by-word reading	Provide a fluent model by using echo reading. In echo reading the teacher reads the sentence fluently and the student rereads it using expression and intonation echoing the teacher's model. Provide a model of reading with correct phrasing and ask the child to repeat the reading, phrase by phrase.
Reading past miscues without self-correcting	Stop the reader and focus on the miscue if it changes the meaning of the sentence. Support the reader in the use of phonics, meaning, syntax, and context so that the use of multiple cues is modeled and stressed.
Inability to answer questions after reading	Support the reader in looking back at the text to find the answers. Focus on the meaning as the text is reread. If the question is inferential, support the reader in finding clues that may help him/her to make guesses related to the question. Discuss the possibilities and agree on a likely response. Try to find ways to connect the questions and answers to the reader's background knowledge.

Figure 39.2 Guided Reading Strategies

EXAMPLES OF APPROXIMATION BEHAVIORS RELATED TO THE TESOL STANDARDS:

Pre-K–3 students will:

- respond to teacher questions to make sense of text.
- use a balance of cueing systems to unlock unknown words.

4–8 students will:

- use self-questioning to make sense of text.
- monitor self-reading to evaluate personal comprehension.

9–12 students will:

- periodically stop and self-evaluate for metacognition while reading.
- use active "fix-up" strategies when reading comprehension breaks down.

References

Cowley, J. (1996). *Where's Tim?* Auckland, NZ: Wright Group.

Fountas, I., & Pinnell, G. (1996). *Guided reading: Good first teaching for all children.* Portsmouth, NH: Heinemann.

PEER TUTORING: Students Supporting Student Learning

40

This strategy addresses the following TESOL Standards:

Goal 1: To use English to communicate in social settings

Standard 3: Students will use learning strategies to extend their communicative competence.

Goal 2: To use English to achieve academically in all content areas

Standard 1: Students will use English to interact in the classroom.
Standard 2: Students will use English to obtain, process, construct, and provide subject matter information in spoken and written form.
Standard 3: Students will use appropriate learning strategies to construct and apply academic knowledge.

Peer tutoring (Thonis, 1994) is a strategy in which a student who has already achieved certain skills works with a classmate to help him/her to acquire the skills. It differs from partner work because partners work together, sharing the responsibilities. Peer tutoring is effective with English language learners for several reasons. A peer who has mastered a higher level of proficiency in academic skills and English usage can often support learning by explaining the assignment in the student's first language or modeling what is expected. The peer tutoring situation often lowers anxiety for the learner because questions can be answered more readily on a one-to-one basis and the students are less likely to be inhibited. Questions can even be answered in the home language when the students come from the same language background. Peer tutoring also provides the tutor with positive feelings of self-esteem and accomplishment as the tutee gains knowledge and English proficiency.

STEP BY STEP

The steps in implementing a peer tutoring program are:

- ***Identifying student needs***—Identify students who are having difficulty in specific academic areas and who would benefit from one-to-one tutoring.

- ***Identifying and training potential tutors***—Identify students who have proficiency in the academic areas selected and who could provide tutoring for other students. Provide training to the peer tutors in:

  - how to pose questions that support thinking.
  - how to break the task into manageable pieces.
  - when to explain in the first language.
  - how to support English vocabulary development.

- ***Matching students***—Match the students who need tutoring with peer tutors considering such things as gender, home language, and personality.

- ***Working with the teams***—Confer with both members of the team—as a team and individually—to celebrate achievements, solve problems, and answer questions. If the team works well, continue to place the students together. Change the teams for various skills instruction.

APPLICATIONS AND EXAMPLES

The fourth graders in Mr. Yamada's class are all busily engaged in reading/writing workshop as Mr. Matthews, the principal, enters the classroom.

"I have a new student for you, starting tomorrow," Mr. Matthews says. "I have just finished talking to his foster mother. He's a new arrival from Bosnia and I know you have a student who came to us from the same area last year."

"I'm glad you let me know ahead of time," Mr. Yamada replies. "I can get Peter ready to serve as a peer tutor. What is his name?"

"His name is Vladimir," Mr. Matthews says. "His new family is calling him Vlad. He's only been in the country for a few days." Mr. Yamada has a short talk with Peter about being a peer tutor. Peter is very excited about having a friend from his own country.

"When will he be here?" Peter asks.

"He's due to start school tomorrow," Mr. Yamada replies. "Go on up to the office to talk to Mr. Matthews, though. Maybe he will give you Vlad's phone number so you can talk to him before he starts school. He might feel more comfortable coming tomorrow if he knows he'll have someone here who speaks his language."

"Great idea!" Peter says as he heads for the office.

When Peter comes back he's smiling broadly. "I talked to him and he's going to play on our soccer team. He plays goalie and we sure need one. They always make me play that position and I hate it."

"What else did you find out about him?" Mr. Yamada asks.

"He wants to be called Vladimir, not Vlad. He's good in math. He likes to read, but he doesn't read English well. His English is way better than mine was when I came last year. We really didn't talk in English, much," Peter says sheepishly.

"That's OK, Peter. You'll be helping him to learn English, but I don't want either of you to forget your native language. It's good that you can practice together."

Mr. Yamada and Peter work together each morning for a few minutes making sure that Peter knows what is expected of him as a peer tutor. Peter and Vladimir sit next to each other and Peter is encouraged to explain assignments to Vladimir any time he needs help. While Mr. Yamada works with small groups of students, Peter tutors Vladimir and helps him understand the main concepts being taught. Peter quickly learns how to give a brief review of any explanations Mr. Yamada gives, supporting Vladimir with English translations or first-language explanations. Vladimir is very proud of his growing abilities in English and Mr. Yamada has to chuckle whenever the soccer team plays. The whole team, no matter what their home language, shouts encouragement to each other in Croatian.

Ms. Bartell's seventh-grade pre-algebra class is studying motion problems. Ms. Bartell is trying to use as many concrete examples as possible since she has so many English language learners in the class. A number of her students are trying very hard, but they are having a lot of problems with the difficult concepts of trains or planes heading in opposite directions and their likelihood of passing each other or crashing. On top of the challenge of the math concepts, Ms. Bartell is aware that the English language is interfering with comprehension.

"I need some peer tutors for my math students," Ms. Bartell says one day in the faculty lounge. "Some of the language in the more advanced word problems is really causing difficulties."

Across the room Mr. Flores looks up from his newspaper and asks, "What are the students' home languages?"

Ms. Bartell looks startled, as if she really hadn't expected a response to her plea. "Most of the students are Spanish speakers," she replies.

"Why don't we set up a tutoring center after school. I have some advanced Spanish students who will be taking the College Advanced Placement Exam in Spanish at the end of the year and they could use some conversational practice. They're all seniors and pretty bright kids. Could you use them?" he asks.

"Yes! Yes! Yes!" Ms. Bartell practically shouts. "Can we set up a meeting so I can review them on the math concepts and teach them some tutoring strategies?"

"I think we can arrange that. I'd want some ways to support their Spanish conversation as a part of the deal. Maybe we should work together on this," Mr. Flores says.

The next day Ms. Bartell discusses the idea with her pre-algebra class and they seem to be interested. "You mean we'll be tutoring seniors in Spanish and they'll be tutoring us in math?" asks Lorenzo.

"Mainly, they'll be tutoring you in math," Ms. Bartell says. "But Mr. Flores wants them to have some Spanish conversational practice as a part of the deal."

Ms. Bartell and Mr. Flores meet the next day to set up a peer tutoring program and decide on the priorities and time line. See Figure 40.1 for their plan of action.

Guidelines:
All students must agree to participate at least two afternoons a week.
One teacher will monitor on Mondays and Wednesdays, the other on Tuesdays and Thursdays.
Tutor and tutee must agree on a schedule and stick to it unless they mutually agree to change.

Tutor Training:
Ms. Bartell will
- train the math tutors, review their math concepts and provide any ongoing training needed as the content changes.
- provide any materials she wants the tutors to review.
- expect monthly reports from the tutors.
- assess any tutees who feel they are ready to discontinue tutoring.

Mr. Flores will
- prepare any materials he wants discussed as a part of the peer conversations in Spanish.
- conduct any training for the Spanish conversations that he deems necessary.

Schedule:
| 3:00–3:45 | Math Tutoring (may be conducted in Spanish, English or any combination) |
| 3:45–4:15 | Spanish Conversations (reciprocal vocabulary building—English and Spanish) |

Figure 40.1   An After-School Peer Tutoring Plan

CONCLUSION

Peer tutoring is a highly effective practice for English language learners. It provides an opportunity for verbal interactions in both English and the home language when tutors are matched by home language. It provides authentic verbal practice in English because of the shared responsibility for studying an academic assignment. Both students benefit from the activity because the tutor is building confidence and self-esteem, learning organizational skills, and refining his/her academic understandings. The peer being tutored gains practice and confidence in verbal and written English and opportunities to have lessons clarified in a less stressful setting.

EXAMPLES OF APPROXIMATION BEHAVIORS RELATED TO THE TESOL STANDARDS:

Pre-K–3 students will:

- verbally interact with a peer to accomplish academic tasks.
- ask clarification questions in an academic setting.

4–8 students will:

- interact with a peer to accomplish a sequence of academic tasks.
- ask for and use suggestions from a peer to improve academic performance.

9–12 students will:

- use discussions with a classmate to clarify difficult text.
- analyze personal academic strengths and needs and seek support from a peer when necessary.

Reference

Thonis, E. (1994). The ESL student: Reflections on the present, concerns for the future. In K. Spangenberg-Urbschat & R. Pritchard (Eds.), *Kids come in all languages: Reading instruction for ESL students*. Newark, DE: International Reading Association.

CLOZE:
Using Context to Create Meaning

41

This strategy addresses the following TESOL Standards:

Goal 2: To use English to achieve academically in all content areas

Standard 1: Students will use English to interact in the classroom.

Standard 2: Students will use English to obtain, process, construct, and provide subject matter information in spoken and written form.

Standard 3: Students will use appropriate learning strategies to construct and apply academic knowledge.

Cloze activities are based on written text in which some words are left out and blanks are inserted. Cloze paragraphs are often used to assess reading comprehension because the word choices students make provide the teacher with an opportunity to evaluate their understanding of the meaning of the text. Cloze activities, when used with English language learners, provide an opportunity to teach English vocabulary and reading decoding skills in a meaningful context. When done in pairs or small groups these activities also provide an opportunity for students to discuss their choices and justify their selection of words.

Teacher-designed cloze activities are especially valuable because they can be adapted to the specific needs and language levels of students. Based on observation of students' oral reading or running records, the teacher is able to identify students who are not using cross-checking of phonological and meaning cues. Creating paragraphs with words left out requires the student to use multiple sources of information, such as context, to predict words that make sense in the paragraph. Cloze sentences can also demonstrate to students that they don't have to be able to read every word of the paragraph to understand the meaning.

The context of the sentence, in combination with phonic and syntax cues, is very helpful in supporting the reader in the identification of unknown words. Figure 41.1 shows the variety of ways one paragraph can be used to provide practice adapted to individual student needs.

Type of Cloze	Definition	Example
Traditional	Leave out words selected randomly.	I went for a walk to the _____. I wanted to _____ a _____. I watched carefully but I was to be _____.
Syntactic	Structure words are deleted.	I went _____ a _____ to the sea. ____ wanted ____ see ____ dolphin. I watched carefully ____ I was _____ be disappointed.
Semantic	Content words are deleted.	I went for a walk to the _____. I wanted to _____ a _____. I _____ carefully but I was to ____ disappointed.
Graphophonic	Some letters are deleted.	I w _____ for a w _____ to the s _____. I wanted to see a d _____. I watched c _____ but I was to be d _____.

Figure 41.1 Cloze Activities to Support Reading and Language Acquisition

Adapted from Gibbons, 1993.

▶ STEP BY STEP

The steps in using cloze activities are:

• **Observing student reading behaviors**—Observe your students as they read and note their use of phonological, meaning, and syntax cues as well as their self-monitoring. Also note the categories of the words that seem to be giving them difficulty. A running record is an easy way to do this. Figure 41.2 presents an example of such a running record.

• **Grouping students for instruction**—Examine your students' running records to determine which students are experiencing similar difficulties, then group these students together.

• **Preparing a cloze activity to meet student needs**—Prepare a cloze paragraph by choosing a selection from a reading assignment at the students' instructional reading level and deleting words using one of the following methods:

  • Copy the paragraph onto poster board or chart paper and cover selected words with wide correction tape. Be sure to use the type of tape that is easily removed.

  • Copy the paragraph onto transparency film, leaving blanks in the text.

  • Copy the sentences from the selection onto sentence strips. Cut the words apart and leave some out as they are placed into a pocket chart.

Passage	Errors	Self-Correct	Errors MSV	Self-Correct MSV
✓ ✓ ✓ ran ✓ to ✓ ✓ Jack and Jill went up the hill	2		Ⓜ Ⓢ V	
✓ find ✓ ✓ ✓ ✓ to fetch a pail of water.	1		Ⓜ Ⓢ V	
✓ ✓ ✓ ✓ ✓ ✓ head Jack fell down and broke his crown,	1		Ⓜ S V	
✓ ✓ ✓ ⌒falling too SC And Jill came tumbling after. ⌋R		2	Ⓜ Ⓢ V Ⓜ Ⓢ V	Ⓜ Ⓢ Ⓥ Ⓜ Ⓢ Ⓥ

Figure 41.2 Sample of a Running Record

MSV refers to the cueing system the child was using. M = Meaning, S = Structure, V = Visual (phonological).

- ***Identifying appropriate words to fill the blanks***—Work with the groups of students, asking them to read the selection silently. Have students write down the words they think would best complete the selection. Ask each student to read the selection orally and insert the words he or she believes are needed to make the selection make sense. After the students read the selection with their chosen words inserted, have them explain how they decided which words to insert. Have them point to or read the parts of the selection that gave them clues. If they selected different words, have them discuss which words seem to fit best and why.

- ***Assessing student growth and understanding***—Using cloze paragraphs to assess student comprehension is very effective. Giving cloze assessments periodically to document growth in the use of context cues is an interesting way of assessing students' abilities to make sense of text. Periodic cloze assessments can easily be included in individual student portfolios to document growth in reading comprehension.

- ***Adding technology***—Cloze paragraphs at various reading levels can be saved on the computer. Students can complete the cloze assignments and then print their work. The paragraphs can then be graded and included in the portfolio.

APPLICATIONS AND EXAMPLES

Ms. Mendez has noticed that some of her second-grade students tend to look at the first letter of a word and then guess. They don't seem to be monitoring to make sure the words they are reading make sense. She designs a cloze activity that will force them to think about the meaning of the words in the passage. It looks like this:

Jack and Jill _____ up the _____. They wanted to _____ some _____. On the way, Jack _____ and Jill helped him by _____.

After the students read the passage, guessing words that make sense, Ms. Mendez shows them the same passage but this time each blank has the first letter of the word displayed. The passage now looks like this:

Jack and Jill r_____ up the r_____. They wanted to f_____ some bl_____. On the way, Jack f_____ and Jill helped him by st_____.

The students read the passage again, using the phonic cues to help them to decide which words fit into the blanks. They discuss how their choices are different. The teacher displays the passage a third time, without any blanks, and the children read it again.

Jack and Jill ran up the rock. They wanted to find some blossoms. On the way, Jack fell and Jill helped him by stopping.

Ms. Mendez and her students discuss how they have to think about what makes sense in the sentence and even when they know the first letter of the word it is still possible to choose the wrong word. Ms. Mendez cautions them to be sure to look at the whole word. After this lesson, Ms. Mendez will remind her students frequently about the importance of thinking about the words they read and the sense they make.

Cloze activities can be used at any level. They force the reader to think about the meaning of the passage and to choose words to insert in the blanks that fit the meaning, structure, and genre of the piece.

Mr. Tompson notices that his 11th-grade English language learners have difficulty making sense of poetic language in narratives. To assist them in making sense of what he calls "tough text," he prepares the following cloze passage:

E_____ for the moment at least from the t_____ of fantasy, Jose in a short time set up a s_____ of order and work which allowed for one bit of l_____: The freeing of the birds, which since the time of their founding, had made m_____ with their fl_____, and installing in their place m_____ clocks in every house. (Marquez, 1970, p. 45)

The students read the passage and discuss what they think it means. Mr. Tompson leads them to the conclusion that, although they can't read every word, they can understand the main idea of the passage. They work as a group to sound out and discuss the words *emancipated, torment, system, license, merry, flutes,* and *musical.* The teacher's goal is met. The students believe they can understand this tough text even without knowing every word. They also learn some new vocabulary as a result of the lesson.

CONCLUSION

As shown by these two examples, cloze activities are helpful in supporting English language learners to focus on meaning in reading. Although new vocabulary may be difficult for the readers, cloze activities help the students to learn ways in which the context of the reading passage—in combination with their knowledge of phonics, syntax, and prior knowledge about the topic—can support their understanding of the text they read.

EXAMPLES OF APPROXIMATION BEHAVIORS RELATED TO THE TESOL STANDARDS:

Pre-K–3 students will:

- supply omitted words in a cloze sentence based on context.
- suggest optional words for substitution in a sentence based on context.

4–8 students will:

- supply omitted words in increasingly more complex text.
- identify words in context that change sentence meaning.

9–12 students will:

- identify unknown words using both sentence context and phonetic cues.
- supply words in context based on syntactic knowledge (word order and parts of speech).

References

Gibbons, P. (1993). *Learning to learn in a second language*. Portsmouth, NH: Heinemann.

Marquez, G. (1970). *One hundred years of solitude*. New York: Avon.

Suggested Reading

Tompkins, G. E. (1997). *Literacy for the 21st century*. Upper Saddle River, NJ: Merrill/Prentice Hall.

ATTRIBUTE CHARTING: Organizing Information to Support Understanding

42

Attribute charting, also called **semantic feature analysis** (Peregoy & Boyle, 1993), is a way of visually organizing information to support students' understanding of the attributes of the concept being studied. For example, if students are engaged in the study of continents, an attribute chart of the continents could be constructed where the students look at maps and note which continents are found in the northern hemisphere; which are connected to other continents; which are surrounded by water; and which are mountainous, flat, or a variety of elevations.

This strategy supports English language learners because the chart they make clearly visualizes their understanding of the main attributes of the topic—in this case continents. By making a chart of these attributes the continents can be more easily compared and contrasted. The students are involved in active research to determine which of the attributes are possessed by the individual continents and they are given opportunities to interact verbally as they construct the chart. The students' chart of the continents is shown in Figure 42.1.

STEP BY STEP

The steps in teaching the use of an attribute chart are:

- **Choosing a concept to chart**—Determine whether the concept you are teaching lends itself to the charting of attributes. If it does, make a list of the attributes, traits, or characteristics that could be charted.

Continent	Island	Connected	Mountains	Flat	Rivers	Desert	Forest	Ice
Africa	−	✓	✓	✓	✓	+	+	−
Antarctica	−	−	✓	✓	−	−	−	++
Asia	−	+	✓	✓	✓	✓	✓	−
Australia	+	−	✓	✓	✓	✓	✓	−
Europe	−	+	✓	−	✓	−	✓	−
North America	−	✓	✓	✓	✓	✓	✓	−
South America	−	✓	✓	✓	✓	−	✓	−

Figure 42.1 The Continents

- ***Discussing attributes or traits***—Involve the students in the discussion of the traits or attributes of the examples that illustrate the concept being taught. Provide the students with a set of clear instructions and encourage them to contribute to the completion of the attribute chart by examining the examples to see which attributes are present in each. Demonstrate how to use a marking system for the task. For example, an attribute might simply be checked on the chart or it could be marked with another symbol showing how closely it fits a given parameter. For example, under the attribute of connectedness, the continents of Europe and Asia would be marked with a plus sign because they are connected across a large area of land, while North and South America would be marked with a checkmark because they are more minimally connected. Australia would be marked with a minus sign because it is not connected to any other continent.

- ***Exploring the materials***—Engage the students in the exploration of resource materials available to support their understanding of the attributes being marked. When charting animals, students might look at pictures of animals. When charting continents, students would want to examine maps and photographs. Give multiple opportunities to view realia or photographs to assure the understanding of the concept and its attributes. Model the use of the academic language being learned and help the students make connections between the academic language, their background knowledge and colloquial language (BICS).

- ***Using the charted material***—Provide a follow-up activity that encourages the students to use the information on the attribute chart. This might be a writing assignment in which they must use the chart to compare and contrast two of the examples. It might also be an activity where the students illustrate and label the attributes of one of the examples from the chart.

APPLICATIONS AND EXAMPLES

Mr. Villalobos and his first graders are looking at pictures of animals and discussing where the animals live in preparation for a unit on the zoo. Since the class will be visiting the zoo, Mr. Villalobos wants the children to understand that the habitats in which the animals are housed are not exactly the same as where the animals live in the wild. Since the class has just completed a study of farm animals, the discussion of the pictures also involves the comparing and contrasting of zoo and farm animals. As the discussion continues, Mr. Villalobos decides that the children will benefit by the construction of an attribute chart. As he begins to draw the chart, he engages the children in discussion of each animal, its natural habitat, and whether it is a farm or zoo animal. The chart they construct is shown in Figure 42.2.

Mr. Villalobos begins the discussion by activating the children's background knowledge of the farm animals they have recently studied and their visit to the farm. He shows the children a picture of a duck and asks, "Who remembers the name of this animal?"

Tua raises his hand tentatively, "A duh?" he asks.

"Yes," Mr. Villalobos replies. "It's a duck. Everyone say 'duck' with me." The children repeat the word *duck* together. "Now, what do we know about ducks?"

As the children reply, Mr. Villalobos writes their words, sounding them out aloud to model the sound/symbol relationships.

"A duck has w-w-ing-s," Mr. Villalobos says as he stretches the sounds of the letters and writes *wings*. He repeats this process with *two legs* and *eggs*.

Next, Mr. Villalobos shows a picture of a horse and the process is repeated. The children say that the horse is a farm animal with four legs and hair. They also add that horse babies, foals, are born alive. They know this because they saw a live birth on their farm visit.

As the children add information about the animals whose pictures they are examining, Mr. Villalobos says, "I have an idea! Let's make a chart so we can remember all about these animals. You have talked about where we see them, on the farm or at the zoo." He writes *farm* and *zoo* on the attribute chart.

"You have told me where the animals live, on land or in the water." He writes *land* and *water* on the chart.

Animal	Farm	Zoo	Natural Habitat land	water	4 Legs	2 Legs	Wings	Hair	Babies live	eggs
Duck	✗		✗	✓		✗	✗			✗
Horse	✗		✗		✗			✗	✗	
Elephant		✗	✗	✓	✗			✗	✗	
Lion		✗	✗		✗			✗	✗	
Pig	✗		✗		✗			✗	✗	
Giraffe		✗	✗		✗			✗	✗	

Figure 42.2   A First-Grade Attribute Chart of Farm and Zoo Animals

"You have told me how many legs they have." He writes *2 legs* and *4 legs* on the chart.

"You have also told me how their babies are born, live or from eggs." He writes *live* and *eggs*. Mr. Villalobos then adds the words *duck* and *horse* under the word *animal* on the chart and explains, "This word says duck. Now I will mark what you told me about the duck. The duck is a farm animal." Mr. Villalobos makes an ✕ under the word farm. "He lives on land and in the water. I have to mark both these words. He has two legs and duck babies come from eggs."

Once Mr. Villalobos has modeled the marking of the chart for the duck, he involves the children in marking the chart for the horse's attributes. The children read and reread the attributes on the chart as they decide which traits should be marked for each animal. Once they have completed the chart they are shown what to do next.

Mr. Villalobos holds up a piece of construction paper as each child does the same. He models folding the paper in half and monitors as the children do the same. He models drawing two animals, one on each half of the paper. The children do the same, choosing the two animals they want to compare. Mr. Villalobos then models the writing of sentences about each animal, focusing on the attribute chart as the source of the words they will need. "The horse lives on a farm. He lives on land and has four legs. He has hair and his babies are born live."

Jeremy adds loudly, "We KNOW. We saw him born. The baby is called a foal."

Mr. Villalobos grins widely. "You can add that to your story, Jeremy."

The children's language and concept acquisition is supported by the use of the attribute chart.

Mr. Villalobos combines the use of the chart with the use of modeling, both writing and resource use, to enable the children to successfully integrate their understanding and completion of a short writing assignment.

Just as young children benefit from seeing their ideas and assignments visualized, older students also gain insight when charts are used to support their learning and planning.

For example, Ms. Vue has noticed that her seventh-grade science students don't always use the strategies they have learned to support their understanding of the science concepts they are using. The science fair is approaching and all the students are supposed to be preparing projects for the fair. Ms. Vue decides that an attribute chart could be used to review the learning strategies involved in preparing a good science project.

"Today, I want to review the steps in the scientific process you are using to prepare your science project," Ms. Vue says as she projects a blank attribute chart on the overhead projector. The chart she displays is depicted in Figure 42.3.

Ms. Vue points to the steps in the scientific process on the overhead chart and reviews what each step means. She then goes back to the top row of the chart to ask, "Why do you think I wrote these particular things across the top of this chart? What do they have to do with doing a science project?"

Rodney raises his hand and Ms. Vue acknowledges him. "I think those are the strategies that are needed to actually do the steps in the project."

"Exactly," Ms. Vue replies. "Each of the steps in the scientific process involves the use of some of the learning strategies listed—and maybe some I haven't listed. Let's talk about how they are related to the steps in the scientific process."

As she points to the first step in the scientific process, Ms. Vue asks, "What does asking a question involve? Do you need to have any prior knowledge of the subject to ask a question?"

Stefan answers, "I think you have to know something about the subject you are going to use for your project or you won't know what kinds of questions to ask."

"Yes," Ms. Vue replies. "That is true. So, having prior knowledge is important to being able to ask a question. We could say that using prior knowledge is a trait or attribute necessary to do this step in the scientific process well. What about *resourcing?* Who remembers what that term means?"

Adriana replies, "It means using resources like encyclopedias and textbooks. You'd have to use resourcing to do a good job of asking a scientific question. If you didn't you may ask a question that has been answered many times."

"That's true," Ms. Vue says. "What about note-taking? Why is that listed?"

Steps in the Science Process	Prior Knowledge	Resourcing	Note-Taking	Planning	Communicating
Ask a question					
Make a hypothesis					
Collect data					
Record data					
Analyze data					
Answer the question					
Prepare a display to share your processes and results					

Figure 42.3 Ms. Vue's Attribute Chart

Adapted from Chamot & O'Malley, 1994.

"You won't be able to remember everything you read," Josef says. "That's why you have to take notes. But I'm not sure you need to do it just to ask a question. That's more what you do later on in the process."

As Ms. Vue works through the steps in the scientific process and relates them to the learning strategies needed to do a thorough job of the science project, the students can see by the chart exactly what they will need to do to complete each step. The last item on the chart—communicating—elicits some spirited discussion.

"You'll be doing all this work for nothing if you can't communicate to others. You need to be able to make your steps and results clear," Alberto says.

"And how do you do that?" Ms. Vue asks.

"By drawing pictures and listing your methods and results in order. Oh, and you have to make sure that you define your terms well so everyone knows what you are taking about," Alberto answers.

"So being able to communicate also takes some planning. Some of these attributes are connected," Ms. Vue says. "That's why I wanted you to get to see them in chart form. Maybe a chart would help you to communicate your steps, methods, data-gathering, and results."

CONCLUSION

Again, by using an attribute chart to demonstrate the attributes of a good science project, Ms. Vue has helped her students to visualize what is required of them. In the process she has taught them an organizational strategy that might be helpful to them as they communicate their scientific processes and results. The students have been given an opportunity to see the fifth and sixth language arts, *viewing* and *visually representing,* in action. This lessens their dependence on *reading, writing, speaking,* and *listening.*

EXAMPLES OF APPROXIMATION BEHAVIORS RELATED TO THE TESOL STANDARDS:

Pre-K–3 students will:

- verbally identify attributes of realia.
- verbally identify attributes of common nouns.

4–8 students will:

- verbally identify attributes of content-related concepts.
- visually represent attributes of content-related concepts.

9–12 students will:

- analyze attribute charts to summarize similarities among concepts.
- write a compare-and-contrast paper using information from an attributes chart containing content-related concepts.

References

Chamot, A., & O'Malley, M. (1994). *The CALLA handbook: Implementing the cognitive academic language learning approach.* Reading, MA: Addison-Wesley.

Peregoy, S., & Boyle, O. (1993). *Reading, writing, and learning in ESL: A resource book for K–8 teachers.* White Plains, NY: Longman.

COHESION LINKS:
Understanding the Glue That Holds Paragraphs Together

This strategy addresses the following TESOL Standards:

Goal 2: To use English to achieve academically in all content areas

Standard 1: Students will use English to interact in the classroom.

Standard 2: Students will use English to obtain, process, construct, and provide subject matter information in spoken and written form.

Standard 3: Students will use appropriate learning strategies to construct and apply academic knowledge.

Cohesion links are the important parts of written and spoken paragraphs that connect sentences so that they form a cohesive whole. These links often appear in the form of pronouns that refer back to a person, place, or thing in a previous sentence or references that require the reader to recall a previously stated fact or condition. Cohesion links that are frequently used in spoken and written English are often confusing to English language learners. This is because the use of pronouns or use of ellipses where words are understood—but not spoken or written—are not always easy to connect to words used in previous sentences. Cohesion-links lessons make these links more visible and understandable to English language learners and are valuable in supporting their understanding of both spoken and written material. The forms of English writing and speaking that English language learners find most confusing are shown in Figure 43.1.

STEP BY STEP

The steps in teaching a cohesion-links lesson are:

• **Using a sample paragraph**—Prepare an overhead transparency of a paragraph at the students' reading level that contains pronouns, conjunctions, substitutions, or ellipses. Start with a fairly simple paragraph and then gradually add complexity in future lessons. Write the paragraph so that you can uncover one sentence at a time.

• **Reading one sentence at a time**—Cover all but the first sentence of the paragraph and have the students read that sentence aloud with you. Discuss any words that substitute for others or refer

Cohesive Tie	Example	Problem
Reference	A tall figure was standing outside the door. <u>The</u> figure turned quickly toward <u>her</u> as Sally stepped onto the porch. As <u>she</u> regained <u>her</u> composure <u>she</u> watched as <u>he</u> turned without a word and walked away toward the bus stop in the rain.	These underlined reference words often refer back to something already mentioned in the text. English language learners often do not recognize the relationship between the sentences and words used to refer back to a previous sentence.
Conjunctions	He worked all day <u>although</u> he was tired. <u>Finally</u> he laid down his hammer. He wasn't finished <u>but</u> his work was getting sloppy. <u>So,</u> he was afraid of ruining his work <u>unless</u> he got some rest.	Conjunctions are key words in helping the reader determine the connections between ideas and the sequencing of events. English language learners do not always understand the connections that conjunctions demonstrate and so they often misunderstand the text being read or heard.
Substitution	He was given a new pair of shoes for Christmas. His old <u>ones</u> were too small.	When one word is substituted for another, English language learners often do not recognize that both words are referring to the same thing.
Ellipsis	He sat down, ✓ stood up, and then ✓ sat down again. He said, "Some people like to dance and others don't ✓."	The checks in the example show places where words are left out but the reader or listener assumes meaning as if the words were present. English language learners may not recognize what is missing or may not be able to supply the meaning because of the omitted words.
Lexical cohesion	The giant was now in a land of tall *trees* and flowing *rivers*. He was still <u>running</u> hard although he was <u>slowing</u> down considerably. He went <u>galloping</u> over an enormous *forest* and on into a huge *range of mountains*.	If an English language learner does not see the connections between the underlined words or the words in italics, this selection will not make as much sense as it should.

Figure 43.1 Cohesive Ties in Written and Spoken English and the Difficulty They Cause English Language Learners

Adapted from Gibbons, 1991; and Halliday & Hasan, 1966.

the reader to another word in the sentence. Uncover the second sentence and repeat the process, supporting the students in making connections between words in the first sentence and references in the first sentence. Use an overhead marker to draw an arrow back to the proper noun that has been replaced by a pronoun or other word that has been replaced to make the connections visible to the students.

- ***Reading the rest of the paragraph one sentence at a time***—Work your way through the entire paragraph this way. Make connections between pronouns and nouns, sequence words, conjunctions, and multiple ways of referring to the same thing.

- ***Practicing in pairs***—Follow up this lesson by dividing the students into pairs and giving each pair a paragraph written on transparency film. Encourage the pairs to work together to draw arrows from pronouns to the words in other sentences to which the pronouns refer. Have them label the conjunctions and circle words that describe the same things.

- ***Reviewing the connections***—Have the students display their paragraphs on the overhead projector and discuss their conclusions after the pairs have completed their work. Have the entire group discuss the connections in the paragraphs that help build meaning as the paragraph is read.

- ***Continuing to review over time***—Regularly review the connections found in future reading assignments by asking questions such as, "To what word in the first sentence does the word *he* in this sentence refer?"

- ***Assessing student growth and understanding***—Periodically ask students to demonstrate their understanding of cohesion links by giving them paragraphs to mark. Ask them to draw lines between the connective as you have demonstrated and they have practiced. After these paragraphs are evaluated, they can be dated and included in individual student portfolios to document student growth over time.

APPLICATIONS AND EXAMPLES

Ms. Collom's kindergarten class is writing a language experience story about their trip to the pumpkin patch. The first sentence they dictate is: *We went to the pumpkin patch*. She stops and asks, "Who went to the pumpkin patch?"

The students respond, "We did!"

Ms. Collom asks, "Who is *we?*"

Philip answers, "Ms. Collom's class—all of us!"

"You are right, Philip. We use the word *we* because it is shorter and easier to say than *Ms. Collom's class went to the pumpkin patch*. When we say 'we', we mean Ms. Collom's class."

The class then dictates, *We saw a scarecrow. He was funny*. Ms. Collom asks the students, "Who was funny?"

The students laugh, "The scarecrow!"

"Yes," Ms. Collom says. "We don't have to say, *We saw a scarecrow. The scarecrow was funny*. We can say *he* was funny because we already said we were talking about the scarecrow."

Ms. Collom knows that pronouns are sometimes difficult for English language learners to understand. She is providing support that will aid their listening and reading comprehension in the future.

Ms. Barnes is teaching a lesson on revising with her eighth-grade writing class. She displays a paragraph on the computer screen, projected on a large monitor so that all the students could see it. The paragraph says:

> I was walking down the garden path when I met a small, round man. The small round man was dressed all in green with pointed shoes and a round bowler hat. The small round man's face was round and his cheeks were red. I felt as if I had seen the small round man somewhere before.

Ms. Barnes reads the paragraph aloud to the students and asks them if there is anything that bothers them about the paragraph. The students reply that the phrase "the small round man" is repeated too many times. Ms. Barnes asks for suggestions as to how that could be fixed. The students help her replace "the small round man" with pronouns so that the paragraph sounds better. After the students help her replace the noun phrase with pronouns, Ms. Barnes questions the students about the pronouns and to whom they refer. The students have no problems understanding the paragraph although many of the English language learners do not know anything about leprechauns.

The students work together to make the paragraph more interesting. One of the challenges Ms. Barnes issues is, "Can you think of some more interesting words to use so that this paragraph isn't so boring?"

Gradually, using suggestions from various students and discussing the meanings of the words added, the class revises the paragraph so that it finally reads:

> I was walking slowly down a winding garden path lined with a wild variety of blossoms in every possible color when I met a squat, rotund man with a shiny red face. He was dressed all in green, emerald jacket and trousers, brilliant green velvet shoes with glittering gold buckles and a round green satin bowler hat. His face was so round that he looked like a caricature of every leprechaun I had ever seen in a book. Even though I knew that leprechauns are usually found in the imaginations of Irishmen and fools who have consumed too much malt, I couldn't wait to get home to describe him to my family. He was the happiest vision one could possibly see on the seventeenth day of March!

As Ms. Barnes and her class revise the paragraph, they discuss the uses of pronouns, the meanings of the words they use, and the images they portray. They connect the sentence "He was dressed all in green" with the phrase that follows, "emerald jacket and trousers" and arrive at the conclusion that the phrase illustrates the reference to "dressed all in green" since emerald is a shade of green.

The students discuss the importance of varying the words so that the readers can envision the sight of the leprechaun and his vivid clothing surrounded by the spring flowers along the garden path. They also have learned that using pronouns helps the narrative sound more natural, but it is important to know to whom the pronouns refer or the narrative doesn't make sense. The students also add a number of new words to their personal writing dictionaries that day.

CONCLUSION

Cohesion-link lessons support students in making sense of the English language, both spoken and written. Teachers help students to understand the formats by explaining the meaning of pronouns, ellipses, conjunctions, substitutions, and other abstract references in text and spoken language by giving examples and by providing students with guided practice in analyzing English text. They also encourage students to take time to analyze the reasons for their own misunderstanding. Demonstrating the connections by writing the sentences and drawing arrows to the words that are needed to make sense of the sentences makes the cohesion links more comprehensible to the reader or listener.

EXAMPLES OF APPROXIMATION BEHAVIORS RELATED TO THE TESOL STANDARDS:

Pre-K–3 students will:

- identify pronoun referents in written text.
- combine sentences with appropriate conjunctions.

4–8 students will:

- substitute descriptive phrases for nouns in written products.
- identify the difference in meaning when conjunctions are changed in a sentence.

9–12 students will:

- use ellipses appropriately in written and spoken text.
- identify similar lexical connectives in text to build comprehension.

References

Gibbons, P. (1991). *Learning to learn in a second language.* Portsmouth, NH: Heinemann.
Halliday, M., & Hasan, R. (1966). *Cohesion in English.* New York: Longman.

Suggested Readings

Irwin, J. (1991). *Teaching reading comprehension processes* (2nd ed.). Boston: Allyn & Bacon.
Tompkins, G. (1996). *Literacy for the 21st century.* Upper Saddle River, NJ: Merrill/Prentice Hall.

LEARNING STRATEGY INSTRUCTION:
Acquiring Self-Help Skills

44

This strategy addresses the following TESOL Standards:

Goal 1: To use English to communicate in social settings

Standard 3: Students will use learning strategies to extend their communicative competence.

Goal 2: To use English to achieve academically in all content areas

Standard 1: Students will use English to interact in the classroom.
Standard 2: Students will use English to obtain, process, construct, and provide subject matter information in spoken and written form.
Standard 3: Students will use appropriate learning strategies to construct and apply academic knowledge.

Goal 3: To use English in socially and culturally appropriate ways

Standard 3: Students will use appropriate learning strategies to extend their sociolinguistic and cultural competence.

Learning strategy instruction (Gagne, 1985) is based on supporting the students in understanding their own learning and in monitoring the methods and results of strategies they use in reading, writing, discussions, and research. Learning strategy instruction helps support English language learners in employing self-monitoring and self-help approaches to succeed in school (Chamot & O'Malley, 1994). Three areas of instruction are addressed in learning strategy instruction. All three areas are self-related. The learners focus on strategies they can use to improve their own success in school. The three areas of learning strategies included in learning strategy instruction are (a) metacognitive strategies, (b) cognitive strategies, and (c) social/affective strategies.

Metacognitive strategies include having a plan for learning, monitoring the learning that is taking place, and evaluating how well content has been learned. **Cognitive strategies** include how to manipulate material mentally or physically to facilitate learning. **Social/affective strategies** include ways to interact with others or control your own emotions in ways that support your learning. See Figure 44.1 for descriptions of some of the strategies included in each category.

Metacognitive Strategies	
Planning	Preview the material to plan a way to organize it for use.
Organizing	Plan the method of study to be used. Parts of the material to be studied and the sequence of study is determined.
Selective attention	Focus on key words or concepts to be learned.
Self-management	Organize a plan for studying, including time and place.
Monitoring comprehension	Check your comprehension during reading or listening.
Monitoring production	Focus on your speech or writing while it is happening.
Self-assessment	Plan ways to check on your learning through such things as learning logs, reflective journals, and checklists.
Cognitive Strategies	
Referring	Use research and resource materials such as dictionaries, encyclopedias, word walls, etc.
Classifying	Organize like materials together. Grouping the knowledge or concepts to be learned.
Note-taking	Write down important information and key words to be learned.
Activating prior knowledge	Make connections between what is being studied and your experiences.
Summarizing	Review the main ideas either orally or in writing.
Deduction or induction	Look for patterns to use a rule or make one.
Imagery	Use mental or drawn pictures to aid in memory or understanding.

Figure 44.1   Categories of Learning Strategy Instruction and Their Descriptions

Activity	Description
Brainstorming	Students suggest ways they have used in studying material. No judgment is made. The list is made and then students can use the list to suggest learning tasks that would match well with the strategies suggested. The benefit of this activity is to introduce the idea that there are many learning strategies and students have choices in approaches.
Partner interviews	Students pair up and interview each other about the strategies they use for studying. After the interviews, each student describes one strategy shared by the partner.
Questionnaires	Teacher prepares a questionnaire about strategy usage, which the students fill out. The results are tabulated and used as a basis for a group discussion.
Task think-aloud	Students demonstrate a task, such as tying shoes, and think-aloud to demonstrate the strategies they use. After one student demonstrates the task think-aloud, a student who has a different approach is given an opportunity to demonstrate it.
Strategy list think	A list of strategies such as note cards, diagrams, webs, and oral review are listed on the board and students give suggestions as to the learning tasks that would be appropriate for their use. Example: Note cards don't work for studying for a spelling test but do work for preparing an oral presentation.

Figure 44.2 Learning Strategy Introductory Activities

STEP BY STEP

The steps in teaching learning strategies are:

- ***Matching strategies and curriculum***—Select the strategy to be taught by thinking about the curriculum to be studied and the demands it will make on the learner. Plan to teach only a few strategies at first, giving the students opportunities to practice the strategies well before introducing new ones.

- ***Reflecting on learning task approaches***—Develop students' self-awareness by having them reflect on how they approach a learning task. Remind them of the cooperative learning activities they have been involved with and what they have learned about their approaches to learning during the debriefing sessions. See Figure 44.2 for suggestions of additional introductory activities.

- ***Modeling strategy use***—Model the strategy you are teaching. Call the strategy by its name each time you model it. Explain how the strategy works to support the students' learning. Give examples of instances in which the strategy will be helpful.

- ***Practicing the strategy***—Provide an opportunity for the students to practice using the strategy while you are available to assist, if needed.

Strategy Use Rubric

Student's Name _____

Learning Strategy _____

Each time you use a learning strategy, place an **✗** on the continuum to show how well you think you used it.

< – >

Poorly	OK	Well
I did not follow the steps well.	I did follow the steps. I didn't give it my full attention.	I followed the steps and was successful.

Strategies used this week:	Subject area:	Effectiveness
_____	_____	1 2 3 4 5
_____	_____	1 2 3 4 5
_____	_____	1 2 3 4 5
_____	_____	1 2 3 4 5

Figure 44.3   Learning Strategy Self-Evaluation Tools

• ***Discussing strategy use***—Hold an evaluation discussion. Ask the students to demonstrate how they used the strategy and what was difficult for them. Provide a self-evaluation tool, or scoring rubric, for them to use in evaluating their strategy use. See Figure 44.3 for strategy self-evaluation tools.

• ***Making visuals for self-help***—Have the students make strategy posters to display in the classroom, which explain the steps in the strategy use. Refer to those posters frequently when making assignments. Help the students see that they have choices in strategies to use and that strategies can be used in many different contexts and learning tasks.

• ***Assessing student growth and understanding***—As strategies are taught, make a checklist with the strategy names and student names to use as you observe them completing assignments. Watch for strategy use and ask students to explain their strategy use. Notes on the checklist can be transferred to anecdotal records documenting student growth in strategy usage over time.

APPLICATIONS AND EXAMPLES

Some of Ms. Hernandez's second graders consistently fail their weekly spelling tests. Ms. Hernandez realizes that some of the students don't have strategies to use in studying their words. She begins the learning strategy instruction by initiating a conversation with the students on Monday morning as she is getting ready to list the new words for the week.

"How are you studying the words for your spelling test?" Ms. Hernandez asks the class.

"I write the words on a big piece of paper and hang it on my bulletin board at home," Amanda replies. "I look at the words every day and spell them to myself."

"I make flash cards and use them to practice writing the words," Carlos says.

"Let's make a list of all the methods we use to study spelling words," Ms. Hernandez says. She writes *Make a poster* and *Make flash cards* on the chalkboard. As the students add suggestions, the list grows. When the students have exhausted their ideas for studying the words, Ms. Hernandez says, "I want to show you one way of studying the words that I used when I was in second grade. You may find it helpful."

Ms. Hernandez gives each student ten 3-by-5 cards. As she writes the new spelling words on the board, she spells them aloud and the students write them on their 3-by-5 cards.

"Now, let me show you how to use the cards," Ms. Hernandez says. "You look at one card at a time. You spell the word aloud as you look at the card." She then demonstrates with one word. "These, t-h-e-s-e, these."

"Next, you look at the word again, turn the card over and write the word." She demonstrates this step.

"You turn the card back over and check to make sure you spelled the word correctly. You repeat the spelling to yourself before you move on to the next card."

Ms. Hernandez then instructs the students to go through the procedure with their new words. While they are practicing, she walks around the room, stopping to give encouragement and to ask questions about the meanings of the words or to ask students to use a word in a sentence.

After their practice session, Ms. Hernandez gives the class a practice test. A number of the students get a perfect score on the test.

"How do you think this method works?" Ms. Hernandez asks the class.

"I think it works great!" Erma says. "I never got a hundred on Monday before."

"You will want to use this strategy several times this week to make sure you really know the words," Ms. Hernandez reminds the students. "I chose these words because they are words you often misspell in your writing so be sure to double-check your spelling of them in your writing this week, too."

Ms. Hernandez is supporting the students' use of learning strategies in response to a concern she has about their study strategies. She introduces the strategy by helping the students recognize that it is necessary to have a strategy for studying. She models one strategy and gives the students practice in using it. She then gives an evaluation exercise, the spelling test, and gives the students an opportunity to discuss their use of the strategy and how it works. She also relates the strategy to their assignments and why they would want to use the strategy.

Ms. Teale has a number of students in her eighth-grade math class who do not turn in homework regularly. She devises a student questionnaire to determine the students' approaches to doing homework. Her questionnaire is shown in Figure 44.4.

Ms. Teale does an analysis of the results of her homework questionnaire, but before she shares it with the class she asks the students to predict what she found when she compared their responses on the questionnaire with their grades in the class. She puts the students into groups of three and asks them to discuss the questionnaire and which of the responses were most important in assuring that homework was done regularly and grades were good. Each group shares predictions that are remarkably similar. The consensus is that doing homework regularly, at a set time and place, is most helpful.

Ms. Teale then asks the students to discuss the barriers they encounter in doing homework. They come up with a list of barriers:

no place to study

younger brothers and sisters interfere

television is always on

lack of motivation

after-school jobs

The students brainstorm ways to overcome the barriers to doing homework. Their suggestions include talking to their parents and finding a place in the house for them to do homework, setting up a schedule, asking that the television be turned off for a set amount of time each evening, and setting up a homework club so the younger siblings are all doing homework, too.

Name _____

Please mark your answer to each question with an **✗** placed at the appropriate place on the continuum or checklist.

1. I do homework assignments

< – < – – – – – – – >

Never   Sometimes   About half   Most of   Always
                                the time   the time

2. I do homework

_____ while watching TV or listening to the radio

_____ at the kitchen table

_____ in my room _____ on my bed _____ at my desk

_____ right after school _____ after dinner _____ right before I go to bed

3. My parents ask me if I have homework

< – < – – – – – – – >

Never   Sometimes   About half   Most of   Always
                                the time   the time

4. I feel the practice I get doing homework is

< – >

a waste   somewhat helpful   helpful   important   very important
of time

5. I feel the weight given to homework assignments in this class is

< – >

too much   about right   too little

Figure 44.4   Homework Questionnaire

Ms. Teale demonstrates a time management strategy in which she shows how she plans the ways she uses her time between the end of the school day and bedtime. She gives each student a daily planning paper that divides the hours from 3 P.M. until 11 P.M. into half-hour segments. She leads the students through a planning activity in which they examine the ways they use their time and helps them find an hour each evening in which they could do homework. Several of the students are surprised at the amount of time they spend watching television or talking on the telephone.

Ms. Teale provides a role-play activity where the students pair up and conduct a conversation as if they are talking to their family about the homework problem and giving suggestions as to how it can be solved. The students practice sharing their daily planning sheets with their families and enlisting their support in implementing a homework hour for the family. Ms. Teale emphasizes how helpful this family approach will be to the younger students in the family.

At the end of the next week, Ms. Teale asks each of her students to write a brief reflection on the homework issue and whether their planning and family discussions were helpful. Those students who carried through on the assignment are asked to share their reflections with the class. Although she still has a few students not completing homework, Ms. Teale thinks the exercise was successful for several of the students. The number of homework assignments being submitted has increased and several of the students are sharing success stories involving their younger brothers and sisters.

CONCLUSION

Learning strategy instruction helps students to become more responsible for their own success in school. Teaching students how to monitor their own understanding and identify, plan, and implement ways to help themselves to understand and evaluate the effectiveness of the strategies being used supports their motivation to learn and their self-confidence.

Although study skills have been taught in school for a number of years, learning strategy instruction introduces the idea that students don't always learn in the same ways. The individual learning style and strong intelligences (see Chapter 50, Multiple Intelligence Strategies) become important in identifying strategies that work for each individual.

EXAMPLES OF APPROXIMATION BEHAVIORS RELATED TO THE TESOL STANDARDS:

Pre-K–3 students will:

- recognize and verbalize when they don't understand.
- employ self-help strategies to correct errors.

4–8 students will:

- use reading comprehension processes and "fix-up" strategies when experiencing difficulty with tough text.
- identify the strategies used to make sense of text.

9–12 students will:

- employ study skills to enhance their own learning.
- recognize personal learning strengths and use them to increase academic progress.

References

Chamot, A., & O'Malley, J. (1994). *The CALLA handbook*. Reading, MA: Addison-Wesley.
Gagne, E. (1985). *The cognitive psychology of school learning*. Boston: Little, Brown.

DICTOGLOS:
A Strategy for Improving Listening and Oral Communication Skills

45

This strategy addresses the following TESOL Standards:

Goal 2: To use English to achieve academically in all content areas

Standard 1: Students will use English to interact in the classroom.

Standard 2: Students will use English to obtain, process, construct, and provide subject matter information in spoken and written form.

Standard 3: Students will use appropriate learning strategies to construct and apply academic knowledge.

Goal 3: To use English in socially and culturally appropriate ways

Standard 1: Students will use the appropriate language variety, register, and genre according to audience, purpose, and setting.

Standard 3: Students will use appropriate learning strategies to extend their sociolinguistic and cultural competence.

Dictoglos is a strategy developed by Ruth Wajnryb (1990) for use with high school students, but it can be adapted for use with all ages. It is especially effective with English language learners because the strategy focuses on fluent academic language and supports learners in listening and recalling good English language models (Gibbons, 1993).

Dictoglos involves students in listening to repeated, fluent readings of English text. At first they just listen but on subsequent readings they take down as much of the text as possible. They then get together in pairs and again in fours to combine their notations and re-create as much of the text as possible. The activity provides an authentic reason for communication and practice in re-creating, rewriting, and rereading English text.

STEP BY STEP

The steps in teaching a dictoglos lesson are:

- *Selecting an appropriate piece of text*—select a content-related text and read it aloud at a normal speaking pace. At first, the students are instructed, "Just listen carefully."

- *Rereading the text orally*—Read the text twice more. The students are now instructed, "Jot down key words and phrases."

- *Pairing to re-create the text*—Have the students work in pairs to re-create as much of the text as possible using the notes taken by each of the partners to write the text as closely as possible to the original text as read by the teacher.

- *Working in groups of four*—Have two pairs meet together and pool their re-creations of the text to reconstruct it more completely. Have the group of four work together to write down as much of the text as possible. Their aim is to re-create it as closely as possible to the original.

- *Reading the re-created text*—Ask one member of each group to read the group's re-creation of the text and ask the other groups to see how closely it matches their versions. Display the groups' re-created texts, and compare and discuss them, noting the sections in the text that were difficult to re-create.

APPLICATIONS AND EXAMPLES

Because Laura Ingalls Wilder is one of her students' favorite authors, Ms. Leonard reads aloud from Carol Greene's biography of Wilder (1990) to her third-grade class. Reading the excerpt from the book where Greene describes how Wilder got ideas for her books, Ms. Leonard instructs the students to listen carefully so they will be able to remember Ms. Greene's words.

The second and third times she reads the text aloud, Ms. Leonard asks the students to jot down key words and phrases so they can recall the author's exact words. Ms. Leonard then pairs the students, instructing them to put their notes together so that they can rewrite the text in Greene's voice. Once the pairs have a text written that combines the words each of the pair was able to recall, the students meet again in fours to try to make their text even more complete. Once the groups of four are satisfied with the text they have re-created, they are instructed to use the text and illustrations to make a big book.

Each group of four is given time to present their big book to the class. The groups then discuss the sections of the text that were easiest to recall and compare and contrast the text of the big books. The groups agree that they used more colorful language in the writing of their big books because they were trying to use Carol Greene's exact words instead of their own.

Dictoglos is an exciting strategy because it gives students a chance to explore literary and academic language in depth. It exposes students to spoken and written English at a level above the everyday spoken English they hear and gives them practice in listening and writing more formal English. This strategy can be used in many curricular areas.

Mr. Estes teaches 10th-grade humanities. In celebration of Martin Luther King Jr.'s birthday, Mr. Estes decides to use dictoglos to support his students in listening to and appreciating Dr. King's "I Have a Dream" speech. The students listen first, and then take notes during the second and third readings so that they can re-create the speech. They meet in pairs to combine their notes and then meet in groups of four to refine the rewriting of the speech. Lively discussion erupts as they struggle to remember the eloquent words. Discussion of the meaning of the literary language is heard throughout the room. At the conclusion of the lesson, one student from each group delivers the group's version

Grade Level	Adaptations	Curricular Areas
Kindergarten	Recite poems and fingerplays, and write their notes interactively	Language arts
Primary	Paragraphs describing content knowledge— re-create and illustrate	Science, social studies
Upper elementary	Literary excerpts, famous speeches, and historical documents such as the Constitution	Language arts, social studies
Middle school	Descriptions of procedures Historical literature linking writing to periods of history Literary language—link to art, music	Science, literature, history Language arts, fine arts
Senior high school	Current Events—famous speakers, speeches Famous literature, poetry, historical literature	Political science, language arts

Figure 45.1   Adaptations of Dictoglos for Different Ages and Curricular Areas

of the speech with dramatic flourish. Although the words are not all exactly right, each group has demonstrated its understanding of the message.

CONCLUSION

Dictoglos is a strategy that can be adapted for use in many different ways. Figure 45.1 shows the ways in which it can be used for different ages of students and different curricular areas.

Dictoglos is not only valuable as a strategy for exposing students to fluent, literary English—it is also an exciting way to help them to study language and its changes over time. By listening to pieces of literature written in different time periods, students become aware of the ways English vocabulary and usage have changed over the years and of the influence of different linguistic groups on the language of the time. The context of the language can also be emphasized so that students begin to appreciate how the choices of words and phrasing are influenced by the purpose of the writing or speaking and the audience for which it is intended.

EXAMPLES OF APPROXIMATION BEHAVIORS RELATED TO THE TESOL STANDARDS:

Pre-K–3 students will:

- listen to and illustrate details from text read aloud.
- collaborate to recreate text in writing after hearing it read aloud.

4–8 students will:

- verbally negotiate with peers to recreate text that has been read to them.
- listen to and analyze contributions from peers in recreating text that they have heard.

9–12 students will:

- verbally negotiate with peers to recreate text based on listening and content knowledge background.
- collaborate to recreate complex text in writing after hearing it read aloud.

References

Gibbons, P. (1993). *Learning to learn in a second language*. Portsmouth, NH: Heinemann.

Greene, C. (1990). *Laura Ingalls Wilder, author of the little house books*. Chicago: Children's Press.

Wajnryb, R. (1990). *Grammar dictation*. Oxford, England: Oxford University Press.

FREE VOLUNTARY READING: **46**
Nothing Helps Reading Like Reading

Free voluntary reading (Krashen, 1993) is a powerful tool for involving students in the reading of English text. Free voluntary reading, or FVR, is a system for encouraging silent, self-selected reading of enjoyable books written at the students' independent levels. It has been found to support reading comprehension, writing, grammar, spelling, and vocabulary development even though the texts read are written at an easy reading level. Series of books in which the reader becomes familiar with the structure, main characters, and setting in the first book of the series and then reads sequels are especially appropriate for building vocabulary and comprehension in readers with limited English vocabularies.

Although free voluntary reading has been criticized (Hernandez, 1997) as difficult to implement because of the large numbers of books required, it has been shown to be effective for English language learners because of the power in exposing them to a large volume of English reading and the anxiety-reducing power of easy reading. A suggested list of free voluntary reading materials is shown in Figure 46.1.

Grade Level	Materials
Primary	*Aliens for Breakfast and Aliens for Lunch,* Stepping Stone Series, Random House. *Animals Ark Pets* Series, Scholastic. *Clue, Jr.* Series by P. Hinter, Scholastic. *Commander Toad* Series by Jane Yolen, Coward-McCann Inc. *Dolphin Diaries* Series by B. Baglio, Scholastic. *Hank the Cowdog* Series by J. Erickson, Puffin Books. *Horace Splattly* Series by L. David, Puffin Books. *Horrible Harry* Series by Suzy Kleing, Puffin. *Magic Tree House* Series by Mary Pope Osborne, Random House. *Pixie Tricks* Series by T. West, Scholastic. *Sweet Valley Kids* Series by F. Pascal, Bantam Books. *The Zack Files* Series by D. Greenburg, Grosset & Dunlap. *Ziggy and the Black Dinosaurs* Series by S. Draper, Just Us Books.
Upper elementary	*The Adventures of Wishbone* Series by A. Steele, Lyrick Pub. *Bailey School Kids* by Debbie Dadey & Marcia Thornton Jones, Scholastic, Little Apple. *The Boxcar Children* Series by G. C. Warner, Albert Whitman & Co. *Dear America* Series, Scholastic *Dinotopia* Series, Random House *Dragon Slayers' Academy* Series by K. H. McMullan, Grosset & Dunlap. *Dragonling* Series, Minstral Books. *Full House* Series published by Minstral Books. *Goliath* Series by Terrance Dicks, Barrons' *The Great Brain* Series by J. Fitzgerald, Bantam, Doubleday. *History Mysteries from American Girl,* Pleasant Company. *Little House on the Prairie* Series, by L. I. Wilder, Harper Collins. *Nate the Great* Series by Marjorie Weinman Sharmat, Dell Publishing. *The Shiloh* Series by P. R. Naylor, Dell/Yearling. *The Three Investigators* Series by R. Arthur, Random House. *Wild at Heart Vet* Series by L. H. Anderson, Pleasant Company. *The Young Merlin Trilogy* by Jane Yolan, Scholastic.
Middle school	*Animorphs* Series by K. A. Applegate, Scholastic. *Babysitter's Club* Series by Ann Martin, Scholastic. *Broadway Ballplayers* Series by M. Holohen, Broadway Ballplayer's Publishing Co. *Eerie Indiana* Series by J. Peel, Avon. *Get Real* Series by L. Ellerbee, Harper Collins. *Goose Bumps* Series by R. L. Stein, Scholastic. *Planet of the Apes* Series by J. Whitman, Harper Collins. *Remnants* Series by K.A. Applegate, Scholastic. *Sweet Valley Jr. High* Series by F. Pascal, Bantam Books. *The Royal Diaries* Series, Scholastic. *Thoroughbred* Series by J. Campbell, Harper Collins.

Figure 46.1 Suggested Materials for Free Volunteer Reading

Senior high school	*California Diaries* Series by A. Martin, Scholastic. *Cheerleaders* Series by R.L. Stine, Pocket Books. *Circle of Magic* Series by T. Pierce, Scholastic. *danger.com* Series by J. Cray, Aladdin. *Ever World* Series by K. A. Applegate, Scholastic. *Fearless* Series by F. Pascal, Pocket Books. *Harry Potter* Series by J.K. Rowling, Scholastic. *Pet Dragon* Trilogy by J. Yolen, Magic Carpet Books/Harcourt Brace. *Sally Lockhart* Trilogy by P. Pullman, Laurel Leaf Books. *Sevens* Series by S. Wallens, Puffin. *Star Wars* Series by J. Whitman, Bantam. *Sweep* Series by C. Tiernan, Puffin. *Sweet Valley High* Series by F. Pascal, Bantam Books. *X Files* Series published by Harper Collins.

Figure 46.1   Continued

STEP BY STEP

The steps in implementing free voluntary reading are:

• *Identifying the independent reading levels of students*—Identify the independent reading levels of the students in your class and gather a number of books at their levels. Organize the books in a way that identifies the reading levels and provides easy student access to the books. To identify other sources of easy reading materials for your students enlist the help of the school media specialist.

• *Explaining the program to the students*—Introduce the free voluntary reading program to the students, explaining that reading widely helps them learn new English vocabulary and improves their writing, spelling, and grammar—even when the reading they are doing is not difficult. Set up a system so they can check out books freely, taking them home to read or reading them during DEAR (Drop Everything and Read) time or free time in the classroom. Provide a celebration system so that the class is keeping track of the numbers of books being read by the class members. Arrange for celebrations as the class reads 100, 500, and 1,000 books. Focus on the number of books being read rather than the difficulty of the books chosen. The object is to get students reading more.

• *Discussing the books in groups*—Schedule informal literature discussions so the students can share their favorite books and talk about favorite authors. Use these discussions to provide positive feedback to the students who are reading a lot of books. Encourage wide reading by introducing new authors of easy reading books and giving book talks about new books as they are added to the classroom collection. Keep these introductions informal, for example, "This is a new book by Mary Grace. If you enjoyed her other books, you'll probably like this one. It's about an ice-skating competition."

• *Adding motivation over time*—Keep the momentum going by adding new celebrations during the year. Add such things as creating video commercials for favorite books, keeping track of the number of students who read a certain title to determine the class's favorite books, and scheduling guest appearances by favorite authors. Holding read-a-thons where students read for a given number of hours per night until they reach self-set goals (10 hours, 50 hours), and then presenting awards such as a 10-hour reader button or a 50-hour reader button add incentive as well.

• ***Assessing student progress***—Have students keep a log of the books they've read to help them see the progress they are making in the volume of reading they're doing. Some teachers have found that just adding a starting and completion date for each book in the reading log helps students see that their reading rate is increasing. Having the students keep a log of new words they're learning from the books they read has also been successful for some teachers. Taking notes and writing anecdotal records of the students' involvement in group discussions of books often reveals increased verbal communication and comprehension of reading material as well.

APPLICATIONS AND EXAMPLES

Ms. Gerrard's third-grade class shows little interest in leisure reading until she introduces free voluntary reading. Ms. Gerrard brings in a series of new paperback books to the class, reads the first book in the series aloud, and sets up a system for keeping track of the number of students who read each book. Students in the class are given a new composition book in which to record the titles of the books they are reading—in school and at home.

There is a tally sheet in the class library where students record tallies next to the books they are reading to keep track of the number of times each book is read by a student. One of the students is appointed class record keeper, and he keeps track of the reading being done each week in two ways. First he posts a list of the week's most popular books, and then he totals the number of books read by the entire class each week.

Ms. Gerrard provides time each day for free reading. At the end of the free reading period she encourages students to share comments about the books they are reading, such as an especially funny part or a reading recommendation. As the cumulative count of books read by class members mounts, Ms. Gerrard gives periodic celebrations. For the 100-book milestone, the class has a cookie party with chocolate chip cookies made and eaten in class. For the 500-book milestone, the students are given free time to sit under the playground trees and read for 30 minutes after lunch. Ms. Gerrard can see that her students are reading more.

Mr. Tibbs' eighth graders are enjoying the introductory day of their free voluntary reading program. Mr. Tibbs begins the program by bringing in a number of comic books to the class. At first, the students don't believe that they are being allowed to read comic books in school. Mr. Tibbs makes it clear that it doesn't matter what they read, reading improves reading. He shares his goal—for each student to read every day. On the second day of the program Mr. Tibbs brings in a collection of easy books that can be checked out for free reading at home and he also makes the comics available for checkout. The students are encouraged to keep a list of the books and comics they are reading. Mr. Tibbs posts a chart where the students place a sticker for each book they read beside the category of the book. The chart he uses is shown in Figure 46.2.

Because Mr. Tibbs realizes that the support of the parents is vital to the success of this new reading program, he prepares a notice for the parents so that they understand the purpose of the free voluntary reading program. He encourages their participation and their assistance in providing time to read, providing a quiet place to read, and encouraging the student to meet his/her reading goals. His parent notice is shown in Figure 46.3.

The eighth graders are a little wary of the intent of this new reading program but they like the reading materials that are available to them. Slowly they relax and enjoy their free reading. Mr. Tibbs gives them a free reading period every now and then as a reward for good work or to celebrate reading milestones, such as 200 books read by the class. The free reading done by the class is showing a steady growth each week.

Category	Place a sticker in a box for each book read.	TOTAL
Adventure		
Biography		
Comic books		
Folktale		
Horror		
Information		
Mystery		
Poetry		
Science fiction		
		Class Grand Total ___

Figure 46.2   The Books We've Read

CONCLUSION

Free voluntary reading is an important strategy in helping students develop a love for reading and a shared literary experience. There are a number of children's and young adult writers producing series of books that build on a common theme or familiar characters. These books are especially appropriate for free voluntary reading by English language learners because the sequels are set in familiar contexts. The authors of these series have created texts that are interesting to readers at certain age levels and yet easy to read and understand. In addition, a number of the classics have been rewritten in simplified language so that teachers can provide understandable versions of these books as class literature studies are conducted. See Figure 46.4 for a list of the classic titles available in this series. Although access to a large number of books is necessary for this strategy to be successful, a number of the book series are available in paperback at reasonable prices.

Dear Parents,

Your children may be bringing home some new reading material this week. We will be encouraging the students to read books—even comic books—to increase their reading enjoyment, fluency, and vocabulary. This program is called Free Voluntary Reading (FVR) and has been shown to benefit students in the following ways:

- It promotes reading comprehension.
- It supports vocabulary development.
- It supports writing, spelling and grammar knowledge.

We know that NOTHING HELPS READING LIKE MORE READING. You can help by:

- Providing time for your child to read each day.
- Providing a quiet place for reading.
- Talking to your child about the books being read.
- Modeling the enjoyment of reading yourself.

Thank you for your support!

Mr. Tibbs

Figure 46.3   Mr. Tibbs' Notice to Parents

EXAMPLES OF APPROXIMATION BEHAVIORS RELATED TO THE TESOL STANDARDS:

Pre-K–3 students will:

- read and discuss books read at the recreational reading level.
- relate events and characters in series books.

4–8 students will:

- express personal likes and opinions of books read for pleasure.
- read increasingly more difficult books for pleasure.

9–12 students will:

- use vocabulary gained from independent reading in speech and writing.
- support opinions about character motivation, by locating and sharing text that illustrates that viewpoint.

References

Hernandez, H. (1997). *Teaching in multicultural classrooms*. Upper Saddle River, NJ: Merrill/ Prentice Hall.

Krashen, S. (1993). *The power of reading*. Englewood, CO: Libraries Unlimited.

Published by Harper Collins: Each book in this series has sections that tell about the author, the book, the main characters, and the setting. The books also contain notes to aid comprehension and a complete glossary.

A Journey to the Center of the Earth
Don Quixote
Frankenstein
Ivanhoe
Joan of Arc
Oliver Twist
Romeo and Juliet
The Adventures of Robin Hood
The Adventures of Tom Sawyer
The Odyssey
The Red Badge of Courage
The Strange Case of Dr. Jekyll and Mr. Hyde

<u>*Puffin Classics published by Penguin Books*</u>

A Tale of Two Cities
Around the World in Eighty Days
Great Expectations
Journey to the Center of the Earth
Kidnapped
King Arthur and His Knights of the Round Table
Moonfleet
Myths of the Norsemen
Oliver Twist
Tales of Ancient Egypt
The Adventures of Robin Hood
The Call of the Wild
The Extraordinary Cases of Sherlock Holmes
The Great Adventures of Sherlock Holmes
The Hounds of the Baskervilles
The Lost World
The Luck of Try
The Red Badge of Courage
The Three Musketeers
Treasure Island
Twenty Thousand Leagues Under the Sea

Figure 46.4   Titles Available in the Wishbone Classics Series

REPETITION AND INNOVATION:

Getting to Deep Comprehension Through Multiple Interactions With a Book

This strategy addresses the following TESOL Standards:

Goal 2: To use English to achieve academically in all content areas

Standard 1: Students will use English to interact in the classroom.

Standard 2: Students will use English to obtain, process, construct, and provide subject matter information in spoken and written form.

Standard 3: Students will use appropriate learning strategies to construct and apply academic knowledge.

Repetition and innovation is the use of a piece of text in several different ways to reinforce the understanding of it and the gradual integration of the vocabulary and concepts into the speaking and writing vocabulary of the students (Tompkins, 1996). The text is introduced and explored in multiple modes with the students finally rewriting the text to create an innovation on the original. This approach is especially effective for English language learners because they have multiple opportunities to revisit both the text and the vocabulary in multiple learning modes. See Figure 47.1 for suggestions of innovations that can be used for this strategy.

STEP BY STEP

The steps in implementing repetition and innovation are:

• *Choosing a book that will sustain interest over time*—Choose a book that you and the students will enjoy reading a number of times. With repetition and innovation you will be revisiting the same text several times; the book should have some interesting vocabulary and action or it will become boring. A book with a pattern or obvious structure makes a good choice for this kind of activity. If necessary, have the book read in the students' first language(s) before reading it in English.

Format	Description
Pocket chart stories	Build stories using the pattern or structure from the focus book. A sentence frame is used with word cards and key vocabulary from the focus book.
Wall stories	The students retell the story and individual pages are written on large pieces of construction paper. The pages are hung from clothesline across the room or attached to the wall in sequence so the students can read the story using a pointer. When the wall story is taken down it is made into a class big book.
Shape books	A cover and pieces of paper are cut into the shape of an animal or object that corresponds to the topic of the writing. The innovation is written and published as a shape book.
Circular stories	A story that begins and ends in the same place is published in a circular shape (see Figure 47.2).
Three-part books	Stories that have a distinct beginning, middle, and end are published in a three-part book format (see Figure 47.2).
Story quilts	Stories are written on individual pieces of paper which are decorated as quilt squares and tied together with yarn (see Figure 47.2).
Formula poems	Students publish poems in different formats. (See Figure 20.3 in Chapter 20, Learning Centers, for additional suggestions.)
Videos	Students write scripts as innovations on their focus book and the enactments of the scripts are videotaped.
Puppet plays	Students write scripts as innovations and the scripts are performed as puppet plays.

Figure 47.1 Suggestions for Innovations

• ***Exploring the story structure***—Explore the structure of the story. If it is a circular story focus on the fact that one thing leads to another and stress that as you read. If the story has a beginning, middle, and end, emphasize that as the book is read. Try to help the students understand the structure and the relationship of the events to the structure.

• ***Playing with words***—Explore the pattern or structure of the book by having the students do some substitution of words using word cards in a pocket chart. Have them change words within the pattern or structure of the book until they can substitute words and make meaningful patterns on their own.

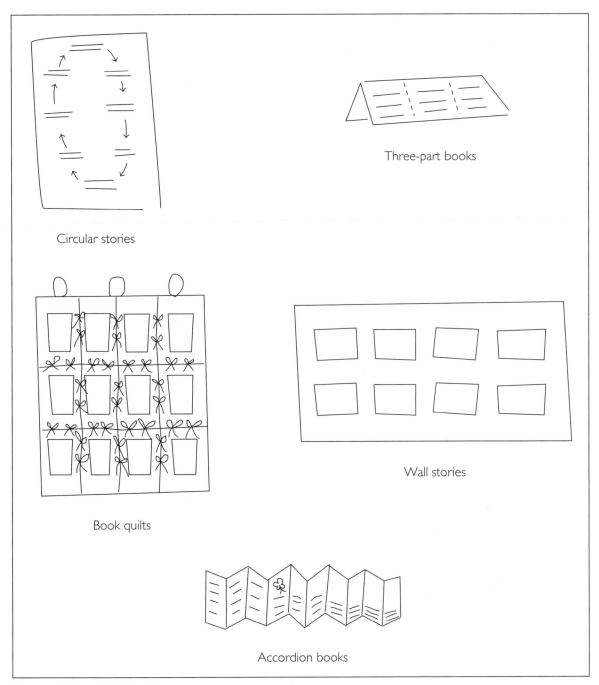

Figure 47.2 Publishing Formats

- ***Creating an alternate text***—Using the pattern that you and the students have practiced on the pocket chart, have students write and illustrate a sentence on a single sheet of paper and then sequence the pages to make a class book. Read the book together, practicing the vocabulary and the pattern orally.

- ***Creating an innovation on the text***—Depending on the structure of the book, write an innovation such as a circular chart (for circular stories); a three-part book for beginning, middle, and end stories; or an accordion book for cumulative stories. (See Figure 47.2 for illustrations of these book forms.) Involve the children in supplying the key vocabulary for the innovation either by doing the writing interactively (see Chapter 38, Interactive Writing), or by taking their dictation.

• ***Creating another innovation or version***—Create another innovation or new version of the same book in another format using the same pattern or structure. This time you could create a wall story using large sheets of construction paper, or a story quilt with individual pages of the book tied together with yarn to form a large quilt. (See Figure 47.2 for illustrations of these publishing formats.) By this time the students should be thoroughly familiar with the pattern, structure, and vocabulary.

• ***Assessing student progress and understanding***—Set up a learning center with materials for the students to create new versions of the story pattern you've introduced. As they complete new innovations or versions, you can evaluate their understanding of the story structure being studied as well as their ability to use a story pattern to create their own books.

APPLICATIONS AND EXAMPLES

Ms. Leonard's first graders are sitting quietly, listening to *If You Give a Mouse a Cookie* (Numeroff, 1985) read in Hmong by the bilingual aide. They watch the pictures carefully and answer questions in Hmong about what the mouse might want next.

After they hear the story in their home language, Ms. Leonard helps them construct a chart of the sequence of things the mouse wanted using realia she brought from home. Ms. Leonard uses this time to review the English names for the household items—straw, scissors, broom, tape, etc. That day at the learning centers, the students sequence the pictures from the book and match the pictures to the real items as one of their activities.

Ms. Leonard has also provided drawings of the household items on Language Master cards for the students. They can practice sequencing the cards so they are in the same order as the story and they get to hear the English words as they slide the cards through the Language Master.

The next day Ms. Leonard uses the pocket chart to display the sentence frame, "If you give a(n) *(animal)* a *(noun)*, he will want a *(noun)*." Using the words from *If You Give a Mouse a Cookie,* the students build sentences by adding word cards to the sentence frame. Ms. Leonard and the students read the sentences aloud after they are built. At the end of the lesson Ms. Leonard and each of the students write their favorite sentence interactively on a sheet of paper and the students illustrate their sentences.

The third day, Ms. Leonard starts the morning showing the students the book she put together from the sentences and illustrations they made the day before. They read the class book together and the students smile broadly when their pages are read. Ms. Leonard then shows them a large sheet of butcher paper on which she has drawn the mouse from the story with blank lines in a circle all around him.

"We are going to try to remember all the things the mouse wanted in the story and write the words on the blanks," Ms. Leonard says. "Do you think you can do that?"

"Yes!" the students declare confidently.

Ms. Leonard has one student at a time help her to write the words in the correct sequence on the blank lines. They have no problem remembering the sequence, the English words, and in most cases the spelling of the English words.

The final innovation on this story is started that day with the students writing about another demanding animal. They decide to write about a pig and all the things he wanted, starting with some mud—and ending with some mud. They are very excited when Ms. Leonard tells them that Laura Numeroff, the author *If You Give a Mouse a Cookie,* has also written a book about a pig called *If You Give a Pig a Pancake* (1998). Ms. Leonard then reads the book to the students.

The word wall in Ms. Avelar's fourth grade is covered with words they have learned in their literature studies during the past few months. The students often use the word wall to find a word to make the stories they write more interesting. Ms. Avelar is planning an in-depth study of the parts of speech with the students based on Ruth Heller's series of books, each of which focuses on a part of speech in an innovative way.

Ms. Avelar begins the study with the reading of *A Cache of Jewels and Other Collective Nouns* by Ruth Heller (1987), which focuses on nouns. The students join Ms. Avelar in finding all the nouns on the word wall and they review the meanings of the nouns as they move the word cards from the word wall to the pocket chart.

As the students arrange the nouns on the pocket chart Ms. Avelar asks, "How can we arrange the words so that we will be able to find them easily?"

"In alphabetical order!" the students answer in chorus.

"Of course. That's the easiest way to find them. But suppose I want you to do something different with the words this week?" Mrs. Avelar asks. "Suppose I want you to make different groups of nouns. One group would be nouns with only one syllable. The next group would be nouns with two syllables. The next with three syllables. Could you do that?"

"Of course we can," the students say.

"You can still put them in alphabetical order within each group," Ms. Avelar adds. "Then you will be able to find them more easily."

Once the students have completed the sorting of the nouns into syllable groups, Ms. Avelar says, "Let's just look at the two-syllable nouns that we have found." She reads down the list: *apple, auto, baby, bottle, butcher, candle, candy,* and so on.

"Let's see if we can think of some more two-syllable nouns for our list. We will want to have a nice variety of them for the project we are going to do this week."

The students add *taco, pizza, sneakers, jacket, pumpkin,* and *catsup* to this list.

"Now I want you each to take one of these little booklets and write one of the two-syllable nouns at the top of each page. After lunch we will work on a new category of words," Ms. Avelar says as she passes out booklets to each of the students.

After lunch Ms. Avelar reads the Ruth Heller book on adjectives, *Many Luscious Lollipops* (1989). After practicing as one group, the students work in cooperative groups, adding a list of adjectives to each noun in their booklets. They are able to add some unusual adjectives working in the group setting. Some of the students have asked Ms. Avelar if they can prepare a second booklet in Spanish and she has given them permission to do that. Several of the students who have asked permission to prepare the Spanish booklets are not native Spanish speakers and this pleases Ms. Avelar.

On the third day of the project, Ms. Avelar introduces verbs and the students practice the actions of the verbs they find on the word wall. Ms. Avelar reads *Kites Fly High* (1988), Ruth Heller's book about verbs, and the class brainstorms additional verbs to add to the word wall.

"I now have a hard job for you," Ms. Avelar says. "I want you to think of verbs for each of the nouns in your word booklets. For instance, the first noun in your booklet is *apple*. What can an apple do?"

"That's really hard, Ms. Avelar," Tino says. "An apple just sits there."

"That's good, Tino. Write *sits,*" Ms. Avelar says, smiling.

"Oh! I get it," Tino says with a grin.

After the students work in cooperative groups to write verbs for each of their nouns, Ms. Avelar introduces them to the pyramid poetry format. "We are now going to use the words we have been collecting into a poem that looks like a pyramid," she says. "The title of the poem is a noun. Let's pick one of our nouns to use as an example."

"Pizza!" Gretchen says.

"Good one," Ms. Avelar confirms, and she writes *pizza* on the chalkboard. "Now we need two words that describe the word pizza."

"Hot and spicy," Tomas says as he licks his lips.

"Great!" Ms. Avelar says as she adds the line to the poem. "The next line has three words and uses verbs that tell about what the noun does. This is a hard one."

"The students all turn to the page in their booklets with the word *pizza* at the top and start reading action words.

"I've got it!" Nikki says, beaming. "Steaming, bubbling, tempting."

"That's good," Ms. Avelar says as she adds the line to the poem. "So far we have:

Pizza

Hot, spicy.

Steaming, bubbling, tempting.

"Now we need a complete, five- or six-word sentence about pizza," Ms. Avelar says.

"How about, 'I like pepperoni, mushrooms, and cheese'?" Tyrone suggests.

"That sounds great," Ms. Avelar says as she adds the line to the poem. "Now we need one more complete sentence using six to 10 words about the pizza."

"Oh, I know!" Nikki suggests. "Let's call Pizza Hut on the telephone right now!"

"That's it," Ms. Avelar says and she writes Nikki's sentence on the board under the other lines. "Let's read our poem." The whole class reads together.

Pizza

Hot, spicy.

Steaming, bubbling, tempting.

I like pepperoni, mushrooms, and cheese.

Let's call Pizza Hut on the telephone right now!

"Can you guess why it's called a pyramid poem?" Ms. Avelar asks.

"It looks like a pyramid," Tyrone responds.

"That's true," says Ms. Avelar. "That's why you have some lines with four or five words and some with six to 10 words. You choose the number of words you need to make each line a little longer than the one before it. It has to form a pyramid shape. Now, you know what I want you to do next." Ms. Avelar smiles.

"Write poems!" the class shouts.

"Yes, I want you to write pyramid poems" Ms. Avelar says. "You may write by yourself or with a partner. You may write in English or in Spanish. You may write with paper and pencil or on the computer. Use the word booklets to help you. Does anyone need a partner?"

The students move close to their partners and some go to the computers to write. Several students go to tables away from the others to write by themselves, but everyone is busily engaged in writing poems using their word booklets.

CONCLUSION

Repetition and innovation strategies provide students with multiple opportunities to learn new concepts. The choice of repetitions and innovations should be based on observation of the students' understanding of the concepts being presented. Each repetition or innovation should build on the last so that the students are experiencing gradually more difficult applications of the concepts. These activities are especially supportive of English language learners because they see multiple definitions and uses of the new concepts and vocabulary they are using.

EXAMPLES OF APPROXIMATION BEHAVIORS RELATED TO THE TESOL STANDARDS:

Pre-K–3 students will:

- illustrate the main events in the story.
- write an alternate ending to a familiar story.

4–8 students will:

- write a sequel for a familiar story.
- write a formula poem based on a familiar story.

9–12 students will:

- write a new version of a familiar plot.
- rewrite a story from an alternate point of view.

References

Heller, R. (1987). *A cache of jewels and other collective nouns.* New York: Grosset and Dunlap.

Heller, R. (1988). *Kites fly high.* New York: Grosset and Dunlap.

Heller, R. (1989). *Many luscious lollipops.* New York: Grosset and Dunlap.

Numeroff, L. (1985). *If you give a mouse a cookie.* New York: Macmillan/McGraw-Hill.

Numeroff, L. (1998). *If you give a pig a pancake.* New York: Macmillan/McGraw-Hill.

Tompkins, G. E. (1996). *Language arts content and teaching strategies.* Upper Saddle River, NJ: Macmillan/Prentice Hall.

GIST:
Exploring Tough Text

48

> This strategy addresses the following TESOL Standards:
>
> **Goal 2: To use English to achieve academically in all content areas**
>
> Standard 1: Students will use English to interact in the classroom.
> Standard 2: Students will use English to obtain, process, construct, and provide subject matter information in spoken and written form.
> Standard 3: Students will use appropriate learning strategies to construct and apply academic knowledge.
>
> **Goal 3: To use English in socially and culturally appropriate ways**
>
> Standard 1: Students will use the appropriate language variety, register, and genre according to audience, purpose, and setting.
> Standard 3: Students will use appropriate learning strategies to extend their sociolinguistic and cultural competence.

GIST or **Generating Interaction between Schemata and Text** (Cunningham, 1982) is a strategy for supporting comprehension of informational text. GIST is especially helpful when students are required to read long texts containing a significant amount of new information. Students work in cooperative groups and read sections of the text silently. After each short section is read silently, the members of the group work collaboratively to generate one sentence that summarizes the "gist" of the passage. In some very dense text, this summary sentence is generated paragraph by paragraph. Once a sentence is generated, members of the group write it on their own papers so that each group member ends up with a concise summary of the text. The teacher circulates among the groups to facilitate and provide support. This is a particularly effective strategy for use with English language learners because the group members have a chance to discuss and clarify meaning as they decide on the best summary sentence for the section or paragraph.

STEP BY STEP

The steps in implementing GIST are:

- *Identifying appropriate text for GIST*—Identify text that may cause some difficulty for the students. Decide whether the text must be read and summarized paragraph by paragraph or section by section and determine logical stopping or summarizing points.

- *Grouping the students*—Divide the class into cooperative groups and identify a leader for each group. Make sure that each group contains a strong English speaker and reader. If possible, group English language learners with other students of the same language background who can provide first-language support if needed. If your main purpose is to facilitate understanding of the text, the discussion of the meaning and the negotiation of the best summary sentence can be done in the students' first languages and later translated to English. If your purpose is facilitating English communication, then the discussion should take place in English with first language translations made only for the purpose of clarification.

- *Demonstrating the strategy*—Demonstrate the strategy by discussing background knowledge and informing the students that they will be working in groups to create a summary of the material to be read. Post the summary points, the points in the reading at which each group is to stop, then discuss and summarize. See Figure 48.1 for an example of a summary point chart. Instruct the students to read the passage silently to the first summary point and then stop and write a one-sentence summary of what they read.

- *Discussing summary sentences*—After the students have completed their summary sentence, ask one of the students to share his/hers with the class. Discuss the sentence as a group and add details that the class thinks will enhance the sentence. Instruct the students to write the summary sentence on their papers. The teacher serves as facilitator and quality controller, making sure that the summary sentences capture the "gist" of the paragraphs. It is important that the quality control be done in a supportive manner through questioning and supporting of the students' understanding of the text.

- *Reading and summarizing paragraph-by-paragraph*—Explain to the class that they will be reading the entire selection in this manner. They will all read to each summary point, as indicated by the chart that is posted. As they wait for the rest of their group to finish reading they should be thinking of the main points in the section and formulating a summary sentence in their minds, or writing it on a scrap piece of paper. The group should then discuss the section and negotiate the best summary sentence they can write. Once the group has decided on a summary sentence, each member of the group writes the sentence on his/her own paper and the process begins again.

- *Reading and comparing summary sentences*—Once the selection has been completed, have the groups read and compare their summary sentences. This provides an effective review of the passage read and gives an opportunity to correct any misconceptions. Again, the teacher serves as facilitator and questions the students to lead them to capture the meaning and nuance of the text.

- *Assessing student progress and understanding*—The group work time in this strategy is a perfect opportunity for the teacher to circulate around the room and listen. This is a good time to

Stop and summarize at these points:
1. Page 3, at the subheading
2. Page 7, at the bottom of the page
3. Page 9, after the chart
4. Page 13, at the subheading
5. Page 18, at the end of the selection

Figure 48.1   Sample of a Summary Point Chart

GROUP	Marcos	Juan	Diana	Carol	Carlos
Listens to others					
Contributes to summary					
Defends own ideas					
Participates verbally					
Takes leadership role					
Presents to class					

Figure 48.2   A Checklist for Documenting Student Interactions and Contributions During GIST Activity

take anecdotal records, documenting student interactions and writing language samples for inclusion in the student portfolios. It is appropriate to create checklists for documenting specific behaviors exhibited by the students at this time, also. See Figure 48.2 for an example of such a checklist.

APPLICATIONS AND EXAMPLES

The fifth graders in Ms. Menashian's class have been studying the American Revolution. They have read the Jean Fritz biographies of the great men and women who lived at the time of the revolution and the contributions they made. Ms. Menashian wants to conclude the unit of study with the reading of Longfellow's poem *The Midnight Ride of Paul Revere*. However, she wants her students to understand the significance of the poem, so she assigns the chapter "A Centennial Celebration" in Augusta Stevenson's biography *Paul Revere* (1986).

Ms. Menashian divides the fifth graders into cooperative groups to read and summarize the chapter. Because her class has a number of English language learners, Ms. Menashian makes sure that each group has a strong reader and several students in each group who speak the same home language. She posts a chart of summary points and the students begin reading and summarizing the selection. As she moves among the groups she hears some interesting discussion.

"I don't understand this chapter. It says it was 1875," Andre says. "That's a hundred years after Paul Revere's ride."

"I think that's why it's called a centennial celebration. That's a celebration after a hundred years," Juanita says. "I think this chapter is going to talk about how they were still celebrating his ride after a hundred years."

"Oh, I get it," Andre says. "What should we write for our summary sentence?"

"How about this?" Tyra asks. "A hundred years after the famous midnight ride of Paul Revere, the people of Boston were still talking about how brave he was."

"That's good," Margaret says, "but it also said that they were proud of him because of his silverwork too."

"But they were more proud of his patriotism," Juanita says.

"What is patriotism?" Mario asks.

"It's being loyal to your country," Juanita answers. "He risked his life to warn the soldiers that the British soldiers were coming." Juanita says this in English and then repeats the explanation in Spanish.

"OK," Mario says. "So the people of Boston are proud of Paul Revere because he was a great silversmith but more because he was a great patriot."

"That's a good summary sentence," Andre says. "Let's use that one. Say it again, Mario."

As Mario repeats the sentence everyone writes it on their papers, including Mario. The group then reads the next section of the chapter.

When they have completed reading and discussing the chapter, their summary looks like this:

The people of Boston are proud of Paul Revere because he was a great silversmith but more because he was a great patriot.

On April 18, 1775, eight hundred British soldiers were going to Concord to seize the patriot ammunition and guns.

Patriot troops had to be warned that the British soldiers were coming so they could move the powder and guns.

John Hancock and Samuel Adams also needed to be told to leave Lexington before they were arrested and hanged for speaking against the king.

The patriots chose Paul Revere to make the ride to warn the troops that the British were coming.

It was a very dangerous ride because British soldiers and warships were guarding the whole area.

Lanterns in the Old North Church belfry would tell Paul Revere how the British soldiers had gone. There would be two lanterns if they had gone by water, one lantern if they had gone by land.

Paul Revere went to the sexton of the Old North Church and told him to put the lanterns in the church belfry when he knew how the soldiers were coming. Then Paul Revere rowed across the river.

Patriots across the river waited with Paul Revere while they watched for the lanterns.

Paul Revere stopped at all the houses between Boston and Lexington and warned everyone that the British were coming.

The Patriots all grabbed their guns and kept the British from getting to the guns. They also gave John Hancock and Samuel Adams time to escape.

Ms. Menashian was very pleased with the summaries the students wrote about the ride of Paul Revere and about the discussion of the importance of the ride that took place as the groups shared their summaries. As she concluded the study of the Revolution with the reading of the poem, *The Midnight Ride of Paul Revere* (Stevenson, 1986), she was sure that the students really understood the words and the significance of the event to American history.

Some of the reading in Ms. Hughes's 11th-grade literature class is extremely difficult for her students to understand. Although she is sure that her students will enjoy the reading of Mark Twain's most famous works, she is concerned that they will not understand the political significance of his work and its place in history. Because of the difficulty of some of the vocabulary in the biographic readings about Mark Twain, Ms. Hughes decides to encourage her students to work in cooperative groups. Being in groups allows them to discuss the vocabulary, to consider the politics involved at that particular time in history, and to comprehend the nuances in meaning that they might otherwise miss.

Ms. Hughes groups her students for the reading of Bernard de Voto's introductory chapter in *The Portable Mark Twain* (1984). She posts a chart that tells the groups to stop and summarize after each paragraph they read and she walks the class through the steps in the GIST procedure. She explains the double meanings of the term *gist* and the procedure name, which connects schemata and text.

"Who knows what it means to 'get the gist of things'?" Ms. Hughes asks.

"It means that you get the general idea," Leon answers.

"That's right, Leon," Ms. Hughes responds. "And today we're going to learn a new strategy for studying that is also called GIST, G-I-S-T, which stands for Generating Interaction between Schemata and Text," Ms. Hughes says as she writes the words on the chalkboard and underlines the letters that create the acronym GIST.

"Using this strategy is supposed to *generate* or cause something to happen. What is supposed to happen is *interaction,* or some action between some things. The interaction is supposed to happen between your *schemata,* or your past experiences that have been filed in your brain, and *text,* which is what you will be reading.

"This interaction, or the comparing and contrasting of your background of knowledge and the text you are reading, will help you to understand what you are reading. You and the rest of your group will work together to figure out what the reading means. Because this introductory chapter is what I call 'tough text,' difficult to read and understand, I want you to stop after each paragraph and discuss the meaning. Your group will write one sentence to summarize each paragraph. When you are finished reading the introductory chapter and writing the summary sentences you should have a good understanding of Mark Twain and his place in American history. We will talk about the chapter after you have completed the reading."

As the groups work their way through the chapter, Ms. Hughes circulates among the groups and occasionally gets drawn into the discussion. Because there are a number of difficult words in the reading, she also gathers words from the groups to add to the word wall. First-language translations for the new vocabulary are added to the word wall as necessary.

At the end of the period, Ms. Hughes asks the groups to share their summaries and they choose the best sentence for each paragraph to create a class summary of the chapter. It reads:

The first truly American literature grew out of the early republic and includes such writers as Emerson, Poe, Thoreau, and Melville.

There were strands of literature and culture that clashed as influences from the South, New England, Louisiana, and the expansion West began to drift together.

A heartland culture, or midcontinental culture, began to emerge and it seemed to be pulling away from the traditional influences of Europe.

Abraham Lincoln was an important advocate of this emerging American heartland culture.

Lincoln's approach to America as an entirely new entity seems to come across loudly as a change from the tidewater republic of the new nation to the continental empire that will be the future.

Walt Whitman expressed his feeling for this emerging nation and its budding literature as "this continental inland west not yet speaking for the people or making images for their spirit."

Actually Whitman was wrong because 10 years prior to this statement, in 1869, a book of humorous travel sketches written by Samuel Langhorne Clemens had been written and signed with the author's pen name, Mark Twain.

Innocents Abroad, Mark Twain's travel sketches book, was an instant success partly because of its obvious disdain for European society.

Because of the nature of this first book, Mark Twain struggled for two generations to overcome literary critics' opinion of him as a clown.

Mark Twain was referred to as "the Lincoln of our literature" because of the many similarities between Lincoln and Twain in their upbringing and humor.

After the groups have read and summarized the introduction to the Mark Twain volume, Ms. Hughes asks the students to think about what they had learned and give an overall summary of the history of the time in which Twain wrote.

"I think the feeling I got was that the new nation had finally gotten past copying things from Europe and was starting to produce humorists and historians who valued America as a new country with a different kind of personality," Monica says.

"Exactly," Ms. Hughes agrees. "Although the writers of the early republic are outstanding and made contributions to literature, they are more like the European writers. Mark Twain is a new kind of voice, a more rustic, more American voice."

"But the literary critics didn't take him seriously," Alberto adds.

"But that happens a lot, doesn't it?" Martina asks.

"I think that happens whenever writers or artists move too far away from the traditional approaches," Ms. Hughes agrees.

After the discussion of the introduction, Ms. Hughes assigns the students the first reading in the Mark Twain anthology and they discuss some vocabulary and background that they will need in order to understand the reading, *The Notorious Jumping Frog of Calaveras County.*

CONCLUSION

Students of all ages benefit from the use of collaborative strategies such as GIST. By placing students in heterogeneous groups, with a strong English reader and writer in each group, teachers can encourage discussion of the reading and give students a chance to clarify meaning and vocabulary. The group task of writing a summary sentence for each paragraph that is read provides an authentic assignment that requires the students to discuss the meaning of the paragraph and agree on a sentence that conveys the important information. Once the paragraphs are read and discussed and summary sentences are written and read, each student in the group has a concise summary of the reading assignment.

When several groups read and summarize the same text and then share their summaries, further discussion of the main ideas and supporting details frequently follows. This gives students another chance to hear the information discussed and new vocabulary clarified.

EXAMPLES OF APPROXIMATION BEHAVIORS RELATED TO THE TESOL STANDARDS:

Pre-K–3 students will:

- collaboratively write a summary of a paragraph.
- support their opinions in a group setting.

4–8 students will:

- identify main ideas in text.
- write summary sentences of paragraphs.

9–12 students will:

- discuss nuances of word meanings and negotiate with peers to accurately summarize bodies of text.
- explore specific word meanings related to content in the collaborative summarization of text.

References

Cunningham, J. (1982). Generating interactions between schemata and text. In J. A. Niles & L. A. Harris (Eds.), *New inquiries in reading research and instruction* (pp. 42–47). Washington, DC: National Reading Conference.

Voto, B. (Ed.) (1984). *The portable Mark Twain.* New York: Penguin Books.

Fritz, J. (1973). *And then what happened, Paul Revere?* New York: G. P. Putnam.

Fritz, J. (1974). *Why don't you get a horse, Sam Adams?* New York: G. P. Putnam.

Fritz, J. (1975). *Where was Patrick Henry on the 29th of May?* New York: G. P. Putnam.

Fritz, J. (1975). *Who's that stepping on Plymouth Rock?* New York: G. P. Putnam.

Fritz, J. (1977). *Can't you make them behave, King George?* New York: G. P. Putnam.

Fritz, J. (1987). *Shh! We're writing the Constitution.* New York: G. P. Putnam.

Stevenson, A. (1986). *Paul Revere: Boston patriot.* New York: Aladdin (Macmillan).

SYNTAX SURGERY:
Visually Manipulating English Grammar

This strategy addresses the following TESOL Standards:

Goal 1: To use English to communicate in social settings

Standard 1: Students will use English to participate in social interactions.
Standard 2: Students will interact in, through, and with spoken and written English for personal expression and enjoyment.
Standard 3: Students will use learning strategies to extend their communicative competence.

Goal 2: To use English to achieve academically in all content areas

Standard 1: Students will use English to interact in the classroom.
Standard 2: Students will use English to obtain, process, construct, and provide subject matter information in spoken and written form.
Standard 3: Students will use appropriate learning strategies to construct and apply academic knowledge.

Goal 3: To use English in socially and culturally appropriate ways

Standard 1: Students will use the appropriate language variety, register, and genre according to audience, purpose, and setting.
Standard 3: Students will use appropriate learning strategies to extend their sociolinguistic and cultural competence.

Syntax surgery (Herrell, 1998) is a strategy that allows students to see the relationship of elements within a sentence that may be confusing to understand. Because English syntax often differs from the word order found in students' home languages, English language learners sometimes encounter difficulty in comprehending sentences they read or confuse word order when speaking or writing in English (Baltra, 1998).

Syntax surgery involves writing a sentence on a sentence strip and then cutting the sentence apart to rearrange it into more understandable pieces. Because the students actually witness the pieces of the sentence being moved, they are more likely to understand and remember the English syntax rules when called on to use them in the future. Syntax surgery is also helpful in refining the students' understanding of the elements of writing and speaking that make their English difficult for others to understand; therefore, the use of this strategy helps them to be more confident in their use of English. Swain (1993) calls this refining of the spoken and written product vital to the development of fluency in her description of output theory.

STEP BY STEP

The steps in implementing syntax surgery are:

- ***Identifying a problematic sentence***—Identify a sentence that is causing difficulty. It may be a sentence that the student has spoken where the home language word order conflicts with the English word order, or it may be a complex sentence encountered in reading that is causing confusion.

- ***Writing the sentence***—Write the sentence on a sentence strip and reread the sentence aloud with the student or students involved in the speaking or reading activity. For example, if the sentence that was written by the student says, "She was wearing a sweater green," take a pair of scissors and cut the sentence apart in the place or places of difficulty. "She was wearing a sweater green," would be cut before the words *sweater* and *green.*

- ***Rearranging the words***—Rearrange the words in a pocket chart or on the chalk rail in the correct English sequence. Place "She was wearing a green sweater" on the chart and say, "This is the way we say it in English," reading the sentence with the correct English word order. Reaffirm the students' knowledge of the home language by rebuilding the sentence in the original order and say, "This would be the right order of the words in Spanish" (or other language) "but we say it this way in English," and put the words back into the correct order for English. Have the student read the corrected sentence along with you and then explain the difference in the word order as simply as you can.

- ***Practicing more sentences with the same pattern***—Write a few more sentences with the same word pattern on sentence strips and have the students read them along with you for additional practice.

- ***Timing the lessons***—Be careful not to use this lesson in a way that interrupts communication with the student. If the message the student was conveying was clear, respond to it modeling the correct English syntax. Write the student's sentence down and return at a later time to use the syntax surgery strategy to support the refinement of the student's English. Be observant of other students who might benefit from the explanation and use the opportunity to give instruction to several students at a time.

APPLICATIONS AND EXAMPLES

Ms. Newsome's fifth graders are reading a series of books by Beverly Cleary when one of her English language learners comes to her with a puzzled look on his face. "Ms. Newsome, this sentence doesn't make any sense."

"Let me see, Jorges," Ms. Newsome says. She reads the sentence aloud, " 'She pushed her bed out from the wall so that something reaching out from under the curtains or slithering around the wall might not find her.' I see what you mean," Ms. Newsome says. "Let's see if we can figure it out. Let's write the sentence on a sentence strip." As she writes the sentence on a sentence strip she reads it aloud with Jorges.

"OK, the first part of the sentence says, 'She pushed her bed out from the wall,' " Ms. Newsome says. "Do you understand what 'out from the wall' means?"

Jorges nods, "It means she moved the bed away from the wall."

"Exactly!" Ms. Newsome exclaims and she cuts that part of the sentence away from the rest of it.

"The next part says 'so that,' which means that the next part is going to tell us WHY she moved the bed," Ms. Newsome says as she cuts off the words *so that.*

"Here's where it gets tricky," Ms. Newsome explains. " 'Something reaching out from under the curtains or slithering around the wall.' Now did the story say anything about something behind the curtains or on the wall?"

Jorges shakes his head, "No. That's why I'm confused."

"The key is the next word, *might*," Ms. Newsome says. "She's thinking there *might* be something behind the curtains or there *might* be something slithering around the wall. She's scared of things that *might* be in her room."

"Oh," Jorges says. "Now I get it." He takes the scissors and cuts *might* and then *not find her* away from the rest of the sentence. He arranges the sentence again to show the relationships among the clauses. "This makes sense," he says as he looks at the new arrangement.

"The words *something* and *might* are important. They give you clues that this is all in her imagination," Ms. Newsome says as she underlines the two words. "You're really good at this, Jorges," Ms. Newsome says with a smile. See Figure 49.1 to see how Jorges arranged the sentence.

Mr. Reynolds teaches 10th-grade English in a high school with a large number of Hispanic students. Mr. Reynolds finds that his students enjoy literature but need a lot of support in understanding some of the more formal language in the classic tales they read.

While in the midst of a study of Arthurian legends, Mr. Reynolds shows a video of *King Arthur and His World* and then shares a beautifully illustrated children's story book, *Young Lancelot*, by Robert D. San Souci (1996) to give the students a feel for the history, culture, and language of the times. The students then read *The Lady of the Lake* and *Excalibur* by Sir Thomas Malory, translated by Keith Baines (1996), which is a part of their literary anthology. The students are reading the tale, taking individual parts and trying their best to read with expression so the story will be as exciting as Mr. Reynolds's reading of *Young Lancelot*.

The language is difficult, however, and they often have to stop and discuss the meaning. Mr. Reynolds has used syntax surgery with his students on several occasions and decides to do it in a shortened version during the reading to move the process along so the meaning of the passage doesn't get lost in the analysis. As the students read aloud, Mr. Reynolds writes sections of a sentence on the chalkboard whenever the reading appears to be choppy or without expression. As Mr. Reynolds writes the phrases or sentences on the board he separates the elements of the sentences that cause difficulty. For example, as a student reads:

> Riding once more through the forest, Sir Lancelot came upon a black brachet, eagerly pursuing a trail. Sir Lancelot followed and soon noticed traces of blood. The brachet

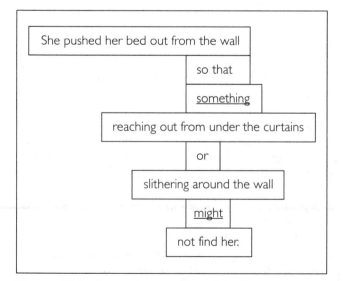

Figure 49.1 Jorges' Arrangement of the Sentence

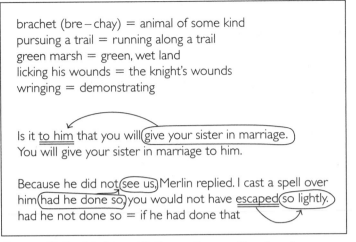

brachet (bre – chay) = animal of some kind
pursuing a trail = running along a trail
green marsh = green, wet land
licking his wounds = the knight's wounds
wringing = demonstrating

Is it to him that you will give your sister in marriage.
You will give your sister in marriage to him.

Because he did not see us, Merlin replied. I cast a spell over
him had he done so, you would not have escaped so lightly.
had he not done so = if he had done that

Figure 49.2 Mr. Reynold's Syntax Surgery Shorthand

kept glancing over its shoulder as if to insure that Sir Lancelot was still there, and finally came to an ancient castle which had been built on a green marsh. The brachet led the way across a shaky bridge and into the hall. A dead knight lay on the floor. The brachet went up to him and started licking his wounds, and then a lady appeared, haggard with grief and wringing her hands. (p. 131)

As the reader is reading this section Mr. Reynolds is writing brief notes on the board. See Figure 49.2 for Mr. Reynolds's notes to the readers. The student watches Mr. Reynolds and rereads the problem sentence using the clues Mr. Reynolds writes. The reading of the Malory tale goes smoothly using this strategy and the students don't lose the meaning in the process.

CONCLUSION

Syntax surgery is a strategy for making English syntax visible to the students. By using written diagrams as Mr. Reynolds does or cutting sentences apart as Ms. Newsome does, the students can both see and hear the differences in the word order in English or separate the thoughts within a complex sentence. By using several avenues to reinforce the English syntax, the students' understanding and memory are supported.

EXAMPLES OF APPROXIMATION BEHAVIORS RELATED TO THE TESOL STANDARDS:

Pre-K–3 students will:

- arrange word cards to create an English sentence.
- add descriptive words to sentences in appropriate places.

4–8 students will:

- expand sentences to include a sequence of adjectives or adverbs in appropriate places within the sentences.
- revise sentences to improve comprehensibility and flow.

9–12 students will:

- visually represent connections between clauses in complex sentences.
- combine sentences with a variety of appropriate connectives.

References

Baines, K. (1996). *Malory's Le Morte d'Arthur*. New York: Penguin Books.

Baltra, A. (1998). *Hispanic ESL students reading in English: The language problem*. Unpublished manuscript. Fresno: California State University, Fresno.

Herrell, A. (1998). *Strategies for supporting English language learners as readers*. Manuscript submitted for publication.

San Souci, R. D. (1996). *Young Lancelot*. New York: Doubleday.

Swain, M. (1993). The output hypothesis: Just speaking and writing aren't enough. *The Canadian Modern Language Review, 50,* 158–164.

MULTIPLE INTELLIGENCES STRATEGIES:

Teaching and Testing to Student-Preferred Learning Modes

50

This strategy addresses the following TESOL Standards:

Goal 1: To use English to communicate in social settings

Standard 1: Students will use English to participate in social interactions.
Standard 2: Students will interact in, through, and with spoken and written English for personal expression and enjoyment.
Standard 3: Students will use learning strategies to extend their communicative competence.

Goal 2: To use English to achieve academically in all content areas

Standard 1: Students will use English to interact in the classroom.
Standard 2: Students will use English to obtain, process, construct, and provide subject matter information in spoken and written form.
Standard 3: Students will use appropriate learning strategies to construct and apply academic knowledge.

Goal 3: To use English in socially and culturally appropriate ways

Standard 1: Students will use the appropriate language variety, register, and genre according to audience, purpose, and setting.
Standard 2: Students will use nonverbal communication appropriate to audience, purpose, and setting.
Standard 3: Students will use appropriate learning strategies to extend their sociolinguistic and cultural competence.

Multiple intelligences (Gardner, 1993) are the ways people are smart—the modes in which they process information effectively. While traditionally teachers have taught only two intelligences in the school setting (linguistic and logical/mathematical) there have been at least five additional intelligences well researched and documented, and others are currently being documented. Although all people possess all intelligences at varying levels, it is helpful for teachers to present content material through a variety of intelligences to make the information comprehensible to all learners.

It is equally important to encourage students to demonstrate their understanding of content in a format consistent with their strong intelligences. Using knowledge of multiple intelligences and being flexible in planning instruction and assessment is one way of supporting students to be more successful in the classroom. Using knowledge of multiple intelligences strategies is especially beneficial to English language learners since allowing them to learn and demonstrate their understanding in the mode in which they are most confident serves to lower the affective filter and boost their self-esteem and motivation. See Figure 50.1 for an explanation of the seven intelligences currently documented.

Intelligence	Definition
Bodily/ kinesthetic	Body-smart, sports-smart, hand-smart—the person has the ability to move through space effectively, learns well with movement, can imitate movements easily.
Intrapersonal	Self-smart—the person understands his/her own ways of knowing and learning, is in tune with his/her own needs.
Interpersonal	People-smart—the person reads others well, works well in groups, interacts effectively with other people.
Linguistic	Word-smart—the person manipulates words and language easily, understands what is read, enjoys verbal interactions.
Logical/ mathematical	Number-smart, logic-smart—the person manipulates numbers and/or logic easily, understands the logical connections among concepts.
Musical	Music-smart—the person expresses himself/herself easily in rhythm and melody, sees patterns and music in all endeavors.
Visual/ spatial	Picture-smart—the person sees pleasing visual/spatial arrangements around him/ her, has the ability to learn and express with visual arrangements, art, and beauty.

Figure 50.1　Multiple Intelligences and Their Meanings

Adapted from Gardner, 1993, and Armstrong, 1994.

STEP BY STEP

The steps to implement the use of multiple intelligence approaches for teaching and assessing are:

- **_Explaining multiple intelligences_**—Introduce the concept of multiple intelligences to your students. Depending on their ages you might use the actual labels for the intelligences, the definitions and examples, or simply talk about people being smart in different ways, while using the "body-smart," "people-smart," and "self-smart" labels to help them understand the concept. Explain that knowing more about the way you learn is one way to help yourself to do better in school. Tell the class that you will be giving them some choices in the way they study and the way they show you that they are learning.

- **_Adjusting lessons and assessments to student intelligences_**—Assume that the students in your classroom have a variety of intelligences and plan your lessons and assessments to allow the students a choice in the way they study and the way they document their understandings. See Figure 50.2 for suggestions on how to allow this flexibility.

- **_Observing and documenting student choices_**—Observe your students during the first few times that you allow them choices in their mode of studying and/or documenting their learning. Keep track of the choices they make and talk to them about their preferences and the ways they would choose to spend their time. You might also want to have them take the informal MI Assessment Survey found in Appendix A. Build a system in your classroom in which the students have regular choices.

- **_Providing self-evaluation opportunities_**—Provide some ways for the students to evaluate their own work and the choices they make about the ways in which they do the work. A self-evaluation rubric is helpful in teaching the students to self-monitor and evaluate their own comprehension and production in different learning and assessment modes. See Figure 50.3 for a suggested self-evaluation tool for multiple intelligence activities.

APPLICATIONS AND EXAMPLES

The students in Ms. Barry's second-grade class are reading and comparing different versions of Cinderella stories. Ms. Barry has chosen *Jouanah, a Hmong Cinderella* (Coburn & Lee, 1996) as the focus book of the week because so many of her students are from the Hmong or Hispanic cultures and the book is available in Hmong, Spanish, and English. After she reads the book aloud to the class, Ms. Barry suggests that the students might want to do some activities focusing on the book in literacy centers this week. Because she has read so much about multiple intelligences, Ms. Barry has decided to set up seven centers, each allowing the children to interact in a way unique to one of the intelligences. The centers Ms. Barry sets up are:

- *Listening Center* (linguistic intelligence), where the children listen to the story in either Spanish, English, or Hmong and look at the pictures in a copy of the book written in the language of choice.
- *Music Center* (musical intelligence), where the children listen to a tape of Hmong music and dress up in traditional Hmong festival clothes. Older Hmong students are invited to teach traditional Hmong dances to Ms. Barry's children at this center.
- *Games Center* (bodily/kinesthetic intelligence), where the children play traditional Hmong games as they are played at Hmong festivals similar to the one attended by Jouanah in the Cinderella tale.
- *Tape-Recorder Center* (intrapersonal intelligence), where the children respond to the Hmong Cinderella story on tape, telling about their favorite part of the story or what they would have done if they had been Jouanah.

Intelligence	Teaching	Assessing
Bodily/ kinesthetic	Introduce motions Encourage role playing Allow movement	Have the students show, not tell Encourage the use of role play to document learning Encourage the use of mime, dance, the invention of physical games to document learning
Intrapersonal	Give opportunity for self-teaching, computer tutorials, Internet, programmed learning	Use self-evaluation rubrics Allow the person choices in ways to best show the learning Encourage the use of self-made multimedia reports
Interpersonal	Encourage group work Celebrate group skills Teach pieces and encourage reciprocal teaching	Encourage group reports Use group evaluation reports Evaluate the products of the group, holding all members responsible
Linguistic	Give reading/follow-up Encourage additional reading/ writing	Use written response activities Oral reports Dialogue journals, learning logs
Logical/ mathematical	Quantify instruction Relate instruction to logical constructs Relate instruction to math/ logic puzzles	Have student design a math or logic game that shows what has been learned Have student design "mind-benders"
Musical	Teach with rhythm, rap Relate instruction to songs, poetry	Have student demonstrate understanding by writing a rap or song
Visual/ spatial	Teach with visuals, charts, drawings	Have student make posters, charts, illustrations, dioramas, constructions

Figure 50.2   Teaching and Assessing Through Multiple Intelligences

Adapted from Gardner, 1993, and Armstrong, 1994.

Name _____   Date _____

Activity _____   Intelligence _____

My understanding of the content of this activity is:

< ->

very   slight   about average   better   outstanding
minimal   than normal

I think that my understanding was affected by:

_____ my background knowledge   _____ the way in which the material was
                                                       presented

To understand the material better, I will need:

_____ nothing, I understand   _____ more practice (in same mode, in
                                                       another mode)

_____ another presentation of the content (in same mode, in another mode)

My ability to convey my understanding in this activity was:

< ->

very   slight   about average   better   outstanding
minimal   than normal

I think that my performance (demonstration of understanding) would have been improved by:

_____ a different choice of response   _____ more practice

I chose to demonstrate my understanding through:

_____ writing   _____ drawing/graphics   _____ music   _____ math

_____ role play   _____ dialogue   _____ personal discussion

_____ group project   _____ other _____

A better choice for me might be:

_____ writing   _____ drawing/graphics   _____ music   _____ math

_____ role play   _____ dialogue   _____ personal discussion

_____ group project   _____ other _____

Figure 50.3 Self-Evaluation Rubric for Multiple Intelligences

- *Story Reenactment Center* (interpersonal intelligence), where the children work in groups, using props from each of the Cinderella stories they have read to reenact the plots.
- *Pattern Center* (logical mathematical intelligence), where the children complete pattern strips based on intricate traditional Hmong patterns similar to the ones shown in Jouanah's festival clothes in the Hmong Cinderella story. Once the patterns are completed, they are used as borders for the bulletin board where the products from the art center will be displayed.
- *Art Center* (visual/spatial intelligence), where the children draw the features and create costumes for male and female paper dolls, which will be added to the bulletin board depicting the festival where Jouanah and Shee-Nang met in the story. The children are also encouraged to create other pictures to be added to the bulletin board.

Ms. Barry encourages the children to use the centers for the entire week. They must keep track of the centers they visit and rate their enjoyment and the work they do in each using a self-evaluation rubric similar to the one in Figure 50.3. At the end of the week, Ms. Barry reflects on the choices the children made in their center use and talks to the class about what she has noticed: "Some of you tried to work in each of the centers this week, others went to only two or three. Why do you suppose that happened?"

"Some of them were more fun," Tong says quietly.

"It's OK, Tong," Ms. Barry replies. "I didn't say everyone had to go to all the centers. What you say is true. Some of you found some of the centers to be more fun than others. Why do you suppose that is true?"

"Well, I didn't do the patterns because they looked very hard," Sia says.

"We like to do things we can do well," Ms. Barry says with a smile. "That is true. We are all better at some things than others. Which center did you like best, Sia?"

"I like the story reenactment center. I like to tell the stories with my friends," Sia says shyly.

"Yes, I know you like to work with your friends," Ms. Barry replies. "We are all different and that's why we need to have different ways of learning. Did you all learn a lot about the Hmong Cinderella story by working in the centers?"

"My mother said that the Hmong men used to steal their brides just like Shee Nang did in the book," Mia says with wide eyes.

"My mother said that, too!" Hou adds. "She says my dad stole her from her family."

"Were they mad?" Jerry asks.

"No, they expected it to happen," replies Hou. "He stole her but it was OK. It's a tradition."

"What's a tradition?" Jerry asks.

And from there the discussion continued. The class was very interested in the different wedding traditions and the students vowed to go home that night and learn more about wedding traditions in their own culture.

Mr. Yoshino's 11th-grade literature class has been engaged in a project in which they are being encouraged to read classic tales they missed reading in their childhood. Each student has identified the children's literature that they most enjoyed as children. Mr. Yoshino has shared some of the classic tales from Japan and others have brought in favorite tales they read or heard told in their homes. If a written version of the story is not available the students have been busily transcribing the oral tales for future generations. Mr. Yoshino is very pleased with the students' work and wants to plan a culminating activity to celebrate their explorations into cultural literature.

"I would like for you to share some of your work with the elementary students next door," Mr. Yoshino begins. "I think some of them have never heard some of the stories you have discovered, and I would like for us to find ways to get the younger students excited about literature the way you have.

"I have been reading about something called multiple intelligences, which talks about how people have multiple ways of knowing and learning, and I would like for you to think about a way that you could share your favorite story with the younger children. Let's brainstorm some of the things we might do," Mr. Yoshino says as he turns to the chalkboard.

"I think my story needs to be reenacted," Marin says. "But I will need to have other people to help me do it."

"That's fine," Mr. Yoshino replies as he writes *Reenactment* on the board. In just 10 minutes the class has created a list that includes:

- Reenactment
- Mime
- Puppet show
- Interpretive dance
- Student involvement
- Read-aloud with finger puppets
- Rap
- Skit
- Storytelling with costumes
- Story told in song
- Show with children taking parts

"This looks wonderful," Mr. Yoshino says as the class appears to be running out of ideas. "If you think of anything you want to add to the list, feel free to add it. I want you to begin to work, either alone or in groups, to plan your presentations. I will talk to the principal at the elementary school and set up a date for our presentations. What shall we call them?"

"Why don't we call it a Literature Festival?" Frederick asks.

"Good idea. Any other suggestions?" Mr. Yoshino asks.

"I like Frederick's idea," Janine says. "We can set it up like a festival and have some booths where the children can be actively involved in dressing up and being a part of the action. Other places they can just sit and listen."

"That sounds like a good plan, since we are trying to support the use of different intelligences and ways of learning," Mr. Yoshino says. "Who wants to form a cooperative group?"

"I need some players for my reenactment," Marin says. "But first I need to develop my script. May I work on that first?"

"Sounds like a good plan," Mr. Yoshino says. "Does anyone need a cooperative group to start work today?"

Soon the room is full of busy noise. Some of the students have begun to work in cooperative groups, dividing the responsibilities among the members. Others, like Marin, will need a group later but have to do some individual work first. A few have chosen to do a solo presentation and are busily planning how they will do it. Everyone is actively involved.

◣ CONCLUSION

The use of multiple intelligences strategies supports the students' learning of new materials because it allows them to use the processing systems in which they integrate knowledge most effectively. By providing multiple ways for the students to demonstrate their understanding, their confidence in their own abilities is fostered and their anxiety is reduced.

EXAMPLES OF APPROXIMATION BEHAVIORS RELATED TO THE TESOL STANDARDS:

Pre-K–3 students will:

- use a variety of learning strategies to enhance understanding.
- verbalize understanding of various ways to learn.

4–8 students will:

- identify personal strengths of intelligence.
- choose preferred approaches to learning.

9–12 students will:

- analyze personal learning preferences.
- use study methods aligned with learning strengths.

References

Armstrong, T. (1994). *Multiple intelligences in the classroom*. Alexandria, VA: Association for Supervision and Curriculum Development.

Coburn, J., & Lee, T. (1996). *Jouanah, a Hmong Cinderella*. Arcadia, CA: Shen's Books.

Gardner, H. (1993). *Multiple intelligences: The theory in practice*. New York: Basic Books.

APPENDIX A

I. Linguistic Intelligence

Reading books makes me feel

Listening to the radio makes me feel

Nonsense rhymes, tongue twisters, or puns make me feel

Playing word games like Scrabble, Anagrams, or Password makes me feel

Using big words in speaking or writing makes me feel

In school, English, social studies, and history make me feel

When people talk about books they've read or things they've heard, I feel

When I have to share something I have written, I feel

II. Logical-Mathematical Intelligence

When I'm asked to compute numbers in my head, I feel

In school, math and/or science makes me feel

Playing number games or solving brainteasers makes me feel

Finding ideas for science fair projects makes me feel

Having to "show all my work" on my math papers makes me feel

Finding errors in someone else's math or logic makes me feel

Measuring, categorizing, analyzing, or calculating makes me feel

Watching science and nature shows on television makes me feel

III. Spatial Intelligence

When I am asked to "close my eyes and visualize," I feel

When I'm asked to draw in pencil and not allowed to use color, I feel

When I read a book without pictures, I feel

When I read a book with actual photographs as illustrations, I feel

When I do jigsaw puzzles, mazes, and other visual puzzles, I feel

When I have to find my way in an unfamiliar building or neighborhood, I feel

When I have to do math without writing it down or drawing pictures, I feel

When asked to draw something from "a bird's-eye view," I feel

IV. Bodily-Kinesthetic Intelligence

When I play sports or other physical activities, I feel

When I have to sit for long periods of time, I feel*

When I work with my hands at concrete activities such as sewing, weaving, carving, carpentry, or model building, I feel

When I spend time outdoors, I feel

When I have to talk without using my hands or body language, I feel*

When I have to look at something without touching it, I feel*

When riding on a roller coaster ride, I feel

When asked to try a new physical movement, I feel

V. Musical Intelligence

When asked to sing "Happy Birthday," I feel

When someone is singing off-key, I feel*

When listening to music on radio, records, cassettes, or compact disks, I feel

If I had to take music lessons, I would feel

If I had to listen to music without tapping my fingers or feet, I would feel*

When someone asks me to sing a tune, I feel

If I had to study without listening to the radio, I would feel*

If there were no more music programs in school, I would feel*

VI. Interpersonal Intelligence

When someone comes to me for advice, I feel

When we have to play team sports at school, I feel

When I have to work out a problem without talking to anyone about it, I feel

When my friends are all busy and I have to spend time alone, I feel

When I have to teach other people something, I feel

When I have to be the leader of my group, I feel

When I go to a party with a lot of people I don't know, I feel

When I have a chance to join a club, I feel

VII. Intrapersonal Intelligence

When I spend time alone reflecting, or thinking about important things, I feel

When I don't get picked for something, I feel

When I spend time with a hobby or interest that I have to do by myself, I feel

When I think about important goals for my life, I feel

When I think about my own strengths and weaknesses, I feel

If I had to spend time alone (safe) in a mountain cabin, I would feel

When my friends want to do something I don't want to do, I feel

If I had my own business, instead of working for someone else, I would feel

Adapted from *7 Kinds of Smart* by Thomas Armstrong (1993). New York: Putnam.

Scoring Instructions

All people possess all seven intelligences in some combination, and this exercise gives you an idea of the relative strengths of your personal intelligences. For most of the items, add the total of your points for each question in each section using the scale of 0–1–2–3–4 (from left to right, crying to big grin) for the face you marked. For the items marked with an asterisk, simply reverse the scoring from left to right, 4–3–2–1–0. Add the total points scores in each section. The sections in which you score the most points indicate your strongest areas of intelligence. The lower scores indicate your weaker areas of intelligence. The stronger areas of intelligence are those in which you will learn and demonstrate understanding most easily.